In Warm Blood

Privilege and Prison,
Hurt and Heart

Other books by Judith Gwinn-Adrian:

Because I am Jackie Millar (2007),
Jackie Millar and Judith Gwinn-Adrian,
Los Angeles: Golden (The Press)

Other books by DarRenMorris:

Goal Setting Guide for Urban Students (2010)
guidebydarrenmorris.blogspot.com

In Warm Blood

Privilege and Prison,
Hurt and Heart

*Judith Gwinn-Adrian and
DarRen Morris*

HenschelHAUS
Milwaukee, Wisconsin

Published by
HenschelHAUS Publishing, Inc.
2625 S. Greeley St., Suite 201
Milwaukee, WI 53207
www.henshelhausbooks.com

Publisher's Cataloging-in-Publication Data:
Gwinn-Adrian, Judith.
    In warm blood : privilege and prison, hurt and heart / Judith Gwinn-Adrian and DarRen Morris.
        pages cm
    ISBN: 978-1-59598-273-5 (pbk. black and white)
    ISBN: 978-1-59598-272-8 (pbk. color)
    ISBN: 978-1-59598-274-2 (e-book)
    1. Prisoners—United States—Correspondence. 2. Ex-convicts—United States—Biography. 3. African American prisoners—Biography.   I. Morris, DarRen. II. Title.
    HV9467.8 .G85 2014
    365.6—dc23   2013952782

Art photography by Nataraj Hauser: www.eyeDance.biz

Book design and typography by The Roberts Group: www.editorialservice.com

Cover design by Carolina Gwinn: www. cargocollective.com/carolinaAD

Cover art by DarRen Morris, "Trapped by Freedom"

DarRen's letters often arrived with decorated envelopes. This rose garden was my favorite, and part of the image has been used for chapter-opening graphics. —Judy

A portion of the proceeds from the sale of this book goes to purchase books for prison libraries.

Printed in the United States of America.

Make me laugh. Make me cry. Tell me my place in the world. Lift me out of my skin and place me in another. Show me places I have never visited and carry me to the ends of time and space. Give my demons names and help me to confront them. Demonstrate for me possibilities I've never thought of and present me with heroes who will give me courage and hope. Ease my sorrows and increase my joy. Teach me compassion. Entertain and enchant and enlighten me. Tell me a story.

—Dennis O'Neil
writer and editor, author of *Batman, Green Lantern,* and
other superhero stories

DEDICATIONS

DarRen dedicates this book to the victim in his case, Johnny Lee Fish and the entire Fish family. *To all the people I have hurt or harmed in any way. To all victims, especially children.*

Judy dedicates this book to her father in hopes that telling the story brings peace.

TABLE OF CONTENTS

FOREWORD

The authors describe *In Warm Blood* as "epistolary stories." But perhaps this book should rather be described as powerful interwoven searches, through letters and memories, of two lives shaped by the realities of their families and incarceration.

For Judith Gwinn Adrian, the search began with the knowledge of her physician father's unlikely imprisonment as a young man for armed robbery. What had his experience been like? What role had his memories played in his subsequent research with prisoners and his alcoholic death? Seeking an understanding, Judith joined a prison ministry group. DarRen Morris was among those the group visited. Her visits were terminated as a result of a violation of visiting rules. Their relationship was sustained in letters, by Judith from a college campus and by DarRen, initially in a segregation cell for a year for the violation.

For DarRen Morris, the search in his letters, sometimes in response to Judith's questions, explored the realities of living in the segregated "hood," the experience of familial abuse interwoven with the presence of a supportive and protective mother and the violence of the streets. Incarceration is a continuation of that violence, but also a sustained opportunity for growth, reflection and understanding.

In Warm Blood provides insights not frequently found in either academic studies of prison life or in prisoner memoirs. Instead, it provides, through the reflections of two persons in dialogue on their relationships inside and outside of the razor-wire barriers, a look at the humanity on both sides of the walls we have erected in fear.

The final sentences contain a recognition that "the system is broken and out of control" with a sense that nothing can be done. But in response, it ends with the statement: "Maybe the stretch of the pen—this pen—is part of the answer."

Esther Heffernan, O.P.
Emeritus Professor
Department of Social Science
Edgewood College
September 22, 2013

ACKNOWLEDGEMENTS

DarRen: I want to acknowledge the efforts of my mother, who did her best to love and protect us and teach us what we needed to survive. It was by her that the gift I was given was shaped. Thanks to those in my family who have always loved and supported me, here and across the seas. To the women and young women who have been there along the way that have helped me move from one phase to another or to just survive the one I was in. In the corrections system, there are so few people who actually care; I have been fortunate to meet a few of them and am the better for having known them: George Kaemmer, Jamyi Witch, Alice Acore (R.I.P.). To Wegner for shedding a tear during our mutual shame. To Kate, Jerry and Gina; you were great friends when I needed you. To Peg Swan, who has stood with me repeatedly. To my son and his mother—despite my difference with her—for the first few years she stood up and stood with me in a way that most women could or would not. To my son, who is a very smart and beautiful young person and I am really proud of him. To those who do not see their name here, you have not been forgotten or overlooked. I am appreciative of what I have gained from everyone that I have come into contact with, be it the good, the bad or the ugly.

To Judy, it has been a long road. We have experienced a lot. Some good, some bad. Had you not been so patient and loving, we would not have made it long enough to get past half of this book. I am blessed that we have evolved into family. That is unique and clearly I picked the right person—no one else could have told the story as you have. For everything we have shared, it has been an honor. Thank you.

To H.I.M. Haile Selassie I Jah Rastafari, I give all thanks and praises for seeing me through and keeping my heart open, my mind and spirit free.

Judy: I acknowledge and thank all—family and friends—who have helped me see and understand the implications of the unearned privilege that framed so much of my early life. I offer special thanks to you, DarRen, for your patience, as well, in aiding me in beginning to understand the worlds of your youth and adulthood—our parallel universes. We have both grown, and continue to grow, through this process; I hope we have been able to capture some of that growth in this writing in ways that will help others on their journeys.

And we both thank Mark Anthony Rolo, most recently author of the award-winning book *My Mother is now Earth*, for his perceptive and masterful editing, Nataraj Hauser for capturing every essence of color in the painting photos, The Roberts Group for patient and expert typesetting, Carolina Elaine Gwinn for her fun-loving and professional cover design, and our dedicated, experienced, and kind publisher, Kira Henschel. This team has brought these words and pictures to light.

Thank you, too, Sr. Esther Heffernan for adding wisdom to this story to help us all understand.

DarRen's and Judy's families

Gwinn family members referenced:
Judy Gwinn Adrian
Rodney Gwinn—Judy's father
Weldon—Rodney's beloved older brother
Bunny—Rodney's half-sister, Judy's aunt
Gardner—Rodney and Bunny's father, Judy's
    grandfather

Morris family members referenced:
DarRen D'Wayne Morris
Vonn—DarRen's brother
DarRen's mother
TwoLips—DarRen's friend
Granny—DarRen's grandmother
DarRen's son
Carl—DarRen's eldest sibling
DarRen's father

Prologue

That last time I left the prison discussion session, I scanned the gap-toothed razor wire, repeating like an ominous grin in a fun house mirror. As I had on earlier volunteer visits, I wondered who thought to create this wire shaped solely to shred flesh.

Across the street from the prison, two boys tossed a baseball. They wore clean Brewers' caps. Daffodils softened white pickets and a dog, warming itself on a blacktopped driveway in the afternoon sun, snapped at a fly. Or a bee. I studied the incongruity of this small-town Wisconsin scene, knowing I'd not be returning to this maximum security institution, or this wire, for six months. After that required break, I should be allowed to visit DarRen as a friend.

Later I learned that the six-month visit would not happen.

Safe. That is what I had felt each week going into the prison where I was a volunteer in a church-sponsored group. I'd sit among mostly brown faces and hear stories of life struggles, inside prison. Weighty topics, like trying to be a dad when you have little contact with your kids, and less clout. Or being present for a frantic cellmate grieving his mother's death. Or forgiveness, forgiving yourself for hurting another.

I teach at a Catholic college and share its social justice mission, yet follow no personal religious script. I did, however, recognize this church group's authentic compassion as I joined them. Entering the prison, we would pass through sensitive metal detectors. (No underwire bras.) Each week the tightly-reined inmates sat in a line, gray hall passes visible in every hand, waiting until we volunteers were all in place so they could enter. Once inside the sterile cement block room, we were allowed to greet each other with a handshake. Antique fans hummed in the clean beige space. Hot in summer. Cold in winter. We leaned in over the noise to hear shared stories.

There were regulars in the group during the three years I volunteered, but over time, I leaned in more closely to one prisoner. It wasn't because of his hearing impairment. DarRen's demeanor, intensity and quirky humor reminded me of my father's accounts of boyhood pranks and, frankly, his smoldering violence. DarRen leaned in toward me as well. I admit to doubts while reaching toward this young man, whose leonine presence filled any room he entered. Although I didn't yet understand why, I saw how he came into a space, always on the balls of his feet, dreads swinging, surveying the scene. Ready for action. He would scan a room, determining where danger lay and where safety stood. Always alert. Slowly he would settle his 6'3" frame onto one of the stackable plastic chairs, sometimes smiling his Jamaican prince's grin. Sometimes not.

After each week's discussion circle, time for individual personal goodbyes was limited. Fifteen seconds, thirty at the most. But after one session, he offered, "Would you like me to do a painting for you?" I hesitated, vacillated. To say yes was to violate rules. I get to live among people in the *creative class*, as one writer has dubbed us in Madison, a community that can survive and prosper in uncertain times while we sip our lattes, yet too often slide into the safety of eternally discussing issues. We can neglect to act.

I had come to prison to act. I came to learn more about inmates and life on the inside, to better understand my father, his crime, and what that meant in his life (and mine).

So I wrote and mailed my response to DarRen's question:

Hi DarRen,

I say yes to a painting. What do I want? Something in blues and greens. Something with waves. I love the sound of seagulls along that Lake Michigan shoreline we shared growing up, at different moments in time. Can you draw the sound of a gull? Something that shows connections, since I believe that relationships are the answer—links between and among people, links with the natural world, links across ideas. How, I ask with a smile, are you going to translate these words into a painting? Well, my friend, that is your problem, not mine! I look forward to seeing what you create.

CHAPTER 1

The Painting

A foolish choice, I suppose, to have written as I did, challenging the rules of the maximum security facility. My father had always taught that we were beyond the rules. It seems the prison did not know that I wasn't used to being denied. Fraternization and enterprising (conspiring to sell his paintings) were the crimes we were accused of two months after I had stopped volunteering—stopped so DarRen and I could share stories of prison and incarceration. Prior to this, I had had no particular feelings about the Department of Corrections.

I was barred from the prison for six months and DarRen was sentenced to a year in isolation. Segregation. I did not realize that he could be disciplined for this recklessness. He did, having lived in maximum security prisons for eighteen years, more than half of his life.

In the subsequent weeks, we corresponded. I wrote from a cozy, safe college workplace with an ergonomically designed chair pulled up to a computer. And he? Crouched in the various levels of segregation on cold concrete beds six inches off the floor, always switching positions to accommodate his size-fifteen feet and whatever was numb or hurting. DarRen's words were thick, as he wrote only with the allotted pencil.

"Day of Rest"

Driving home from the college one day, I stopped at the Madison post office box I had rented for my correspondence with DarRen. In my original going-to-prison orientation, we were told not to give out personal contact information and I followed those rules. He mailed my painting before being sent to segregation, but its journey was exceedingly slow. *Had my painting arrived?* I wondered.

Nowhere to park; a floppy portable orange fence stretched carelessly around the parking lot. This was surely not razor wire.

There was the smell of fresh blacktop and a scuffle of kids on bikes, celebrating the start of summer vacation by playing on the smooth new surface. I paused by the driveway, leaving the car flashers on, as if that would do anything other than attract the parking police. Inside the building, a pink slip informed me a package, too large to fit in the mailbox, had arrived.

The clerk slid a homemade (prison-made?) cardboard container across the counter. My painting! The container was carefully crafted from several boxes, torn and reassembled by hand, fused with an equal mix of clear tape and cardboard. A rose was painted on the outside.

No ticket on the car. I moved it, parked, rolled down the windows and cut through tape. Inside, a letter.

Dear Judy:

I am drawn to lions.

When I was a young boy, I was at a rummage sale with my momma and a couple siblings. I seen this velvet painting of a lion in a wood frame. 24" high and about 36" long. $2.50. I loved it. My mother didn't think it was a good painting. It was my first and only painting that I paid for. It hung on the wall in the room I shared with my brother, Vonn, over my bed. I had started out on the bottom bunk although I've always been bigger. After a few late night incidents, Vonn took the bottom.

Had he sent a painting of a lion on velvet? Well, I too am drawn to them, more the lion than the velvet canvas, but wait, the painting DarRen sent was called *Day of Rest*. That could capture the call of seagulls on my beloved Lake Michigan, the blues and greens of summer.

. . . This painting was based on my memories of my time in Jamaica. It was like a picture on my granny's wall. I was thinking of what it would be like to be at home, sitting there on the cliff, enjoying a smoke (green is my favorite color) and drawing and dreaming.

A painting of a Jamaican scene? I asked myself.

No time, no time. I wanted to get home and make dinner for my family. Although my husband was always home, living the retirement he had earned, I was the cook this week. I'd finish reading and look at the painting more carefully, later.

Strange to me, I thought as I drove—the traffic was moving along well—how comfortable I felt writing DarRen. I would tease him about sending me a painting of Jamaica rather than Lake Michigan. I teased him in much the same way I had done with my father when he would give us loud answers to soft questions. "Affirmative," he would sometimes say. Or, "Negatory," when he slid into his physician or military modes, as though he had forgotten he was home with us, his family. But he was always attentive to my questions, always the teacher.

Was I putting DarRen in a similar role as I asked him to teach me about prison life, even though my early questions seemed to swing more toward his personal stories, stories that I had heard bits of over time, leaning in to the discussion circle? I had gone to prison to learn more about my father and in many ways, felt I was becoming reacquainted with him through this easy correspondence, because the two men did share irreverence, a risk-taking spirit, funky sense of humor and the charm of the bad boy—something I must have learned to value from what I knew (and was yet to learn) of my father's improprieties.

And, yes, embers of violence smoldered in both men—coals that could flash.

In one of the prison discussion circles, an inmate (I later learned he had raped boys and men) entered the room. DarRen glowered, then spoke. The other man challenged and then tried to interrupt the escalation. "Bro, bro, no harm, no harm," he said, arms extended, palms supplicated. With stabbing eyes and no further words, DarRen stood, whipped up his much-washed dull green prison-issue coat, nearly tumbling the plastic chair that was not built to hold big men, and steamed out the room. There was harm. Pride was disregarded and I knew the import of prisoners' demands for respect. I did not know what the issue was but subsequently learned how that exchange—that individual—had triggered DarRen's memories of his most cruelly abusive sibling. "Had I not left that room when I did," he later confided, "I would've been forced to hurt him."

At dinner that evening, I displayed the painting for my family and talked about the letter exchange. Polite responses. As the dishwasher sloshed with steamy water and my husband cozied up to a TV golf tournament, there was yet time for me to take an evening bike ride, alone. I love the freedom of being totally alone. As my sister once said, "The best thing about being alone is that the company is always good." I rode the bike that had transported me over 1000 miles through two, week-long, fund-raising AIDS rides.

I often choose the lake-side bike path, breathing in the throaty scents and watching the progression from spring-yellow daffodils to mid-summer crimson roses. This time, I saw tight rose buds with predictable thorns. Thorns: the razor wire of the plant world.

A fellow prison volunteer once told me, "After you have been inside, a part of your spirit can never leave." It is true. Even though some of the men I had gotten to know had committed awful crimes, there remains the comparable horror of locking humans in tiny cages. (As they say, an eye for an eye and we all end up blind.) Zoo lions have more room.

I needed time to think about the day's events, celebrate the inviting summer warmth and, well, to think about DarRen's letter and painting. As I had requested, the painting was about relationships with the natural world, albeit a Jamaican cliff rather than Lake Michigan. And the distant person dressed in white lace and standing by the house in the valley—was that me?

My mind drifted to my father. *He was an artist, too—a musician—*I thought as I pedaled along the quiet street.

I miss the father of my youth; his death took him too far away from me and sometimes I fear I won't remember the beautiful complexity of the man. That man I sat next to on the piano bench before dinner as he played the notes of *Nancy with the Smiling Face* accompanied by the tinkling of ice shards in his martini glass. He loved that song. My sister, Nancy, had been a tomboy in lace.

After family dinners, I'd often perched in my father's basement workshop on the tall stool he kept there for me (well, I believed it was for me), learning the particulars of woodworking, oxyacetylene welding, electronics, Morse code (which I later realized he had learned while incarcerated) and, well, also how to discipline our German shepherd with the whip my father concocted from strips of flaccid deer hide nailed to a hand-sculptured wooden handle. The violence of the man oozed out in some unconventional ways, as if it had to be released somewhere.

I never feared this man, my father. I never questioned my safety. Not only did he never hurt me, he never threatened to do so. I could see respect—or was it fear—in some of his co-workers. He was the man in charge. Did I unconsciously feel the same thing—safe—in a maximum security prison, knowing my father had once been on the inside? Having safety is a kind of privilege, but so is entering a prison and asking for favors from people who do not have a full range of options in their lives.

Later on, I would learn that my father had struggled with this precise issue—asking favors from those who could not give *informed consent*. Did he feel this same moral conflict that tugged at me? Did I dare allow myself to know prisoners as humans? Was the conflict, in fact, a major factor leading to my dad's ill-fated relationship with alcohol?

My father had had options. After my parents' separation (never any talk of divorce because that just wasn't done), I remember him arriving at my mother's hilltop home to the hostility of his last Christmas dinner. Another family holiday. Scowls filled the living room as he drank and drank more. It wasn't a question of whether he knew his limit for alcohol; it was whether he had any. Excessive drinking was not a new pattern; it had been impetus for their separation. Before dinner, he tried to pick up a cutesy cocktail napkin with the mocking message *Go Away* printed on it. It had fallen to the floor. He tipped in slow motion, first to one knee and then to both hands, and finally his forehead touched the thick white carpet. He wasn't noticeably embarrassed. Was he even aware? The others pretended not to see as they finished setting the table.

Before dinner, he had pushed me toward the picture window with stumbling urgency saying, "Do you see them? Do you see?"

"What, Daddy? What?"

"Them. Them. The ashen bodies stacked like cord wood."

I looked out at the banks of snow. When I turned back to him, he had moved away from the picture window and the warmth of family. There was nothing to say in response.

He ate with us that night, glistening eyes unfocused. Pupils dilated. Mostly he drank, wine on top of his customary martinis. "Skip the Vermouth."

The dinner conversation was superficial, interruptible.

"Only the Packers could have a Snow Bowl."

"Yeah, 36,000 no-shows at Lambeau Field, I heard."

". . . A snowy winter. . . "

My memory drifted. Family members chewed and half swallowed, waiting for the next awkwardness. As children of an alcoholic, we had long learned to stuff our emotional responses; we were collectively good at that—at compartmentalizing. Possibly my father was able to sense the tensions or maybe he just longed to drink without distraction. After dinner, he lit his pipe and embers fell on his saggy slacks, adding more burn holes to the existing pattern of what we children had long lightheartedly called his "pipe piddles." Better burns on his slacks than on my mother's forest-green linen tablecloth.

Before dessert—perfect pears sliced thin and spread like fans, with chocolate mint dribbled over their white flesh—he stood, staggered. Ready to leave. No one else moved. I couldn't bear to have my father walk away like that. Alcoholism or not, I loved the man. He had to drive several miles to the home he shared with the gray and now feral cat that lived in the cavity between the living room floor and the basement ceiling, a cat as traumatized by the DTs as my father was. As the oldest child, I debated whether my father (and others) would be safe as he drove home, although driving drunk was nothing new for him. I rationalized there was hardly any traffic on this cold Wisconsin night. As the family sat, watching him out of the corners of their eyes, I put on my coat. At least I could walk him to his car.

His stained coat was unbuttoned. His face was red, more from broken capillaries than temperature. The snow squeaked under our boots. His slow, once-confident surgeon's hands hung by his sides like arthritic clubs. He fumbled, reaching into various pockets.

"Where are my keys?"

"Here, Daddy." On the key ring was his worn Phi Beta Kappa key, a symbol of past academic glory.

I pulled the keys out of his unbuttoned coat pocket and placed them in his warm hand. He seemed to have no memory of how to open the car door. I assisted, smelling the recognizable blend of stale tobacco and sour juniper-berry breath that was him. Should I offer to drive him home? It would sting his pride and pride was about all he had left.

The two of us stood on the dark hill, overlooking the distant icy glint of Green Bay. Moonlight accentuated the rolling snow patterns. Before getting into his car, my father stopped. He turned slowly and faced me fully. We stood, me looking up to this man I had forever adored and tagged behind with such pride. A physician. A medical researcher. An inventor. A gin-soaked drunk. He slowly reached out and put his hands on both of my shoulders. He bent down and kissed me full on the mouth. His lips were warm, soft. He had never done this before. He was not a man who shared his feelings. He knew many things, but understanding the ordinary stuff of life seemed to have passed him by. My tears welled instantly. He eased back and said clearly, "You will never know how much I love you."

He got into his car and started the engine. Then he turned the key a second time. The starter motor ground. I knew his anger would have flashed if anyone else had done that, at least earlier in his life. Not now. He slowly drove down the hill. The car seemed to stagger.

I would never see him again.

He died three months later at age 66. His kiss that night has held and embraced me, while also allowing me to glimpse another layer of this man I thought I knew so well. I didn't, but would come to know him more as my journey to understanding continued. You see, my father robbed a department store on the eve of his society wedding, not simply because he was broke but also because of family pride.

He was used to privilege. He had been accustomed to having the world stand and praise him. He felt he needed the money to honor his bride and his reputation.

The reflections about my father's life ended abruptly as I pedaled to the end of the bike trail.

Enough of being in winter when the sun was warm on my shoulders and the lake glistening as I biked past the crimson rose buds. Their thorns seemed to hold less threat now. I was writing DarRen to learn more about my father's incarceration and prison experiences, writing to learn more about what may have led to his drunken end. My motives were clear.

I confess to putting DarRen's painting, carefully, in a closet. I told myself I had minimal wall space for new art and the colors clashed with my decor. Interesting to me that he chose to paint himself and his world rather than the blue/green lake we both knew growing up, the canvas I had anticipated.

My letters to DarRen continued. I'd send one to the prison. He would write back. One a week. Two. Sometimes even three. Did I debate whether to continue this correspondence? Not really. I greedily wanted the stories and had a collaborator willing to share. The deeper question was *should* I have continued the correspondence? Harder to answer. Was it fair to him to ask questions about his life even though I, too, was sharing my own tales—in most cases, admittedly, hiding in my father's tales rather than my own. Ethically, is it right to ask this of a person whose options are limited?

Dear DarRen,

The painting arrived. Thank you! Interesting choices you made. It is a painting with blues and greens, yes. And water. Jamaica rather than Lake Michigan, you say? Are there like a lot of seagulls calling in the wilds of Jamaica? I'm teasing you. I assume you are the dread sitting on the cliff, smokin' and

*painting. And the lacy woman in white, far below (by the water);
what is the significance?*

*I cannot really picture you as a kid tagging along behind
your mom. Did you have a bike and ride it on smooth blacktop?
What happened to the velvet lion painting? Has your mom kept
your things for you? And tell me more about your brother, Vonn,
and late-night incidents. What does that mean?*

CHAPTER 2

The Ramp Held

Have you ever watched a cat become liquid?

When I walked into the house, Kasey (my long-hair calico) surged past me with fur flying, ears flattened and whiskers akimbo. She was headed for the safety of the basement. I remembered anew that it was July 3.

DarRen had sent me his own brand of fireworks as well in the long letter I had picked up that day and quickly scanned. I was learning that he could be mercurial and that I could often get a vibe about his current mental state by reading the opening lines. This time, however, his mood changed mid-letter, going from boyish play to a lion's growl. I thought to myself, this man is locked in segregation, a six-by-nine-foot cage, for twenty-three hours a day. Who would I be in that situation? Mercurial could be a mild euphemism. I wondered if I would melt down. I had folded the letter back into the envelope for the time being. Some letters were too full of fire to read when there were any other distractions.

I was looking forward to my few days off and the family barbeque coming up. If DarRen were invited to my barbeque, I suppose he would be disappointed in the limited creativity of my cooking, the BBQ sauce coming from a jar and all. Well, and no pork in his diet either. He and his fellow Rastafarians chose an Ital diet (food that is natural and pure from the earth), when they are able, he had explained to me. It was, in fact, a sad day for him when he found out that Skittles were considered a pork product, but then, they may not have been pure to begin with. No candy for him in segregation anyway.

Since my family was off golfing and there were moments to relax, I sat on the porch, with my glass of Merlot and my feet on the paisley cushion, to read DarRen's letter more carefully.

Judy,

Did I ride bikes on blacktop as a boy, you ask? Sure.

There was Lil' J. He was a ugly kid. He looked like a thirteen year old version of JJ from Good Times, *the TV show. He was slick in a way that was non-threatening. There are some people who are slick in a way that spells trouble and you can sense it right away. He wasn't that kind of slick. He had simple logic. It sounded as if it could be true.*

Adults thought Lil' J could do no wrong.

We built this ramp. Lil' J seen it on TV and had come up with a design that would work. This thing, when finished, was about eight feet high. You know them pallets they use to stack things on in the warehouse so the fork lift can lift all this stuff at once? We had a bunch of these stacked up and some wood nailed to it to make a ramp. I tell Lil' J, "I don't care how slick you are, I am not dumb enough to try this one." So we see this other kid, RR. We called him over. Lil' J smiles as soon as he sees him. Somebody had to test the ramp.

Lil' J works on him and works on him. RR finally gives in, but only if he can use one of our bikes for the test. Mine was the Frankenstein of stolen bikes so I gave him mine. He takes off. We're cheering. He's going real fast. He hits the ramp. This dude was about ten or fourteen feet off the ground and then he landed and the impact caused the bike frame to snap. RR went tumbling. He was bleeding pretty good from about four places. But the ramp held.

Then D, a tall older kid who looked like a rapper, punched Lil' J in the face and took his shoes. He couldn't even wear them; D was like sixteen or seventeen. I carried this pipe that was once the pole to a bike seat. I had taken it and wrapped it up with black electrical tape. This will sound nuts but it was called a nigga beater. I didn't make this up; it was a common phrase around where we were for a small stick or pipe.

I go with Lil' J to find D. Me, my brother Vonn and M. M was a pussy but he looked mean. We find D at school playing basketball and I jump off the borrowed bike and walk over to him and the other people with him parted like the Red Sea, mostly because they knew my older brother. Right away he puts up his hands, palms up, a sign he doesn't want to fight me. I pull the pipe from my pants and I whack him with it. He tries to dip to avoid my blow. He ducks one, but catches the other. He goes down. I stand over him threatening him with the pipe and said to Lil' J, "Get your lick back."

Just then the school door pops open and my sixth grade teacher, Mrs. B, comes out. I was in like eighth grade at the time. I hide the pole; this was at about 4pm in June or July. No one should have been in school but there she was. She questions us and, of course, no one said anything, but I'm concerned about M; he's a rule follower and he may crack. But just when it looked like he might, Lil' J speaks up. "See, D had fallen and hit his head. He was dizzy. DarRen was trying to help him up."

She glares at me, but then she looked at Lil' J and softened. She knew something else happened, but Lil' J. . . Lil' J was telling the story and adults thought he could do no wrong.

I assumed that even though RR was "bleeding pretty good from about four places" that he was okay and perhaps a bit proud of his demonstrated courage. Brain intact. Soul intact. No bleeding from the heart. Yes, the ramp held.

DarRen's stories were rich. They were filled with action and intelligence and insight and humor. Well, and increasing violence.

Who was this boy who became this man, this boy who would hit another with a pipe to stand up for a friend? Who was this older brother whom the other kids so feared? Who were these boys who had each other's backs, no matter what? Had my father been such a boy? Was the knowledge that my father's violence had never been aimed toward me what allowed me to continue to walk with DarRen, through his stories, without fear?

DarRen had written that he had always been tall for his age and his facial hair began to come in by fourth grade, when he was yet again in another new school. He got a bright orange lunch ticket. "I didn't care that that meant I got a free lunch. After all, I was getting lunch." Then another boy made fun of him. In art class, DarRen tried to paint the ticket white like the tickets for kids whose parents paid for lunches. "The school didn't make a big deal out of it. They gave me a one-time free replacement and told me not to do it again."

I shifted position as Kasey came to sit on my lap. Apparently the fireworks were ended for the moment and she felt safe coming back upstairs. Her fur was hot against my legs.

DarRen was writing about many things, but he was skipping the questions I had asked. I would have to repeat them in my next letter. I read on.

... *We lived miles apart—you just north of Chicago. For me, Kenosha was Mom. Waukegan was Dad. Kenosha roots is small town so any growth will be from that. There was hardly ever anything to do, that we wanted to do. Waukegan was a little bigger and had more of city feel to it. Both places benefited from being so close to Chicago. Clothes, music, guns and drugs. Goin' to Waukegan, there was a rib joint named Hillary's. Anyone black knew about Hillary's. There were Sweetest Day, Juneteenth and Afro Fest: more celebrations of blackness.*

Inside the hood in Kenosha there seem to be more of family environment and disputes weren't as violent. Waukegan had more people in a small space and many were from East St. Louis and Chicago and the disputes were over what many whites called turf. There was more racism in Waukegan than Kenosha. But in the midst of all of this guns, drugs and violence was a sense of togetherness. Inside the corners of our hoods we weren't niggers. We weren't anything but who we wanted to be. In the hood, we could be important. We could have status. Inside our own little world we weren't descendants from slaves. We were on our own concrete island.

What is good about the hood in the midst of all the bullshit? One word, well two. It's ours. It is the only place where we are accepted as we are for who we are. Outside, when we go to school, we are told the way we talk is wrong. We go to the store, we are suspected of something. We get pulled over when driving. When we do get a job, we have to be other than who and what we are usually so not to offend white folks. In the hood, you can drink sweet Koolaid from recycled mayo jars. We can eat greasy fried chicken without fear of being judged for some stereotype (some of which are true). We can be loud. We can dance, sing, rap, make fun of or rough house without people panicking and thinking a gang fight is about to happen.

Outside the hood, we cannot easily spot the dangerous people. In the hood, we know who and what to stay away from. In the summertime, girls playing jump rope and, when I was younger, they had drill and dance teams or stomp contest. Girls would work out these steps and songs (sonnets) and they would get together and they would pop, giggle and wiggle. Boys playing basketball or football. Music pumpin' from here and there. The smell of a grill and usually every hood had at least one grill master. When I smelled it, I usually knew who it was. There was family reunions. The hood was full of life everywhere you went. Old heads sittin' around, some playing dominos and talkin' shit. Some standing around over the open hood of a car engine. Within them blocks we were able to do as we please because, for the most part, we knew we were covered. The hood was like that.

My family barbeque, scheduled for the next day, was sounding pretty staid. No dominos. No talkin' shit. No open car hoods. It would be proper and the glasses would match, although I suppose recycled mayo jars could also match. DarRen once teasingly commented that Merlot sounded like something you would drink out of a glass rather than the bottle kept in the brown paper bag they put it in at the store. He was right. We had grown up in parallel universes, mere miles apart. We shared views of Lake Michigan, from two vantage points. Our stories connected at the level of humanity, but would I remain the woman in white lace at the bottom of the Jamaican cliff—so far from the reflective painter in dreads sitting, smoking, thinking?

Is it ever truly possible to connect with another person who has lived in a profoundly different parallel universe?

Kasey stood to stretch and I gently pushed her hot body off my lap. "Is your water bowl empty, kitten? Time to start making dinner." I put the letter on the floor and went to the kitchen. I filled the cat bowls, got out my red baking pan with the lid, separated some pork chops, added a bit of garlic powder, and put them in the oven to bake. I refilled my wine glass and returned to the porch to continue reading the letter.

Had I subconsciously noticed that DarRen's handwriting changed in the next section? The curled cursive suddenly became wide. There was more space between the lines on the paper. There were exclamation marks and words angrily crossed out.

> . . . *They are trying to feed me nutriloaf again. It looks like a block of shit molded to the shape of a loaf of bread. It smells and tastes just as bad. I kicked it back through their fuckin' window. I ain't eatin' this shit. And I ain't eatin' their other shit which is why I didn't return the dinner tray. There isn't enough food. I'm always hungry. At least now I'm hungry on my own terms.*

I remember the day—a perfect summer day like this one—when I was working in Allied Drive (a lower-income area of Madison). The local government had intentionally separated such neighborhoods into about seventeen different areas of the city. The pockets of poverty were small (and organizing for power couldn't happen as readily). It had been late afternoon. Hot. Friday. I was dropping off some papers in the first-floor apartment that a landlord had assigned to become the makeshift community center while a newer facility was being discussed. I walked quickly into the building, smelling the humid mustiness. Graffiti and tagging on the door. Torn carpet. No one was in the office, so I left the papers and was rushing to get onto Madison's bantam Beltline highway before the traffic backed up. As I walked past a dark stairway, I glanced up and was startled. A tiny girl, maybe seven years old, sat halfway up the stairs, arms hugging her legs. Her eyes glistened and she was completely silent. I nodded. She did not respond. I went on my way.

. . . The room I'm in is filthy; same size as the regular cells but designed for discomfort. I'm in here by myself. There's a metal light at the top of the wall near the ceiling, pointing down and a window that has a hole in it or is not properly sealed so outside air blows in.

My days in seg? They are pretty full. I lay here until I get warm and I'm woke. I get up, wash and brush my teeth for breakfast. Then I wait till they come get the tray (well except for yesterday). Then I get medicine (the door sign you made about me being hearing impaired seems to be helping; at least they pause by the door). Then they pass out toe nail/finger nail clippers or floss. All personal, but can't be kept in the cell. I floss. Then I take the back of the writing tablet and sweep the floor. For some reason there's a lot of dust in here which is strange since the door never opens; in some of the cracks I can see the remains of what I imagine is fecal matter that was smeared around. Anyway, then I take a sheet and spread it on the floor and I practice on yoga: Warrior I. I want to be able to hold it a little longer and find the correct balance before I move on to another. Then my floor exercises to strengthen chest, arms, stomach and back. In between I do jumping jacks to keep the heart rate up; it builds lean muscle faster.

I pace and read—they have books like The History of DNA. *I can sleep anytime I want; no rule against that. Dinner is at about 3:30pm and nothing else to eat until 6am. Staff use meals as punishment. There's a rule that if you are not at the door when meals, medication or other services are passed out, you are passed up. So there have been times when I've made staff mad at me and I'm standing there waiting for the meal saying I want to eat. "Morris, you not eating? Okay." They walk off.*

Showers? They use only one set of handcuffs but the design is to mentally attack you and degrade you. We are forced to kneel in order to be handcuffed. One in the shower at a time. They close the door and take the cuffs off. Showers are cold; no hot water which makes the showers go faster. Every weekday except officer training days, furlough days and when the weather is bad, they offer one hour of rec, which isn't rec. It's a big ass dog kennel—no ball, no bike, no equipment. Nothing but fresh air and sometimes sunshine.

Right now I'm under attack. I opt not to engage or respond. Well, except to this white guy who asked me, "What's it like to have skin the same color as fresh dogshit?" I said, "It's probably the same as having skin the color of an uncooked chicken." Several people laughed.

This wing became the quiet wing after they moved a few people around so the officer said they needed to spice things up. He seemed to get a attitude because I made a complaint over his head about being denied meals and medication due to my hearing. He puts me next to this new guy who knows me from '95. I don't remember ever doing anything to this cat but he has decided to launch a series of comments at me, saying the same thing almost nonstop. "Ren, you bitch nigger. You homosexual fag was living with the other fag." He's very fond of the nigger word. I don't cell fight. That's what it's called. He just came out for a phone call and seen the note in the window, "Hearing impaired. That's why this bitch won't fight. . . nigger's deaf."

Allowing a rumor to go unchallenged means it must be true and then you have to be on the lookout to be sure that does not set off some other stuff. They moved two real negative boys across the hall. In Jamaica there's a term known as blackheart, meaning that person is evil or unfeeling. Within days there was verbal attacks—name calling. We're all in segregation, locked behind the doors, so no immediate physical threat. But when I didn't respond or keep the argument going, then came the threats of physical harm. Try to imagine this noise for months: when you sleep, when you wake up, when you pray, meditate, even when you masturbate. The tactic is to take something hard and bang on the metal toilets all day and throughout the night to keep you from sleeping. The banging causes others to bang. The pipes are connected so it's very loud. They keep working on a guy's mental until he breaks. At that point most either fire comments back or check off the tier which is a sign of weakness, allegedly. "You're not going to sleep you filthy nigger; I'm going to make you kill yourself or check out. Either way I win." The guards find this funny. "Play nice," they say as they laugh and walk off. (Rules are in place to prevent this.) Well, my disadvantage becomes an advantage and I sleep nicely. I take out my hearing aids and I'm left in a muffled silence of sorts.

Seg is uncomfortable and hard, but not hard the same way I experienced as a kid. I am okay. I tell myself I'm made stronger by this.

On the last page of this letter, DarRen sketched a face bunched close to a tiny mesh window. Wearing glasses. It was the man in the segregation cell across the hall.

What can I do with this information, these insights into the prison world? A funny, quirky, angry human I care about is living in a cage being teased and humiliated, being forced to kneel before an oppressor. No, I'm not this liberal who thinks only with her heart (well, a bit perhaps). I know that DarRen has done bad things, evil perhaps, things that could make me cry. But inside him is the core of

"Josh in DS2"

a shy, silent boy who doesn't hear what many of the rest of us do and who painted his lunch card white so he would fit in. How do we work to free that boy rather than just castigate the man?

I drop the letter and sit staring. Kasey comes and sits on the paper. Why do cats do this? It is like they have to take possession of the space all the time. I get up, leaving the letter there, and go to bake some potatoes to accompany the pork chops.

Dear DarRen.

Seg sounds cruel. Sometimes I get afraid for you, knowing you aren't exactly a good rule follower. But I was glad to see you are sketching, even if you have only that pencil and typing paper. Next level of seg, do you get a pen? How much does the nutriloaf confrontation set you back, if it does?

You haven't answered all my questions very fully but maybe it makes sense to wait until after segregation to have those talks. Your call. You could tell me more about your Jamaican heritage though and why you chose to paint that scene rather than Lake Michigan, not? More about your family possibly. Tell me more happy memories. I've been thinking about my father's boyhood and how I know virtually nothing about who he was as a kid and young adult. I know he had an older brother he cherished. They were inseparable like you and Vonn. Maybe I'll travel to Seattle during the fall semester break and meet his one living sibling. Perhaps she would tell me his stories.

CHAPTER 3

Seeds of Compassion

The liquor corner in the grocery store was crowded with folks preparing for upcoming Labor Day festivities. Mobbed, actually. The young clerk's nearly white shirt had *Ryan* written in cursive across the pocket. He was fussing with a customer who insisted the advertised price on his twelve-pack of wine coolers differed from the cash register price. I should have just given him the dollar, but was in no rush, so watched the drama play out. The two walked back to check the display; the customer was right. Then the electronic cash register locked up and no manager was available. I turned to the stranger behind me with whom I had chatted earlier as we danced past each other looking for wine.

"How did I get in line in front of you?"

"You are more decisive than I am, I guess." He edged his left shoulder toward me slightly.

Ryan was apologizing for the delay, turning redder by the moment. The check-out drama moved to the front of the store as he tried to pin down a manager. I turned more fully toward the stranger, lightly flirting.

"Happily none of us has any place to be this day." I smiled, nodding toward the ever lengthening line.

"Good thing," he replied with a touch to my shoulder and a sunny grin. No gap tooth. I glanced down into his cart and saw a pre-made meat loaf in an aluminum pan. Likely I was the only one within shouting distance thinking, "Nutriloaf."

The image took my mind back to DarRen's most recent letter. Good time stories, well, mostly. He was out of segregation early. No reason given, but that is the nature of prison, I was learning. No reasons had to be given.

> *Judy,*
>
> *I have been moved back in population early even though I remain on cell confinement. I am relieved to be out of seg. Praising Jah for answered prayer. But is it over? Lying here I can feel that sadness, darkness deep inside me. Something tugging on my soul. I left a piece of me, again, over there in that hole because my mind has not settle. In some ways I am still in the hole. I am not eating any better. My cellmate does not have a TV or radio so the room is a silent place except for the clicking of the typewriter as I paint this (word) picture for you.*
>
> *Damn, you bossy. Do you know that about yourself? Questions, questions, questions—unending questions. So it sounds as if you want to hear more of my life story. It's not very interesting, lots of darkness, physical and sexual abuse. Some really bad stuff has happened; I've done just as bad or worse. So you need to be sure you want to know that. I wonder though, how does it change a person to hear this? I've come to embrace it all; it make me who I am today. But what will it do to you?*

Bossy! I'm bossy? Am I bossy?

Back at work, I walked to the nearly empty pre-holiday coolness of the college library where I curled up in one of the barrel chairs to re-read parts of Richard Wright's *Native Son* in preparation for the following week's literature class. The book was a dog-eared paperback that had taught many a reader more about life on the rough side of the mountain. Bigger, a young black man, was pressured by Mary, the heiress daughter of his new employer. In her zeal to treat him as an equal, she put him in a place beyond their shared experience. Embarrassed, confused and frightened, he unintentionally killed her. Her desire had been positive but her method was arrogant and elitist.

Bossy? Is bossy another kind of unearned privilege?

Native Son rested on the table in front of me as I pulled the day's letter back out to read further.

Stories continued in spite of DarRen's fleeting reprimand about me being bossy. I had asked for more of the joyful stories but he was cautioning me about bad experiences in his life and I began to see the ruthlessness sprinkled between his good memories.

He mentioned he was one of eighteen children, nineteen if you count the one who died early. My mind locked on that fact. *Eighteen children?!*

. . . This journey began when I was just a young boy. I vividly remember the first time I saw her. She had such a bright and warm smile. When she smiled her eyes looked like little lanterns, all full of light. I had not even noticed that she was missing her front teeth.

Every day we played together. Every day we would go to a place that was our space. It was a place that physically existed at the end of the lagoon by the perfectly placed bridge. It was our place and space.

I have always loved bright colors. On the other side of the bridge was a sitting park that had these very clean pathways, and neatly trimmed hedges and them bright colorful flowers everywhere. I use to wonder how the gardens got that way and why would anyone plant them there inside a world that was so ugly. I would later find out that my father's whores turned dates in this park at night.

"Gap Tooth Girl" and "Sketch of a Girl by Bridge"

The little girl and I would sit in our space. We would laugh and make up stories. Sometimes we just watched the water that was so inviting, but swimming in that water was not a good idea. I could hear it calling my name. No fantasy. I do believe that was true. It called out to me and I would listen.

She told me that someday we would get married in that park. She said we would be together forever.

It was summertime and she asked how come I never wore shorts when it was so hot outside. One day I showed her. The next day she broke a piece of her mother's Aloe Vera plant and rubbed it into my wounds.

I cannot remember her name. At times I wonder if I made her up. She has been with me forever.

Yea, right. Who is bossy, I thought. Who is the tease? A story about color in a park and two children playing together on summer days. Whores in the park? My father's whores? And he says "my wounds" as if this is something other than rough boys playing on bikes in the school yard on a summer day. Teasing me. He is a flirt. A story flirt. He sees what I want, so doles it out in measures just large enough to keep me coming back for more. Well, it is cute. Playful. I can participate. No wonder women have always been a major part of his life. Protecting him. Teasing him. Loving him. Soothing him.

Native Son is a stunning read and I remembered the story clearly so didn't feel I had to go back to the book right then. The sun edged around to my chair. My choices were to curl up further and take a nap or to get up and find some coffee. I opted for the second choice. I continued reading the letter in the college café, with my coffee. And a peanut butter cookie. Why not?

His grannies. I read about these women of strength who were centrally part of his growing-up years and thought back to my maternal grandmother, the only grandmother I had known. A thick-waisted suffragist, she was determined to invoke discipline and respect for austerity on us the one summer we spent in her Seattle home. It was okay for us to laughingly spend a day riding horses at the arena or running track at the day-camp. But come evening: "Bread and milk for dinner. Children should not have too much fun. They require discipline."

"Grammy, can I eat the bread and milk separately, please?"

"No, the milk goes on the bread."

I watched the bread disperse and gagged. I suppose we three kids required discipline though I couldn't see it, frankly.

DarRen's maternal granny differed from mine.

. . . More fun stories about my family, you ask. Even from here I can feel Granny's fits of laughter. She's love, she's fun, she's safety, she's (belly full) food, she's wisdom. She loved playing games with us: Hungry Hungry Hippo, Connect Four, Sorry, Trouble, *and more. She has two stories about me as a four or five year old that she tells every, I mean EVERY, time I talk with her; one or both of them.*

"You and me were headin' to Arkansas, to visit family. It was dark out and you were falling asleep. I made a wrong turn and did a fast U-turn."

She whipped the car around and I popped up. Now you have to understand that I was a silent, fearful and shy kid. Few words—hardly ever talked. She would say, "Even as a baby, lil' Ren didn't cry a lot or do much fussin'. We could leave him in the room thinkin' he's asleep, come back and you'd be wide awake, just layin' there."

But this whipping of cars around brought it out of me.

"Whoa, Granny, cool it." She tells the story and throws back her head, laughing. I can't help but join her.

Granny's other story is about her cooking fish or chicken or whatever. She would save the grease in that way people do when they have lived poor. She would strain it back into the canister. Maybe this went back to the clay dish of fat and a rag wick used by slave families that could not afford tallow candles. Maybe not.

Yes, it gave flavor but at a certain point it isn't a flavor you want. Then the grease had to be taken out back behind the house and dumped. Looking back I can only imagine what that has done to the earth over the years.

Well, she called me and told me to take out the trash. I did and came back and washed my hands. And then she tells me to take that can of grease out back and dump it. "You should have told me that before; get somebody else to do it. I just washed my hands."

Yes, the silent and clean child.

Granny loved those two stories.

Wait. How does a silent, fearful, shy boy end up in a maximum security prison, with bubbling anger and an ever-present potential for violence? I felt bipolar as I swung between these gentle stories and what I know about where and how DarRen now lives, and has for more than half of his life. I see the boy inside the man. There is so, so much more to this story. Every letter raises as many questions as it answers.

I thought about the prison being so concerned with public safety and protecting me from DarRen (inmates in general). Did they ever think about protecting him from me and my endless questions?

But this time we were focused on happy childhood stories and seg had ended, so I relaxed and read on—reading carefully, not scanning.

. . . My father's mom was a blend of everything: Shango (the Voodoo god of thunder and weather) and Catholic. She lit candles and prayed for the saints' guidance. She smoked weed and talked of Jah and Rastafari. She believed in a black God and black peoples' redemption.

I was helping her with the animals in the garage. My uncle had turned it into a barn. Exhaust fans, sectioned off, chickens and hens down low and a separate section in back for the big cock and goats up top—three female and a male. The male was Chuck. I know you are going to ask, Ms. Bossy, but I have no idea why she called him Chuck.

My friend TwoLips come by. He was called that because as a boy he had lips that the rest of him had not grown into. He use to play with me all the time. So one day I take TwoLips with me and he loved it—feeding and playing with the goats. Then every time I went, he went. Chuck seemed to like him too. Months go by and it's time for the love feast, around summer's end. It can be any time, we had them in each season so four a year. We could invite two friends (lots of food). I invited TwoLips. We sing. We laugh. We eat. My aunt fixed our plates.

He said, "Man this chicken is good."

I looked over and said, "That's not chicken."

"Pork?"

"Nope."

"Beef?"

"Nope."

"What then?"

"Chuck."

He smiled and I looked at him and I pointed to the table where what was left of Chuck sat. His eyes got big as plums and his mouth fell open. He didn't finish his Chuck. No worries. Good goat won't go to waste. I took care of Chuck one last time.

DarRen's family is vast, I learned. They may or may not be related biologically; they were not allowed to ask and it doesn't matter. He is connected to others in ways I never have been in my relatively isolated world, where I don't even know the neighbors two houses down.

Reading about DarRen's extended family, I thought about my own. Most were in Seattle. West Coast, at least. I did not know them growing up, do not know about them. I met my father's father once in my life. No warmth, not even curiosity about who we were. He did not care that I just ran faster than all the other kids at my father's pharmaceutical company picnic race and won the tennis racquet that I then moved from box to box with me for years, never testing it on a tennis ball. I remember how my father had beamed and been congratulated by the other men all day, me walking tall by his side.

Growing up, we took several trips a year as a family; they did not involve visiting relatives. Often the spring break trips were to Midwestern cities. At the time, I did not wonder about that, but who goes to Detroit or Joliet or Indianapolis on vacation? Well, we did. And one summer, we drove down south. My siblings were sleeping in the Dramamine-induced fog that my father prescribed to keep us from vomiting, in rotation, in the back seat of his car. The silent child, I was playing my game of pretending I was a horse running along the side of the road with the car. When there was a ditch, I would jump it. When there was a barrier, I would pretend to duck out onto the road for a minute. Mile after mile.

On the outskirts of Atlanta, my *horse* stopped at a rural street light. There I saw children my age. Black children. Dusty children. They were playing in the unpaved street. None wore shoes. (I didn't like shoes, either.) Some were naked. That would never be allowed on my street. I looked at the line of houses. Even my child eyes could see that the clapboard houses were breaking apart. *Winter winds would surely get through those cracks*, I thought. The car started moving again and my horse left. But I remember being distracted and wondering why those children *wanted* to live like that.

I was taught privilege. I did not know that, but see it now. We children attended New Trier High School. My parents moved us to this affluent area because of the famous school district. Big deal, though I didn't know that. When it came time for my sister's graduation, there wasn't room at the school to house the nearly 1,000 graduates in one space, so there were two graduation ceremonies. Even at that, tickets were restricted to four per graduate. No exceptions.

The five of us arrived for the ceremony and my father told us to use the tickets and go in. He would join us and, a few minutes later, he did. Impressed, I asked how he had done that and he explained that he had simply told the ticket taker that he had been called out on a medical emergency and was now re-entering the building. No ticket needed. The subtle message was that if you do something with enough composure, the world will not question you. What did I feel? Pride in his cleverness at circumventing the rules. What would DarRen call this same cleverness? He would say my father *be street enough* to deal with whatever came. DarRen clearly *be street* as he embraced the opportunities for joy his life presented to him.

. . . I do have love and I'm not afraid to use it. One last little good-times story, well, not so little. . . So I'm sitting there looking at her. She's tall, long legs. She's like 5'8". She had these thick calves. She turned around and caught me looking at her legs. Of course she's exaggerating her movements. I see where this is going so I asked if I could take a shower. In the trunk of my car I kept a kit. All my hygiene products and two change of clothes in a gym bag. I went down, took a shower and before long she came and asked if it was okay if she got in with me.

Of course.

After a long sensual shower, we went to the bedroom. I wanted to lotion her down. So I went back to the bathroom looking for lotion and seen a bottle and seen "lotion" on it. I went back in. She had turned the lights down. I always enjoyed lotioning a woman's body after a bath or shower. Her whole body—hands, arms, chest, back, everything. Of course I use this as a form of foreplay so I'm adding extra lotion. We go ahead and enjoy the night. Fall asleep. Wake up in the middle of the night, another shot at the title and again in the morning. I'm heading for the shower, turn on the water and I hear her scream. I grab my robe, rush in. She was laughing. Her whole body was orange. It was all over the sheets. I looked at my hands. Orange. I opened my robe and yep, orange. Self tanning lotion.

Cute story, I told myself, as I returned the letter to its envelope and walked toward the panel discussion on adjustment to college life. It occurred to me that DarRen had been incarcerated at age 17, younger than the freshmen I'd shortly be meeting in the auditorium. So he got an early start.

DarRen.

I loved the stories about your grannies and the compassionate women.

Your letters tease me. How can I help but ask more questions when you leave half written sentences—well, not sentences, but stories—the way you do. I'll try to restrain myself. Poor TwoLips. He had Chuck on his plate and in his gullet before he knew. Well, at least no goat went to waste. Where is TwoLips today? See, I know how to ask safe questions. . . teasing you back.

I do recognize this about you; you love to eat. You asked, have I ever been hungry because there was no food. I've thought about this much lately. My answer is no. No. I have never lacked food to eat at any point in my entire life. It is something I had never even thought about, never had to think about. I did think about it for you when you put the nutriloaf back where it belonged. I saw a pre-packaged meat loaf yesterday in the grocery store. I had to look away. When you are free and you come to my house for dinner, I promise I will never serve meatloaf. In fact, I may not ever eat it again.

CHAPTER 4

Catch a Flatbacker and Slide Down This Blade

Seventy-some percent of the students at the college where I teach are young women, many away from their rural Wisconsin communities and in *the big city* for the first time. I had just left my first fall class where we participated in the small school ritual of introductions. A new semester always brings a purr of excitement. A new beginning. A fresh start. All things seem possible, at least for those of us outside the razor wire.

Fittingly, DarRen's and my letters were focusing on concepts and big questions. What does family mean? What is a parent and what does parenting mean? What does relationship mean? DarRen had recently written about his dream for college and the woman who was the closest he ever had to a wife.

. . . What were the images I had for my life after college? It is almost silly to me now. College was a dream—not a realistic goal so I had no real plans. The only two times I ever gave that much thought was with my girlfriend who talked about wanting more than what existed in that moment so we talked about kids and a family. We would role-play; our entire relationship was fantasy.

I do not think we ever had a conversation without being in character. I played a doctor and I thought about what it would have been like to be a doctor. But it was just a fantasy. I did not think I would live to be thirty-five and after I came to prison I had not given the future much more thought.

The young college women I knew gave careful thought to their futures. Our first class that semester had focused on the art and culture of Trinidad, in preparation for traveling to that country the following January. I wondered if DarRen had actually been to the nearby island of Jamaica, land of his roots. A Trinidadian woman, who would be a speaker in the class, told me, "Stay away from Jamaican men. They beat the stew out of their women." I protested the comment, but she had delivered her cultural stereotype and couldn't hear me.

Dear DarRen,

Man, now that you have forever ruined meatloaf for me, what's next? Well, that isn't really a problem since meatloaf wasn't high on my list to begin with. Every time I think deeply about eating ground-up animals, I swerve toward vegetarianism (and hope vegetables don't feel pain). And then a good steak catches my eye and, what to say. . . such is the yin and yang of life. Roast. That was my father's favorite. And mashed potatoes, actually about half butter and half potatoes. I connect the smell of a roast cooking with my father playing the piano after he'd return home from work. How about your dad? He came from Jamaica, right? You haven't written about him.

These words just fit on the postcard I purchased in the college bookstore and mailed after class. The flurry of meetings continued all week so it was Friday morning before I again checked the mailbox. DarRen had written about his dad.

. . . I've been thinking about my dad too as we write about what it means to be a father. Here is a poem I wrote about him:

"Some say I'm a pimp."
That was the answer he gave when I asked, "What do you
* do?"*
I was eager to tell my teacher that my father dressed as slick
* as a black preacher.*
He smiled like a model.
His dark purplish skin sparkled in the light.
His steps were easy and smooth like some sure footed big
* cat.*
He kept his ___ clean
* and perfected the gangsta lean.*
"But I'm not a pimp.
Some think the pimp is the top hustla,
But a pimp is a victim.
He's a victim to public opinion.
Subject to be his own best ho,
To keep up his image for public view.
What I do is love, guide, and help to discipline."

I thought about this. He loved me. He guided me. When I learned to ride my bike, he sat on the banana seat behind me teaching me how to guide this bike. When I acted up, he disciplined. Yep. Sounds about right.

"But what do you do. How do you make money?"

"With proper guidance these ladies learn to love and with the greatest expression of love they want to see me happy and want to see me have nice things and will do what needs to be done to make that happen. Always remember a woman will show you what you are worth to her by what she's willing to sacrifice to make you happy. A woman that will not sacrifice for you does not love you and cannot be trusted. Love is not a noun. It's a verb. Action."

I watched a young college couple walk past me, hand in manicured hand. Does she sacrifice for him? Likely. And him for her? Yes, again. I turned back to DarRen's poem about his father.

> . . . *"So I be myself and do what comes naturally. . . I'm a*
>   *gentleman of leisure.*
> *This is a lifestyle.*
> *I live.*
> *Breathe.*
> *Eat.*
> *Sleep.*
> *Shit and shower.*
> *This is life."*

This gentleman, this handsome, smooth-talking easy-going Jamaican gentleman of leisure got me high when I was three years old. I passed out and had a seizure.

This man of love beat my beautiful mother, swelling and bruising her light yellowish skin. It seemed she would scream for hours. I never seen him hit her. They went in the room and closed the door. What went through her mind as she sent us outside and turned on the stereo knowing what was to come next? Always and Forever. The music done nothing to muffle the sound. And then he would have sex with her battered and bruised body. When he had sex with her would he force her or did she seduce him to soothe him?

How could this be the man that put me on his shoulders and ran around the house with me?

Wrestled with us.

Cooked for us.

Wiped asses and changed diapers.

How could this be the man that taught me how to avoid snakes, spiders and scorpions? Taught me how to climb a coconut tree.

A banana tree.

My father never raised his voice to us that I can remember. He had a way of speaking when he was serious and his eyes changed and you knew to get in line.

This was normal in our house but I didn't want to tell my teacher that my father was love, guidance and discipline. So when asked to write about the most influential male in my life, I wrote about my uncle. He was a drug dealer who never hit his woman and was always good to me.

How do I make sense of this? DarRen has told me that everything that has happened in his life has been a part of making him who he is. I was beginning to understand some of what the boy inside the man had to negotiate walking through childhood. I remember a time in elementary school—some sort of parent's night—when I was told to introduce my parents. Painfully shy, I still stood tall and said, "My parents: Dr. and Mrs. Gwinn." With pride. What did DarRen do in that same situation? Maybe there was pride. Was it easier for him to tell me this story of his father's livelihood through poetry? He did write earlier that his father's whores turned tricks in the park that was lined with brightly colored flowers. That story was poetic, too. Maybe the poetry is his way of painting the pictures for me. Yeah, well, I'm not here to psychoanalyze (or judge), am I.

The young manicured couple had settled at a nearby campus picnic table. Books open, they studied. But what they were studying had seemingly nothing to do with words on a page. Each other. That was what they are really studying. Sitting at a picnic bench near them, I wrote.

Dear DarRen,

Thank you for writing about your dad. I know virtually nothing about prostitution—have only one story that I'll get to in a minute—though I have to wonder what the women get out of it. Reading your description—a poem really—I thought back to my high school years. My sister and I would head out for a good time, cruzin'. We would drive north along Sheridan

Road (that road connected you and me just as Lake Michigan did) past the mansions. There were staid, silent oaks on both sides as we snaked along the roadway. Peaceful beauty. After a slow hour or so (only twelve miles), the tree shelter ended and the roadway widened into four straight lanes. We knew we were coming into Highwood then and the havoc of Fort Sheridan Army base. We would drive past the lines of bars and the men hooting at us in our mother's powder-blue car. I don't know about my sister, but I never stopped to talk with those overly eager men, though I did wave back. Thinking about that place now, I realize that your family lived another twelve miles north. Fort Sheridan would have been a ripe field for the family business you described.

I didn't *get out of the car* in Highwood when I was a teen, but metaphorically I did now. I asked more about prostitution. Perhaps a tiny piece of me doubted the poetic description of his father. I hadn't ever personally known anyone involved in prostitution. The following week, DarRen's subsequent letter erased any doubt about his knowledge of the family business. Just as I had perched on the stool in my father's shop learning about woodworking and welding and electronics, DarRen had learned about his family's work.

Dear Judy,

Prostitution is about more than sex. Prostitution sex is not like regular sex in most regards. A flatbacker is one who has sex for money. Believe it or not, not all do. There are tricks to lessen the damage to a workin' girl. Most ladies forbid kissing on the lips. Kissing is very intimate and private. It builds connections and it's the only thing she can share with her someone special that no one else can get. Good hookers learn that if you dominate his mind and his fantasies, he'll be easier to handle. She has been taught how to get him off quickly which saves time for her and he is not able to just pound away, draining energy. Depending on the size of his piece, pounding away is something they want to keep to a minimum. There are tricks to the trade that makes things go very fast. Verbal. The pre-conversation, getting him so worked up he's ready to bust before he even gets in. The sound effects once he is in; you know. . . it's very exciting for us men. We are ego driven and the more joy she has, the more pleasure we have.

The kind of prostitution depends on the type of pimp. A workin' girl must find her specialty and work that. It's best to make a client list and schedule high-end Johns for $400 or $500 an hour. A street walker will likely only get $40 or $50 for sex. Some women are paid to hurt the men, to pee on them or to dominate them. One lady had a regular who'd pay her to serve him dinner and treat him affectionately with all the pet names. No sex. His wife would never cook for him and her pet names were not words of endearment.

DarRen did not know about the prostitute I saw in Amsterdam, my one story about this subject. We had taken a group of college students to Ukraine and on our way back, took a day for R & R in Amsterdam.

The group wanted to see the Red Light District and we agreed, but were not open to letting them go alone. The students were making fun of the place with its cornucopia of sex shops and other enticements. As lights and sound flashed all around us, we turned a corner and saw a row of very small shop windows with glass from sidewalk to roofline. A woman stood just inside every window. There were curtains behind each one, allowing minimal privacy for the bed behind them.

Again the students were pointing and laughing nervously and the teasing was two-way as the prostitutes flippantly offered themselves to our group. This was outside the students' range of experience and mine too, frankly. We walked past about twelve *caged* women.

There was one final window, so we walked to the end. A girl stood in the last cell, same age as our students. She looked awkward, as though she was unaccustomed to wearing high heels. One foot supported her while the other leaned out slightly. She was gaudily made up with crimson lipstick and a seamy yellow dress that tugged across her breasts and hips. As we had been with all of the women, we were two or three feet away from her, separated by thin glass. This woman had no teasing banter. In fact, she was crying. She looked at us full face, her mascara running. The fun of the evening ended in that moment as we turned away. I felt helpless sympathy. The students asked to go back to our hotel and the decision was unanimous.

I felt I knew DarRen well enough to know that what the students and I experienced in Amsterdam would trouble him today. I also recognized how deeply important family is to him and thought about how easily I forgave my father's crime when he told me he had committed an armed robbery. A human tension. I turned back to DarRen's response to my question about what the women get out of prostitution.

. . . What the ladies get, I'm not sure. It seemed that they loved the pimp and loved when he loved them, which came when they played their part to the fullest. He'd take nearly all of their cash but then spend money on them. He took care of them.

There are many sorts of pimps. Gorilla Pimp (beats or uses force and threats to control), Bootleg Pimp (gets young girls hooked on drugs—usually something strong like heroin it's the hardest to kick, and keep them hookin' through their need for dope), Chilibowl pimpin' (uses smooth talk and love). He's one who uses a mastery of words and affection to entice. The visual starts with the style of his clothes. Hence the big hats, the bright colored suits and the big cars. He has to stand out (Peacock).

For example, if a pimp in Chicago or southeast Wisconsin meets a young white girl, she's most likely unfamiliar with the level of attention he offers. If she's running away—possibly looking for love, safety or the adventure of the big city—he promises all of these. He says her dreams will come true if she will be down for him as he'll be down for her. For the first couple of weeks, if she's new, he'll be the perfect gentleman. Money, *clothes, expensive trips out of town. At some point, he'll ask her to do him a solid—a favor. Make this guy happy so <u>we</u> can make this deal. By this time she's floating and with his mastery of words, he has created in her mind a visual of how this makes sense and what her role is. The pimp game has a sharp edge like a razor, so slide down the blade would be join the stable. . . join the team.*

Some of my relatives ran girls—worked the girls together. One had a mobile home that he called Pussy on Wheels where he would provide small-town entertainment. He put in extra beds and dividers and would park in spots he knew the girls could make some money.

My family has many well-known pimps. I would often make fun of them. They would sit around, get drunk, and tell pimp stories kinda like people who swear they shot a 30-point buck or wrestled a bear and lived without a scratch. So I created a character—role played—a name, voice and style: I was Big Daddy Woo Woo and in my teens, some called me, Woo.

But I could never be a pimp because I could never do that to a woman I loved.

This letter was disturbing to me, though I felt confident DarRen was truthful saying he could never be a pimp. I was thinking of the young college girls I work with. DarRen was writing about their peers. Possibly about them even. Unexpectedly, my mind returned to the dusty children I had seen on the outskirts of Atlanta, so many years prior. Then I felt myself to be a strong, capable horse navigating each bump or (admittedly) small barrier that life presented with relative ease. Wondering why the children *wanted* to live that way later led me to see that not everyone had the same choices.

DarRen was taking me to a new level of understanding, seeing more deeply into the world-as-it-is rather than the place I liked to hide in, the world-as-it-should-be.

My galloping horse was slowing to a walk. I was trying to understand in a different way. I did not skim his letters any longer, searching for his state of mind. I was trying to put myself more deeply into his world. To understand.

Then came an offer.

I was invited to meet DarRen's mother.

CHAPTER 5

Her Beauty Was Ageless

I rang the buzzer a second time and continued to wait for my get-together with DarRen's mother. The apartment buildings were indistinguishable so I had some trouble finding the right address. After parking, I jogged across the street around the flurry of trucks and un-muffled cars, carrying the bag of cookies I had purchased before leaving Madison early that morning. I was right on time and rang the bell, but no answer. Had I arrived on *white people time,* so was far too early? What to do. Should I leave? I didn't want to. DarRen had done the preparation to allow me to visit his mother. I both didn't want to disappoint and did want to meet her. I had her current cell number in my phone, so called. She answered, sleepily.

"Hi, it's Judy."

"Who?"

"DarRen's friend, Judy."

"Oh, yeah."

"I'm at your front door."

A pause. "Wait a minute."

My fingers tightened on the paper bag holding the cookies. I had selected oatmeal raisin, chocolate chip, molasses and two peanut butter cookies, thinking one of those might be her favorite and knowing I would want a peanut butter one. Oil stained the bottom of the bag.

There was the sound of footsteps coming down the hallway. The door opened. The man was tall with dark purplish skin that sparkled in the light from behind me. He gestured for me to follow and turned. *His steps were easy and smooth like some sure-footed, big cat.*

The apartment was just a few doors down the hallway. We entered into darkness. The window was draped with several layers of curtains. The TV was loud. The apartment was hot. The kitchen was immediately to the left with a dividing wall separating it from the living room. A double bed stood on the far side of that wall and DarRen's mom rested on the bed, propping pink pillows up behind her and moving to a sitting position with some effort.

"Turn on a light. I had just gone to sleep. Have a seat."

"I brought you some cookies." I held out the bag.

"Get us some soda to go with the cookies," she said to the tall man.

"I got different kinds of cookies; didn't know what you'd like best," I said, needing to add something else to the conversation. We sat making very small talk while he served sodas.

I furtively glanced around the room. There was a shelf with glass collectables—little figurines I couldn't identify from a distance. There were photos and paintings in frames hung on the light gray living room walls. One photo showed a beautiful woman—high cheekbones, artful make-up, open-mouthed smile—wearing a deep coral dress with matching fur around the collar and a teasing hint of cleavage. A thin chain showed at her neck and she sat next to a pumpkin-colored boy about six years old, a boy with sad eyes. He was dressed in a conservative black sweater over a muted plaid shirt. Another framed photo showed an older woman with shine in her hair, sitting cheek to cheek with a child who looked to be one or two. I thought of what DarRen once wrote about photos, "When people took out cameras for parties and things, we would scatter like roaches when the lights come on. I don't remember smiling much when I was young. That picture of me and my mom is about right. A dull expression."

"My two children," she said.

"Beautiful." I meant it.

"He likes cookies," she said, gesturing toward the man. And he did. He ate one cookie, politely asking where I had gotten them because they were quite good.

"I brought them with me from Madison."

"Oh."

Not everyone is equally enamored with Madison, I thought.

He stood by the divider wall between kitchen and living room for some minutes and when he had determined she was safe with me (I think), he went off to pick up her prescription for pain medication.

Talking got easier.

"DarRen suggested some questions for me to ask you. Is that okay?"

"What are they?"

"When did you love DarRen the most?"

She smiled, remembering. "From the minute he was born. That baby is so dependent on you. When I was shot, I was determined to get well because I didn't want anyone else raising my child. I was seventeen when he was born so we were friends even more so than mom and son. He grew up too fast; got all his teeth in one year. He walk at nine months and was very smart."

The second question DarRen had sent with me was,"When did you realize DarRen had some kind of mental illness?" I asked it.

Her brow furrowed slightly as she painfully changed position. She nibbled on a piece of her oatmeal raisin cookie that rested on a napkin, on the bed covers.

"DarRen would flip out. One night, he was screaming my name and saying, 'Get these people off of me.' Imaginary people. I was scared of him. I thought he was putting me on. I'd say no to him and he would get so mad, he'd blow up. For two years, I slept with my door locked. I believe he was having problems, in part, because he could not hear well."

"DarRen wrote down a question about the abuse for me to ask. Do you want to talk about that?"

"He say he was sorry about the abuse. He was not the man he should have been and didn't know how to act then. I don't know how that abuse affected DarRen; he was so young. How does he remember all of that? The abuse was the reason I left; I don't need to take that shit. I was raped at age fourteen by two men and again at age fifteen by six men."

I changed the subject. "You left to move to Green Bay?"

"I regret moving to Green Bay. Was part of what happened there my fault? The murder, I mean. I don't understand why DarRen doesn't have to serve 50 percent of his sentence, given he was sentenced under the old law? Do you?"

"No, I don't."

One of DarRen's early acrylic paintings hung on the wall showing a muscular white unicorn, standing with its head turned to the rear. The background was dark with what looked to be menacing clouds behind the horse.

And, on the floor, prominently displayed, was an acrylic portrait of family members, showing DarRen in the upper left corner and his parents, his sister, his son and baby, and his brother, Vonn, pictured. There was a trio of lion heads at the bottom of this painting.

Pointing to the family portrait, I wondered aloud, "Are these Jamaican Rasta lions?"

"I don't know nothin' about Jamaica. DarRen wasn't ever there, was he?"

Changing the subject again, "May I take a couple of photos of these pictures and paintings to send to DarRen?"

"Yes."

I emailed the photos to myself from my cell phone.

I felt as though my interview time had ended. It had been good. I enjoyed meeting this strong, shielding woman. I asked if I could take her photo to send to her son as well. She agreed and slipped into her wheelchair. She looked at me pleasantly but with no gap-toothed smile. I could see a white T-shirt under her checked purple, pink and lime green housecoat. I saw both the sternness and the sparkle within her.

Her beauty was ageless.

Driving home from Kenosha on the winding Wisconsin back roads, I had two hours to reflect on who this woman was and the yoke she bore, sometimes with determination and sometimes with annoyance. Still, she marched.

Lake Geneva, Elkhorn, Whitewater, Fort Atkinson. White people. I've heard it said that our churches are the most segregated places in America. Small towns, too? Wisconsin state voting maps show the sharp edges of our difference, or indifference, to the other. As King once said, "There are two Americas."

And my mother? I thought to myself. She taught us how to survive the northern Illinois and southern Wisconsin of my youth. We kids used to tease each other about violating table manner rules. "I saw you use your salad fork to scrape off that Hollandaise sauce!" That would have been the single year my mother decided to try gourmet cooking and spent hours making fragrant sauces for family dinners. (We were brats.)

I wrote a quick letter after arriving home from my long day on the road.

Dear DarRen,

I visited your mom on my way home from seeing my brother. I hadn't realized how close they live to each other. About thirty miles. I was nervous going to your mom's apartment, but she and your dad were very kind to me. He liked the cookies I brought. Your mom is recovering from the surgery on her leg. I felt she trusted the decision to have me come to visit, obviously because of your introduction, though they were not exactly sure what to make of me. I know you have had other friends like me since you have been incarcerated but don't know if they have been to your mom's apartment. It was evident that your parents value the friendship you and I have. You are clearly loved.

Your mom is a beautiful woman. Do tell me more about her and—back to our discussion about parenting—what kind of mom she was for you.

CHAPTER 6

Be Warned, I Love My Momma and I Place No Blame on Her

Several times a week, I would pick up DarRen's letters from the post office box and then read them when I got to work, often over a cup of coffee in the campus café, as I did this fall day.

His next letter began with a roar in his mom's defense as we continued weaving stories about our mothers. I did not know what had triggered the emotion.

Dear Judy,

My mom was a contradiction but be warned, I love my momma and I place no blame on her. She done the best she knew how to do, so don't you blame her either. She could have been better, but with all things considered, she done good.

"Stay out of them streets. Them streets lead to death," she would say. She taught us to survive northern Illinois and southern Wisconsin, the best way she knew how.

I called her Money; couldn't say Mommy. She and the others called me Pumpkin. I was so light, the color of a pumpkin and a little round. We had fun then—me, her and Vonn. All of that changed after the shooting.

DarRen's mom had also said, "After I got shot. . . " I tore a corner off of a blue college memo and made a note to myself to ask more about this shooting, hiked up on one hip, stuck the note in the back pocket of my jeans, sipped my coffee, and continued reading DarRen's letter.

. . . I'm not sure my mom put that much thought into our physical punishment. Mom said that when we broke the rules we'd get a spanking and if we didn't mind getting spanked, she didn't mind spanking. When we were really small, her cloth-top shoes with the rubber bottoms was her weapon of choice. We thought it was funny 'cause after she was finish we would have welts that showed the pattern of them shoe soles on us. We were always punchin' and tusslin' either for real or for play in our house and Mom would get in on it sometimes. If she popped you too hard, she would claim it was a love tap.

Anything that cost her money—suspension from school or coming home in the police car—automatic whippin'. As we grew, the brown electrical cord became her weapon of choice. I assume you don't know what it feels like to be hit with an extension cord.

A couple of stories.

I was in elementary school when a Jewish family moved in. There was a boy about my age, nine or ten. His older sister was fifteen or sixteen. Everyone said he was a Jew, as if he had done something wrong. I'm ashamed to say now that it never occurred to me to ask any questions like, "What's a Jew?" or "Why am I mad at him?"

We picked on him every day for weeks. There was a crab apple tree at the other end of the block. On the way home from school we'd chase and pelt him with these apples.

"Kike," we'd yell.

"Nigger," he'd yell.

When he said nigger, I don't know why, but somehow the way
he said it, it stung.

This one day he stopped and picked up a rock and slung it
and of course, out of six or seven people, it hit me and split my
knee open. I was on his heels as he ran. He made it home and in
the door with my fingertip nipping his collar. I pounded on the
door. His sister answered,

"Tell him to come outside and fight."

"No. Get off our porch."

I banged and banged again. The door flew open and she
step forward, pushed me in my chest. I went tumbling back and
landed on my ass in the dirt. Back in the apartment she went.
The crowd that had gathered hoping to see a fight, laughed. I
went and got a brick out of the pothole and went back. Banged
on the door again. It popped open and I let it fly. The brick hit
her in the head; within seconds, her blue Smirf shirt was red
with blood. It was pouring out. I took off running. I ran home.

My momma asked me, "What the hell you done did?"

"Nothing."

"Hell, nawl, only time you run yo' ass in this house when you
done did something;' yo betta tell me."

"Nothin', I swear."

She asked me what happened to my knee.

"Some boy hit me with a rock. I don't know who and I don't
know where he stays."

She got out this stuff in the brown plastic bottle and cleaned
my knee. But the worse was the next part, the small green bottle.
It looked like oil but it smelled like bug spray and it burned.

"Get back outside."

I pause in my reading, thinking about the time I locked my sister
in the hall entryway. She could have turned and gone out the front
door but chose, instead, to crash her fist through one of the glass
panes on the inside door. The glass cut a deep horseshoe shape out
of her upper arm as she pulled back. Blood everywhere. My dad put

her on the kitchen table, injected some numbing medication into the wound and sewed her up right there as she cried and I cowered on one corner of the slate-colored living room couch, holding my Steiff stuffed lion—a toy so special to me that most of its fur was worn off by the time I was in my early teens. My father said the wound came close to leaving my sister with a withered arm but luckily there was immediate medical attention. The large scar was forever a reminder to us both of that thorny day.

I think about DarRen's word, "stays." He told his mom he didn't know where the boy who threw the rock "stays," not where he "lives." One word implies stability to me and the other impermanence. The differences in our worlds were so subtle. I turned back to DarRen's story.

. . . I wondered if the girl was okay. I walked past the apartment but all the lights was out. I never thought it would actually hit her. I thought she'd duck or move or if it hit her it would hurt and leave a knot but nothing as serious as bloodshed.

Later, when I got back, our apartment was quiet except the blues was playing. All the house lights were out. Mom kept her "before-I-kill-this-child" drink on the shelf near her collectables. Crown Royal. I learned firsthand that if you done something wrong and you wanted to see how bad it was to be, look for that bottle. If you seen that bottle missing, yo' ass in trouble. I walked in. Mom was sitting at the table with the double up—a joint burning in the ash tray as she poured another shot in the shot glass.

She asked in the most sweet and loving voice, "You hungry?"

I'm almost always hungry. My line is, "I could eat."

"Anything you want to tell me?"

"No."

"Gon' in there and take a bath before you eat," she said as she opened the oven.

I seen and smelled the roast and potatoes (mashed, my favorite). I had my eyes on that roast and nobody else was around. I could take my time and eat. I went, stripped, and jumped in the bath tub. Suddenly the door was kicked in like a SWAT team was out there. I swear it look as if she was six inches taller. Seemed to have a lot more muscles than I remember and I think I heard her growl like a bear or lion. Her eyes had no white part, all black. Then I seen it. The brown electrical extension cord wrapped around her hand, dangling in a loop.

I was naked in the water. I tried to hide behind the shower curtains. She snatched them down and, well, she done to me the same thing she done to that roast. She warmed that ass up.

Lesson learned. But sometimes I question what was the lesson I learned. I hurt someone and that cost my mom money so she hurt me. I remember the cord wrapped around my body and it hit me on my penis. I hollered,

"My penis, Momma, you hit my penis."

She said, "I don't care about that. I told you about throwing them rocks; you gon' learn when I say something I mean it."

She meant it. I had welts over my back, my ass, my legs, my chest, my arms and stomach.

At times she would abandon physical punishment saying she'd try something else because beating me didn't seem to work. Once, when I'd gotten suspended from school, my punishment was housework. I had to wash and iron all the curtains and drapes. Wash all the sheets and blankets. I had to wash all the dishes, pulling them down from the cabinets, washing all the walls, kitchen and bathrooms, from top to bottom and all the laundry and I was her personal errand boy. Plus all my school work.

My days were full.

The discipline of my childhood? Unlike what DarRen was describing, I have never been hit, much less whipped. Never once in my life. Discipline involved things like being grounded or having more household jobs added to the customary Saturday list of chores— things like, "Clean the third floor bathroom" or "Mangle the sheets" (there actually was a mangle in the basement for ironing the sheets, which was a large machine small children wouldn't be allowed to touch today and, yes, we got burns from that contraption all the time). Sometimes one of the jobs on the Saturday list would be, "Get a Coke and take a break." Back to DarRen's mom stories.

. . . Then the time I was in the 7th grade—not sure, maybe my second time—suspensions. They kept calling home complaining 'bout my behavior. So one day, after another suspension she says, "You get suspended again, I'm gonna come up there to that school." I don't remember exactly what I said but it was some kind of disbelief. "Yeah, right," or something. That comment sealed my fate. "Oh, you think I won't come up there with my boots and yellow rollers in my hair?" Of course I didn't believe her.

I got suspended again and my three days went by without a word of her going to school with me. We went through our routine. I took my ass whoppin' and done my chores. So on the day I'm to go back she says, as I'm leaving to go catch the bus, "Where you goin'?"

Puzzled, I answer, "School."

"You can relax, we got some time yet."

I couldn't help but catch the, "we."

She's sitting there watching TV. She's got on this head scarf, a checkered or polka-dot pink and white house coat, and these thick 80's style purple leg warmers. She had these big winter boots I think were mine that she liked to wear 'cause they had fur on the inside. She turns off the TV and gets this coat from the closet. I'd only seen her wear it twice maybe. It's brown and it's got like dog fur on it around the collar and sleeves. It had to be dog fur. No other animal had fur that looked that bad. It was the ugliest coat I've ever seen.

She likes to chew ice (there's even a clinical name for it). And she gets her two big ass Super-Size-It cups, the kind they gave away at the fast food places to promote this or that, and fills them.

So off to school we go. She got the radio going; she's singing and crunching ice. I'm still not believing she's going to go in there with me. We park. She's, "Oh, let me take this scarf off so they won't think I'm crazy." All she's worried about is this scarf? Off it comes. Her hair is a mess, dry and uncombed. She takes her fingers and rakes it all to the back. I'm still thinking, okay, she must have a meeting with them. Out comes the cane and she sets the ice down into the deep pockets of this dog coat.

"Okay, let's go." I take long strides and try to make some distance.

"Where you think you going, nawl playa, slow down and wait for me."

She has to go to the office and sign in for a visitor's pass. She walks me to my class and sits down at a table in the back. She's crunchin' ice and sitting there without a care in the world. Every single class. 'Til lunch.

At the time I resented her for doing that to me. I may have gotten the point then if she would have dressed normal, but because I was so embarrassed it was further proof to me that she hated me and blamed me for giving her such a fucked up life. That only led to more problems. She never wanted this for us.

I'm remembering when I threatened to do exactly the same thing to my son that DarRen's mom did to him. I didn't follow through, didn't actually have the courage to *humiliate* myself in front of him and his peers. Interesting difference. DarRen's mom was tougher than I. Well, I tell myself, maybe she faced more in dealing with this spirited young man. My son responded to the threat and we both sighed with relief. I never hit my son though I did roughly stand him in the corner a few times and then had to turn away to smile when his dog joined him, also facing into the corner. And I grabbed his teenage chin once—my son's, not the dog's. I had to reach up to do that and remember the flashing thought, *he could squash me like a bug.*

He did not.

How do I understand this violence and these messages to a young man? How do I understand them without judging? Because she did not parent the same way my mother or I did doesn't necessarily mean she was wrong. She was trying to save this boy, this young man. Save him from "them streets," from death. I read on.

. . . My mom has stories like mine of going to school sore and hurting from beatings. She left that to be with my father, a charming pimp from Jamaica. He made a nice living and gave this young girl money, clothes and status. She wanted what she was scared to get. Love. She was so (afraid of him) in love with him. I never fully understood why she allowed all of that to happen to her.

My dad established a safe place for himself away from the street life. There she raised the children—all the children. She wanted more in life but didn't know how to get it and she unfortunately gave us what she knew. When my father was "away" (in prison), the women left us for the most part though ever so often some would drop by to give money. My mom was good with budgets. She would delegate funds and juggle bills, paying off the most important and just enough to keep the others from being turned off. She sold icy cups. An icy cup is extremely sweet Kool-Aid poured into Styrofoam cups and frozen. We'd sell them for $.25 for the small and $.50 for the large. She made pretty good money at that. Well, and a few regulars.

One night, a drunk jumped on her. He pushed her down and got on top and started trying to pin her arms down. He hit her a couple times. I got a paring knife from the kitchen and stabbed him in the shoulder. This knife was very small but large enough to get his attention. By then others were woke and he seen it was best that he make a quick exit. I was praised for stabbing him.

Leaving the office, carrying an armload of student papers covered in blue ink (I don't like to use red ink; it feels insensitive to me as if it is about authority-over rather than learning-with), I stopped in the college bookstore and picked up another postcard with a Madison scene on it.

Dear DarRen,

I'm still thinking about how resilient your mom is. She is a survivor, as you are. Tell me a story about a good time you all had together. What did you feel? I saw the sparkle in her eyes when she talked about you, so know there are happy shared memories.

By week's end, another letter arrived, this one offering a happy shared memory. Well, and more. Several things were becoming clear to me. DarRen and I were both enjoying the respectful exchange of stories and were seeking to authentically understand the other's life experiences across the prickly barriers that divided us in nearly all possible ways. Mostly, however, I saw us building trust in each other as we walked, through correspondence, toward a new level of openness.

I glanced at the calendar by my desk. October. The picture was of a human form created from building blocks stacked up randomly and the quote, "There is a sun within every person..." Building blocks. Story blocks. Stuck together with shared openness, I think.

Judy,

A happy memory with Mom? There was one Christmas I wanted this inner tube for sledding. It was black (bottom) and yellow (top) with a picture of a grey bobcat or some other big cat in the center. Mom got it for me. It was the only time I can remember I got what I asked for. She took us to the park and we went sledding for the whole afternoon. She had a big four gallon jug full of hot chocolate. She wouldn't take a turn but still, no fights and no funny stuff. Nice time. We tried to make a snow man but we couldn't figure out how to get the second big ball onto the other big ball. We lifted it and it broke a few times. Finally we gave in. But still we had fun.

About this same time, Mom started this thing where ever so often she'd take us out in the winter time and we'd go to what we called the white folks neighborhood to see the Christmas lights. I loved them lights. In our house we were being yelled at to turn off lights or TV's. To not waste money and here these people had lights all over their house, blinking and flashing and figures in the yard that seemed to stay lit all the time. Me and my brother Vonn use to dream and talk about someday we'd see the inside of one of those houses. Not own, but see.

It had been my mother's idea to decorate the front of our three-story Colonial house. I was a young teen. On the jigsaw in his basement workshop, my father had taken two sheets of plywood and cut out life-sized British soldier figures. My mother painted the uniforms and tall plumed hats red. Each held a full-sized candy cane instead of a gun. The wooden soldiers were stored in the garage attic until the appropriate time each year and then brought out to be attached to the wrought-iron pillars by the front door. Windows were outlined with understated white lights and an electric candle was placed in every front-side window—all twelve of them. Maybe there was something about the twelve days of Christmas, but I didn't catch it.

I shook myself back to reality. It wasn't winter here, now. Fall was inching toward us. There were more pages to this letter from DarRen about his relationship with his mom.

. . . I was in Lincoln Hills juvi for selling drugs when I actually felt like Mom loved me. I don't mean the general love, which is what I assumed, but actual love.

This other guy in juvi had a nice watch and really expensive shoes and had a room full of all sorts of snacks and goodies and every week he got a visit from his momma and he rubbed it in. I knew that watch was his pride and joy.

For months my mom had been telling me she was going to visit but always had an excuse why she couldn't make it on a certain day. I was pissed off for not getting my visit this day and there he was bragging. He talked tough but I could smell the softness on him. So I smacked him and took his watch. He told on me and I went to the hole.

Two days later Mom came and, well, segregation in Lincoln Hills was not very good and visits were in the hole. So she had to come down there and smell the stale, musky, piss and shit filled air. There I stood in a belly chain that went around my waist, cuffed both hands and a chain went from my hands to the leg irons around my ankles. No comb. Those cells are dry cells—no sink or toilet in the cell. So that means I looked a mess. I had been sleeping and was not able to wash my face or brush my teeth.

She seen me and burst into tears and as she hugged me she said she was sorry and told me she loved me. At times my mom would kiss us on the lips. It was a way to tell how things were. If the bills were paid and she had money and nobody was bleeding or in jail, we could get a kiss on the lips.

The first time I actually remember getting that sort of kiss though was in that Lincoln Hills seg. She kissed me on the lips with true love. It freaked me out when she kissed me like that, not because it was a bad kiss. I just was not ready for it.

That was both great and horrible. I didn't know what to do with that so I got into more trouble. It's not fair to say that's why I got into trouble, but it weighed on me and it added to things.

I was fifteen.

My mother doesn't know what all has happened to me so I can't tell her the whole story without telling the abuse part. She is in a bubble. Either she knows and never said anything or she did not know. Part of why I didn't tell her is shame and part of it is that I believe her heart has been broken enough. Every time she's ever expressed regret or sorrow, I chase it away. It does no good for her to feel that way.

The reality of where we were demanded that we learn to survive. Then, I didn't think she loved me. Now, I know she does. She's all I have really. When no one else has been there, she has, in her way. I had to come to understand that. She could not be who I wanted her to be. She was her own person and her way of expressing herself is unique to her. I also see that she made me tough mentally and physically. She is strong and she is loyal and do what she needs to to survive. I am my mother's son. I call home every Sunday. My mom is still battling her addiction; she's been good. So I cherish the time and do my best to squeeze the most love out of every moment. I really wanted that hug as a child and teen. And I still feel that way now.

I saw a new tension in DarRen's and my writing. I had begun to ask how he *felt* about the experiences he had lived through. He flared at that. I could see his frustration in the underlined words and wide spaces.

. . . I could not afford to show emotional reactions when I was growing up. Anger was the only acceptable one. But I did not need to express emotion to fight, for example. I could be cool as can be and then attack without warning. I don't think you really grasp how insane we were, the level of hood that was in us does not go away on its own. It is like a demon; it has to be forced out. The way of the hood.

We agreed to include emotion in the storytelling when it made sense but I learned I was not any better at that than he was. Too many years of taking emotions and submerging them—albeit for different reasons. His was about protecting the family, I think. Mine? Some sort of British restraint.

Dear DarRen,

I get that part about always wanting a hug. My mother was proper and always socially correct. Not a hugger. She was smart. She was beautiful, too, like your mom. My mother loved dogs and called them all George. That was both odd and problematic, since her father's name was George and her estranged brother-in-law's name was the same. She had started medical school in order to marry a doctor, saying it was possible to fall in love with many different men so why not fall for one who was going to be successful. That worked for her to a point and she had some very good years and some very good dogs. I'll tell you one story that sums up much about her.

Toward the end, Alzheimers clogged her brain and she was living in the memory impairment wing of the Evanston Presbyterian Home, locked away from the chandeliers and formal dining rooms she had always coveted. She no longer spoke. She stopped speaking when she confused the word hospice with hostage and a knowing look flashed across her face quick as a hummingbird darting between flowers.

My siblings and I were with her one day when aides came in to change the bedding. With difficulty she was helped into a chair as we three watched. The bed was stripped, new sheets brought in, and then the staff was called away. Mom gestured that we should make up the bed so she could lie down. We were eager to have something to do in that room crowded with the last riches of her life, including the tiny pirates' treasure chest my father had made for her in the prison woodworking shop.

We spread the bottom sheet on the bed. She stopped us and gestured toward the corners of the sheets, pointing and shaking her head. Oh. Hospital corners. She wanted the sheet to be properly placed on the bed. The right way. We untucked the bottom sheet and redid it with the corners folded just so. And then the same with the top sheet. We were giggling at her demands, playful puppies nudging each other.

She watched us, sitting regally in her white cotton eyelet robe. We folded down the top sheet, fluffed up pillows, and moved to help her get back in bed. She shook her head, half-frowning, half-smiling at our antics. She gestured again, holding one hand high with fingers pinched before pretending to drop something from her hand. We paused. Then figured it out. She wanted us to drop a penny on the sheets to see if it would bounce, ensuring they were perfectly tight on the bed. She was teasing us.

Thinking about my mother and all she kept secret took me back to the original purpose of this journey into prisons, where I met DarRen. I had gone to prison to better understand my father's incarceration, his work as a medical researcher, and how these events might have contributed to his alcoholic end.

On my sixteenth birthday, my father sat me down at the writing desk in the dining room where I could smell paste from the new, trendy, hot-pink burlap wallpaper that gave definition to crisp, chalk-white lace curtains at each window. He told me—his oldest child—the secret of his incarceration for armed robbery. At the time, I felt nothing, distracted by adolescent introspection.

Now I wanted to know more about my father's story. DarRen and I were still waiting to hear from the prison about being able to visit face to face after waiting another six-month interval, but our letter writing was helping me understand how youthful experience could frame later life decisions. It seems obvious, I admit.

I wanted to learn the back-story of my father's crime. After wrangling an invitation from my father's last living sibling, I went to Expedia.com and booked a flight to Seattle to coincide with the college fall break.

I had questions.

CHAPTER 7

The Gang's All Here

ORD to SEA. E-ticket confirmed. Carry-on only. Chocolate in my pack, in case of emergencies. Someday a domestic airline will come up with the novel idea to have gourmet food as part of its flights and I'll probably scrape off Hollandaise sauce then, too. My father's sister would host me in Seattle. I knew this would involve meeting many relatives. Strangers. My father was the one who had slithered away from his family after the viperous newspaper headlines on his crime, so I'm the stranger, the other, to that cohesive crowd.

Before leaving Madison, I picked up two letters and after the plane circled over the lakes and leveled off above the clouds, I apprehensively opened the first, stamped with the prison warden's return address. Having waited the required six months, DarRen and I had reapplied for visitation rights. This time, I had even sent the warden an accompanying letter explaining that I was not a felon, had no misdemeanors on my record, and was a stable community member who had been teaching for nearly twenty years. I explained that DarRen and I had had two op-eds published nationally and a Letter to the Editor in the local daily newspaper. All focused on mental illness and incarceration. I had orchestrated a prison art show that included DarRen's work. And I was sorry about those phone calls DarRen made and I accepted; it wouldn't happen again. The warden wrote, *Ms. Adrian's past actions as a volunteer have demonstrated her willingness to circumvent policies and procedures of. . . Institution. I am responsible for the safety and security of staff, inmates, and the public. . . apply for reconsideration in six months.*

As I said earlier, I had had no opinions about the Department of Corrections before entering prisons as a volunteer. Now I was feeling like a child being disapprovingly sent to her room. What I found strange was that no one had ever asked me about my part in writing the original letters or whether I had understood the seriousness of those so-called *enterprising* violations. Being a teacher, it was very clear to me that nothing that was happening was about teaching or learning or rehabilitation. It was about punishment. . . and power.

The other letter was more interesting. DarRen continued our writing theme on relationships. The gang, his gang.

Dear Judy,

Even as a kid I drifted from one extreme to the other. In the nearby field, my brother Vonn and I often played as Native Americans—outlaws fighting for justice. One day my mother had taken and dropped us off at the library and I seen this book, black and white with all kinds of squiggly lines on it and other designs. I picked it up and it was about Shaka Zulu, strong black African warrior.

Who knew?

We were no longer Native Americans in the forest; we were African warriors protecting the village.

Boys, we are wired different than girls. I think that all boys, black and white, reach this point when they have the same desire—the desire to be the warrior, the protector, the hunter awakens. When I was about thirteen or so, this desire to do something, to accomplish something, came. I got the tattoo on my chest. I had joined the group and I had developed this desire to please my mother so I combined the two things that were important to me. The guy who was one of the group leaders

"Shaka Zulu, strong black African warrior"

came to the apartment and told my mom I was no longer her son (only), I was now...

DarRen left out the specific terms here. As he had done with his family, he was protecting the gang, I realized. That was fine with me. There were things about gang involvement I didn't want to know, in detail anyway. At least initially the gang had evidently offered DarRen the caring family he was seeking.

. . . He (the gang leader) liked that I had heart. There are nine symbols that represent various aspects of the group. My brother, Vonn got the tattoo first. He got the same symbol I did but his was on his back and smaller and he didn't get mom's name. He said it hurt too much. So, of course, to show my courage I told

the guy doing it to make mine thick and make it big and so he did. No gun, just a needle with a piece of thread around it.

What people don't realize is it's not about the allure of guns and drugs in most cases that draws people to the gangs. For me, at least, it was the positive message about being a family, about taking care of one another and having someone care for and love us and protect us. The organization I use to be a part of was called Growth and Development; it use to be Gangster (master or leader) Disciple (humble enough to follow). Our literature taught us that we were suppose to take care of our own people, not just the gang members but the neighborhood. We were suppose to be our own government, police, and teachers of morals and family.

Nothing in there supports violence, drugs or disrespect. We thought these people were our core family members and the hood was our distant cousins. I wanted a family. I wanted kids to be safe. I liked the idea of protecting and providing although I did not have them words. And the other part—the occasional violence—was okay with me as well. To protect the family. Things like Vonn and I did were what we were suppose to do; things like giving money to the Boys and Girls Club to get lunch meat, bread and chips to give them kids something to eat. (Some never got to eat because we were getting all their parents' money, selling them drugs as part of the gang.) Now, I've discovered I really like helping people, teaching them not to deal with each other wickedly.

Tensions rose and a gang war was started because many of us branched off and created Deuce Ace Family. In the fall of '92 and the summer of '93, I lost sixteen of my homeboys in a war. They lost many as well, in four different cities. They said we were spreading poison. We figured out we were being used and they were getting rich. At first it seemed like we had enough to fight; money is the backbone of war. You need it to win. We had little.

The flight attendant offered two packages of gourmet cookies and a coffee. I saved my chocolate.

Clouds whipped past below the plane. Fast. Yes, DarRen was in a hurry to grow up even from his earliest days, as his mom had told me. Was that about him or about survival? It was clear he dealt with "adult themes" as a youth. Me at age thirteen? I still had some girlhood toys with me, like my stuffed lion. No dolls though. My mother grounded me for taking the head off of the one special doll I had been given. I wanted to see how the doll's eyes worked, opening and closing like that. So I was dissecting a doll while DarRen was driving his first car. One of us was precocious.

. . . I got my first car then too—a Chevrolet. I paid $80 bucks for it and Vonn went half. We had it for about a week. A brother took it from us. He asked to borrow it and we said, "No." He took it anyway and then he claim to have left it when the police got behind him. But later I seen someone else driving it and found out he lost it in a dice game. Later that same year I got a '81 Toyota Tercel (automatic) two-door with the hatch back. I had that for about six months. The brain box went out and it would cost about $600 to get it fixed. I only paid six for the car. Then I had a Olds Cutlass Supreme 84 or it may have been a 88, four-door. And then I had this green Delta 88 (four-door) with gold trim. I had the grill and the bumper painted gold also. The guy I bought the car from had had Rent a Dad air brushed across the back window. Instead of having it removed, I put my pager number up there.

Cute story. In another world and time, I might well have called that pager number just to see what would happen. An ex-friend once told me she could no longer be friends with me because I made her too nervous, taking risks she wouldn't take. I was so surprised at that. I don't think of myself as a risk-taker at all. I'd never jump out of an airplane, for example.

I let my eyes rest on the front eastern edge of the Rocky Mountains—the "Front Edge" to those of us who live *in the land between the mountains,* as I once heard a Californian condescendingly describe the Midwest. I wasn't shocked that DarRen had been a gang member. It was clear to me that the gang affiliation had hurt him as a boy. A very young boy. From what I was learning, he had been fairly high up in the organization so that the "occasional violence" he wrote of was likely more than I knew. Who was hurt? In what ways? For what reasons? What had he learned from the experiences? How was he changed by them? As always, I had questions to both ask and ponder, but I did not push further on this sensitive topic.

At the very moment he was searching for a family to hold him, the gang was there to offer that. This did not happen accidentally; gangs saw the vulnerability, or perhaps the pain, in these brave young boys who wanted to take care of their families and homes, only to discover that doing so led to more destruction of families and themselves as young men. DarRen wrote about his desire to escape the gang. The bloom had faded for him.

> . . . *We learned very quickly that we were being used by the gang and we were not benefitting from our actions which caused us to branch off. I went over to a friend's house; he had a son about five or so. He called him. The son came.*
>
> *He said, "Tell the creed." and the son said it word for word, about 800 words. He knew all sorts of stuff. It broke my heart. He was being robbed of his chance to be more than what we were. I left. There's nothing. Nothing cool or acceptable about children being anything other than beautiful, smiling, laughing, happy, world-exploring little people.*
>
> *We had met a man from California who had a drug connection. At this time I found out that my mother was tweeking—losing her battle with drugs (crack cocaine). The apartment was in very poor shape. So this new venture seemed to be the answer. We decided the best thing was to move from Lake County (Waukegan) to Kenosha because there was more*

*daily going from the shoulders (fighting) in Kenosha but more
gun play in Waukegan. We could turn a faster, safer profit in
Kenosha. And then move to Cali.*

I put both the warden's and DarRen's envelopes back in my pack,
ignoring the chocolate again. I'd write DarRen later after meeting
with my Seattle family; he would have gotten the same letter from
the warden, so no surprise there. Happily, the man next to me on the
plane was not a talker; I could continue reading uninterrupted as I
snuggled into my window seat corner.

The other pages I had brought for in-flight reading were yellowed.
After my mother's death, I had become the keeper of family papers.
Folded in a long-sealed envelope, I had found my father's forty-
some-year-old prison journal. I brought it along to re-read as I
moved toward his family and their memories of my parents' society
wedding that none of them had attended, because it never happened.
As I began reading my father's journal, on the heels of DarRen's letter,
I immediately saw the link in being part of a gang. Being one of the
boys. My father's prison journal began.

*I was sent down to the outfitting room, given clothes and then
stripped, showered, and stepped out as Convict 12027. They gave
me three blankets, sheets, pillow slip, tooth brush, comb, and
regulations, and showed me to my cell. It is hardly the bridal
suite... About 9' x 6', a cot, small table, toilet and basin. Come to
find out, I got off to a very bad start because the Superintendent
had showed my dad and brother, Wel, around before I got here.
Then they ate in the Officer's Quarters and of course, the news
spread immediately, everyone thinking Wel was me. That's
straightened out, and I'm part of the gang now.*

The privilege of having a well-connected, wealthy father who could
visit the prison before his son was sent there put my dad in a unique
place. He both wanted to be one of the guys—part of the gang—and
he wanted to be separate.

Newspaper headlines on my father's robbery

. . . I am not an inmate. I pity them. I don't regard myself in any way as superior mentally, socially, or in any other way (except the superficial education), but I don't want their concepts pounded into me.

My father had been at the mid-point in medical school when he committed the armed robbery on the eve of his wedding. That plus the wealthy family was headline fodder for the *Seattle Times* newspaper. Had my father even been aware of the newspaper headlines?

I read on in his journal.

. . . I made 100% on my I.Q. test—that is perfect, for here. 143. She said the highest ever before was 121—but I feel no pride in that—rather shame that I'm not using that I.Q. in better channels. But that will come. The test was the original Alpha Army Exam. My I.Q. grade has gotten around—I'm either Brains or Doc—but guards and trustees are still doing their best to help me.

He was deeply unimpressed, even mocking, of the medical care offered in the prison.

> ... *We fish were herded over to the hospital for physicals, which are merely serological, and weight, height, etc. The doc is a quack—using big words which meant nothing, to impress us—and not even enough technique to prevent hematomas on each of us.*
>
> *Later, the would-be Doc came by again and he looked so damn funny. He had all white on, a full-length dissecting gown and rubber gloves, white mask, etc. Boy was he decked out. He stopped and asked me if I'd seen a new man—a soldier—he had a bottle for a urine sample. So I said, "Say Doc, what tests do you run?" He said, very mysteriously, "Oh, everything: sugar, albumen, creatine, etc."*
>
> *So, knowing he was lying and feeling mean from sitting all day, I asked, "How much creatine do you find?" I was very innocent. He walked right in. I questioned him on his procedure, how long he autoclaved it, etc., as if I hadn't done several hundred of these tests last summer. He began to squirm and finally admitted he didn't run them. I felt sorry and we had a laugh over it. Anything to pass the time.*

As my father's writing continued, it was clear he was fighting depression.

> ... *A guy would be sunk if he ever really got sick in here. So many (99%) of these inmates suffer severely from deficient disease of all descriptions—hives, acne, rashes and itching—it's a mess. They claim a year in here will ruin the best set of teeth and head of hair. I believe it, and would add disposition, digestion, and sense of humor.*

And not all the guards honored my father's *privileged* status. I could see a bit of his wry sense of humor shine through, though.

. . . At noon today, we had horse meat. Actually—and I couldn't make it. So the guard made me sit there and eat the whole thing. It was cold and half raw, and even though I got down enough to get out, I didn't keep it down. Never will be able to look a horse in the face again. I got the saddle and stirrups. Oiy.

Addressing the journal to my mother, he continued but couldn't hide the growing sadness.

. . . About 6" of snow fell which is plenty to keep us inside the rest of the week. The melting snow and darkness added to a general depression in here which everyone obviously felt. Tempers are getting short and I've seen two fights today and "mute" evidences of several more. So far I've kept clear but I can't promise to always. I will try to, but there are times when one must, and even though I know you wouldn't approve, I may have to. Don't know if you'd understand that. If I walked away from some remark, I'd have to fight the next day, while if I stop it immediately, I'll have fewer. Sometimes I think they see me as meek because of my upbringing, which translates into weak. I don't want to—it's very childish the things they argue over, but not to them. I'm getting so very tired of this filth and crudeness and swaggering attitude. You could never understand the mental strain of this environment. Those who go into segregation—the dark, damp, sewer-like hole— living on bread and water, come out more animals than men. A criminal is born. It's easy enough to say snap out of it and forget the outside and do "easy time," but it's as tough a job as I've ever undertaken. It's so hard it makes everything else I've ever done seem simple in comparison. If I can—and I will come through this—life will be simple—guess I'm a baby.

As I continued reading, I saw my father's growing compassion. Barriers were breaking down and he became more open to showing his care for others. During his time behind bars, he moved from focus on his own pain to that of his fellow prisoners. Was it this compassion—later muffled by *professionalism*—that eventually led to his alcoholic decline when his job took him back into prisons, in a new role, as a medical researcher?

. . . Something pathetic happened—I had just come back from our twice weekly Glee Club practice and stopped by to say hello to Shorty next door. He's a little fellow—five foot—that is in on a phony beef. He's been doing tough time today. He has no folks, no friends, no money, and his wife just divorced him and took their baby. And he overdrew his account <u>three</u> dollars. We started talking and he broke down and cried like a baby—gosh I felt sorry for him. We talked for about ½ hour and finally I encouraged him a little. I'm going to help him if I possibly can. He needs a friend very badly. I have decided a friend is the most valuable thing in the world.

And another.

. . . A strange thing happened tonight. Jack, who is the fellow in charge of the fish tank and who has made things bearable up here for me by being friendly and helpful, suddenly fell, paralyzed from the hips down. My neurology is sadly deficient but I never even heard of such a thing—no feeling or movement. Seems like he was injured some time ago in the small of his back and at that time was paralyzed and blind for a period. Why it should come back with apparently no reason is puzzling. Gosh I feel for him. It's bad enough to just be here without having that added worry. He, of course, is afraid it's permanent this time—and it may be, but he'll never hear that from me.

In the three months he was incarcerated, my father's prison journal showed this changing man. His father and his attorney Frounde met with Washington state Governor Langlis more than once trying to get my dad out of prison, even though he had clearly committed the crime he was locked up for.

. . . I feel sort of rotten. Matter of fact, I feel like hell—mentally and physically. Dad and Frounde are seeing Langlis next week for the added weight (actually accommodation) of his recommendation. Not much has been happening anyway— guess this is what they call doing time. One catches one's self just kind of existing—not thinking or conscious of anything. That is what I have to guard against because you can see that blank look in everyone's eyes—just blank.

This is a Reformatory alright, but their only concern is to reform what good points you may have into a vicious, sneering contempt of everything lawful. Not me, understand. I'm just watching a show and not even getting into the mood of it, but I pity some of these fellows—what a little firm, kindly help would do for them! Jeepers, I'm a radical.

I read that governors were *giving away clemency like candy* during World War II. My father was one of the recipients; being part of his family's "gang" had served him well. Had that not happened, I'd not have been born. Had he not been released early, who would he have become? After serving three months of his fifteen-year sentence, he was sent to the military. And seven years later, his powerful father's untiring efforts earned my father a governor's pardon. A pardon for a crime he had committed.

DarRen later wrote, *These days, it would end a governor's career to sign anything that has to do with allowing a prisoner to serve three months on fifteen years.*

The wheels of the plane touched down with a jolt. Seattle sunshine filled the window as we taxied in. I was to take a cab to my father's sister's home. She was the youngest of the eight children in that blended family. Had I ever met her before? I couldn't remember.

CHAPTER 8

The Family
Was Never the Same

Day two of my Seattle visit. I used the desk in Aunt Bunny's guest bedroom—where my cousins had probably studied—to write DarRen about this journey. I was spending time with two relatives. My father's youngest sister and the wife of one of his brothers, the remaining members of his generation.

Dear DarRen,

My Seattle relatives are taking extra good care of me and seem eager to share the secret family stories. When I first contacted Aunt Bunny, I was clear about why I was coming. I wanted to hear more of my father's story. I sensed no reluctance on her part. Maybe these were stories that had too long been hidden and there was now a need to tell. There may be something about being the eldest generation in a family that I do not understand. Something about ensuring the legacy will be authentically told.

I have also spent some hours in the city's glimmering glass library looking at microfiche articles from the Seattle Times. *(Microfiche makes me nauseous or would that be the content I'm reading?) "Seattle Capitalist's Son Admits Holdup." "Rodney*

79

Gwinn Wedding Off Indefinitely." "Gwinn Gets Fifteen Years Despite Leniency Plea." "Gwinn Charge is Decreased." There was one that must have been agonizing to my mother and her family, "Fiancée Hides From Camera." That was the caption under a front-page photo of my mother (gracefully) holding her long coat over her face as she and my father's father, Gardner, left the King County Jail on what would have been the eve of her wedding.

I remember, toward the end of my mother's life, when we were moving her into the memory-impaired wing of the Presbyterian Home, she said we could take anything left in her apartment. My sister pointed to the engraved wooden chest, lined with royal purple velvet that held the formal silverware and said, "I'd like to have that." Mom bellowed, "You cannot have that!" We collectively cowered, not anticipating the response. Later, I learned that that sterling silver setting for twelve had been the gift my mother's parents had gotten for her wedding, the wedding that was not reported on the society pages of the Seattle Times, *but happened later near a Texas military base, in a Justice of the Peace's office. My parents left foot prints in the red dust. You know, I wonder what became of that silver and I wonder why we were never told these stories. Why didn't we know that the silver represented love, and loss?*

So many family stories—and secrets. Your friend, Judy

My favorite space in Aunt Bunny's house was the family room. From there, I could walk onto the deck overlooking Seattle below and Puget Sound and Bainbridge Island in the distance. To the right was Lake Union where my mother's family had lived. To the east, behind the hill, Lake Forest Park where my father and this sister had grown up. Here lay my biological roots.

I was relieved when breakfast was finished, the TV was silenced and Fox News disappeared. In her demure, yet forceful way, Aunt Bunny began to tell me the family stories. She needed to tell as much as I needed to hear, although it felt as if I had arrived in the middle of Act Two, having missed the opening scenes. The story began bluntly with, "As the second oldest of eight, your dad was one of the children who was not abused by our father. He was one of the blonds." Aunt Bunny continued telling her and my father's story as I tape-recorded her words.

The Gwinn family name was very strong, but not well-loved. That was why the robbery was a major deal. When anything happened to the family, we would say, "Crap, that's going to be the headlines tomorrow." The family was Gwinn Construction, proud and confident. In very high places in Seattle society. Gardner, your grandfather, was quite a shrewd man, having built hundreds of Seattle homes and downtown buildings, including the 350-room Benjamin Franklin Hotel, where he made his sons work. Rodney, your dad, was an elevator operator.

Gardner, had to have grapefruit every morning, therefore, we ALL had grapefruit every morning. Our live-in maid, Francis Walkup, lined up ten half-grapefruits and cut the sections in each.

At dinner, we stood behind our chairs until everyone was at the table and after dinner, all eight of us went to the living room to read the Bible aloud.

"Weldon, Rodney, Ralph, Stanley, Nobby, Dorothy, Bunny, Bill. . . keep them safe throughout the night. Now I lay me down to sleep." That was the prayer we said every night as we knelt by our bedsides. The boys would come to the nursery to pray with us before they went to the sleeping porch. It was the routine. We were together all the time.

Aunt Bunny and I poured another Seattle's Best coffee and she continued with the family story.

. . . The family started the Lake Forest Presbyterian Church. I remember when we first filed in to the pew, in order. By the time they got to me and Bill, the youngest, people were laughing. Your grandfather Gardner's proud moment was his kids all in a

row, perfect, the way they were supposed to be. We attended five separate church events every Sunday. After church, we were not allowed to play tennis on the family court, only croquet on the lawn and basketball at the end of the court.

The blondes (like me) won out, except for Stan. Dad was mean to Stan. He was mean to Nobby. He was exceedingly mean to Bill, saying, "Weak Willie, Weak Willie. Cry for me." And Ralph, he blamed him for his first wife's death following childbirth. He was mean to Dorothy, though he didn't hit her. Just the boys. If they didn't do something right, they would get hit or kicked. He would walk past and give us all a slap on the leg for no reason. He called it a love tap, but it wasn't. One time, he was hitting mother and pushed her into the closet. We were yelling at him to stop. Today you would definitely call your grandfather abusive, physically and psychologically. No one argued with him. We didn't talk back. Gardner may have been bi-polar but he was never diagnosed. That wasn't even in the medical books then, I don't think. Even if there had been medication for it, he probably wouldn't have taken it. Because he was perfect.

Your dad took piano lessons from the best teacher in Seattle. He was a natural. Mother had to pay for it out of her allowance (that covered everything like clothes and food). It was never enough. We would go to Rhodes Department Store, three of us at a time, and buy shoes for the year. And then a month or two later, another group would go when she had more money saved up. She paid for the maid out of that, too.

The boys would go to the local store and steal cigarettes. Those rascal Gwinns. One time there was a kid who beat up on one of the younger brothers. Wel and Rod came out, got him and threw him in the nettles.

But then your dad came home with this gal that smoked and drank. Gardner was opposed to him marrying your mother. She didn't meet the family model. Not demure. Not religious. Not society.

The sharing of secret stories was exhilarating and exhausting. I was trying to make sense of how it was that when the sons of a rich man stole, they were rascals. What had it meant to my father being one of the children who wasn't abused, knowing that others were? No one stood up to his father, Gardner.

Aunt Bunny took me to The Club for lunch, stopping briefly to mail my letter to DarRen en route. We sat on the veranda near feathery ferns overlooking the ninth hole. Three men relaxed next to us with pastel polo shirts unbuttoned at the neck showing an appropriate amount of chest hair. Perfectly braised salmon on crisp fresh greens with a drizzle of lemon. Lime sherbet with a single raspberry. Wine, too. Why not? And then the short drive to another family member's home where there were many photos of my dad, a life I'd never seen. A life revealed.

At that relative's home, I explained some about DarRen's and my writing project. "How do you know him? What was his crime? What was his sentence?" As I answered these questions, I could see fear in their faces. Without even knowing DarRen, they were afraid of him, afraid of what he represented to them. Had they been afraid of my father during his incarceration or was that not an issue because they knew the person beyond the crime?

On the way back from The Club, we skirted the Home Depot store, where groups of brown-skinned workers waited for someone to hire them for the day.

"We would never hire these men. You can't be too careful," Aunt Bunny confided.

Back home, we sat on the back deck, lazy in the Seattle sun. There were more answers and questions. Aunt Bunny kindly continued with the stories about my father, Rodney, and the seven other siblings, as I again recorded her comments.

. . . After the crime, why did Gardner stand up for your father to get him out of prison? To publicly distance from the crime, the best thing was to get him out of it, right? That would explain seven years of working toward the Governor's pardon. It was

against your dad, but it wasn't really against him. It was against Gardner Gwinn and his proud moment.

Even at that, though, I don't think he would have stood up for the younger boys. Ralph? Stan? He would have left them there. Nobby? Probably a little bit. Bill? Nothing. I don't know what he would have done to the others, but it wouldn't have been kind.

The oldest child, Wel, didn't believe his adored brother had committed the robbery. When you've known somebody that long and you love him, you think the people who are saying things about him are crazy.

Oh, yes, this was a major family crisis. Nobody knew about it ahead of time, within the family that is. All of a sudden someone opens the gates and comes into the yard. The gates were <u>always</u> closed after Gardner got home. . . closed immediately. The police came through the gates in plain clothes, no uniforms.

"Is Rodney Gwinn here?"

"He did what?"

It was so shocking; something your mind, body and soul never forgets. We missed dinner; were all told to go to our rooms. I don't remember if he was arrested then—if they took him away. I mean because of who he was. He wasn't some crook or some bad person. He was just a stupid kid who did a stupid, stupid thing. For as smart as he was, I just don't know how your dad thought he could pull that off. He was desperate, he was going to get married, he needed money. But you don't rob the store you work for!

Every Saturday night, the family listened to Gang Busters*, a radio show about who was being caught for their crimes. It came on with shrill police whistles, sirens wailing, machine-gun fire, screeching tires and even convicts marching in cadence. From that show, we were kind of aware of what happened to people when they did something bad. They were put in jail.*

We kids were so embarrassed. It was all over the newspapers. School was the hardest. I had just started high school. Here I was, this little blonde girl, and her brother had done this, this robbery. People saying, "That is who she is... her brother screwed up didn't he?" It was finger-pointing time.

I was weary after our dinner together that night. The room I was staying in overlooked the Seattle neighbor's garden, down the sharp hill. All was so beautiful and the evening sunset so compelling, I decided to pull the curtains and open the window so the Pacific air would flow into my room. Shortly, there was a knock on my door.

"Did you open the window?"

"Yes."

"We wanted to check because opening a window sets off the silent burglar alarm system."

"Oh, I didn't know. I'll close it right away."

"Thanks."

"Good night."

The next morning, breakfast. Aunt Bunny was a creative cook, I was learning. Another family member joined us, a woman who had married into the Gwinn family. Fox News was again turned off and we all sat around the kitchen table with more coffee. Additional stories. More tape recording. More questions. Aunt Bunny and I listened as her in-law added her personal experiences about my father's crime story.

"The family is awesome so don't let what one child has done influence you when you date his brother." That is what I was told. My college sociology professor used your father's case, which continued to be Seattle Times' *headlines, because of the wealthy family. The professor said your father deserved the sentence that he got, prison-wise, but because of the family wealth, he was able to get out sooner. He talked about how your grandfather, Gardner, intervened. Not that it was that big of a crime, for heaven's sakes. We just thought your dad had flipped his wig when he committed the robbery.*

Armed robbery, I was thinking. Not that big of a crime? From my time inside prisons, I knew anything involving guns was a serious offense. People could get hurt, even killed, in the stress of the moment. Interesting to me how my relatives were separating the crime from the man—what my father did from who he was. They knew him as a human and figured he was simply not himself when he did the robbery. And yet, with DarRen, their initial questions reflected fear. Who was he? What was his crime? I knew that it violated prison etiquette to ask someone about their crime. Even inside, the focus was most often on the human being in the present moment, not what he or she had done in the past.

Aunt Bunny again took over the storytelling.

. . . Your grandfather Gardner contacted legislators, the Governor, and important people in the city trying to get your dad released. He even got the business that was robbed to write a letter of support. The pressure continued for seven years until the Governor's pardon came. How could they pardon? He did the crime. He did it. He was wrong. Maybe he thought he shouldn't be punished in the same way because he was a Gwinn. But you won't find anything in the family history about trying to get somebody out of prison. We did not talk about where your dad was during the three months he was away, but of course we knew what was going on because it was all over the papers. And no one in the family ever talked about it afterwards; we never even told our children, your cousins. All they knew was that your dad was a doctor and vice president in two pharmaceutical companies. That was it. We just figured that was on a need-to-know basis and they didn't need to know. If they found out a thousand years later, that's alright.

But your dad fell apart after that. Away from the church; away from the family; away from everything. I think he felt that he disgraced himself, but he didn't want to be around anyone else who felt that same way. The family was never the same.

Where your dad was wrong—and that is hard to say because he was pretty good—is that he really owed the family an apology. He did not realize what he put us through and how embarrassing it was. Sometimes the most brilliant minds don't think the rules apply to them. Where there are lives without limits, rules are broken and people get hurt.

As Aunt Bunny's SUV pulled up to the airport curb, I could see lines inside the terminal and was again glad I travel light, so wouldn't need to wait to check a bag. I paused to hug my Seattle family goodbye and thank them for their graciousness in hosting me and their frankness in telling me Gwinn family anecdotes I could never have learned any other way. What had it meant to hear these stories of my father and see photos of a boy and a life I had known nothing about? Deepened. I think that is what I felt. Nothing in what I had learned changed my feelings for the father I adored. But I understood some of his actions in new ways. Why did we always have to have a lunch of Boston Baked Beans, cottage cheese and canned brown bread after working collectively doing yard work on Sunday mornings? Because his family had always done that (although on Saturdays). Little things, some delightful. Stories I wished he had told me so long ago.

I slept through the gourmet cookies on the flight home, exhausted. And once back in Madison, I stopped by the mailbox. There was a letter from DarRen and a pink slip for an item too large to fit in the box. The large envelope was from the Indeterminate Sentence Review Board in Olympia, Washington. I had sent them a check and a request for a copy of my father's prison records.

My Madison family was interested in the details of my journey; we talked long.

Later, when alone, I opened the Review Board's package. One hundred fifteen pages of records, mug shots and letters. They were in order by date, so the top sheet was the Governor's pardon—Executive Clemency—which erased my father's felony record. After that, letter after letter from my grandfather, Gardner, or initiated by him. Military letters asking that my father be released to enter

Officer's Candidate School. I couldn't put the papers down and ended up reading late into the night.

One letter haunted (and haunts) me. It was carelessly stapled on top of a batch of *Seattle Times* newspaper clippings on my father's crime.

Dear Sirs. Please read these clippings and see if there is any justice unless one has money. My son was sent to Walla Walla prison on circumstantial evidence, for twenty years. Gwinn's parents are wealthy. I had no cash to pay off. Yours Truly, Mrs. W. Howard.

I now knew my father had been a student at the University of Minnesota when he came back to Seattle for his wedding and stole the money, in the middle of the day, from the department store where he had worked the previous summer. He was afraid to ask his father for money for his honeymoon because he was marrying that woman who did not fit the "family profile"—my mother to be. My dad had said the gun used in the robbery was plastic, but that was not in the newspaper reports. At the time of his arrest, sitting there at Gardner's dinner table, he had completed his Master's Degree and three additional years toward an M.D. My father was released into the military after serving three months of his fifteen-year sentence. He completed Officer Candidate School. Drawing on the G.I. Bill, he finished medical school and then spent his career in medical research—much of the research conducted on prisoners.

Dear Judy,

It sounds like your Seattle family liked meeting you. I had a sense you were putting them down for being afraid. Is that right? I have seen enough and heard enough to know that it is healthy to be afraid. You need to remember those are your people; your heritage. They deserve your ras'pect.

CHAPTER 9

Fear Is a Mothafucka; a Person Can do Some Real Spectacular Shit with Fear on Their Side

Alittle-known gem was offered inside the metal cap on my Snapple Tea as I opened the bottle and turned on the computer to write DarRen. "The muzzle of a lion is like a fingerprint—no two lions have the same pattern of whiskers."

The ground was wet with water that had begun its descent as snow. A cold, gray Midwestern Sunday. I pulled the curtains closed and turned on warm indoor lights. No family members objected. With each passing month, I saw the pattern of DarRen's whiskers more clearly. Following my Seattle visit, we had begun writing about big questions. This series of letters focused on fear and I had a growing sense that bleakness lay ahead of us; the stories were deepening.

Dear DarRen,
Thanks for your letter. So you think I judged and disrespected my Seattle relatives because of their fears? Well, I don't think I

did, but I also recognize I do not feel afraid in my world so may have unintentionally criticized them.

I liked your point that on the TV shows, where animals are attacking someone, the person being attacked is never black. You wrote, "Life is dangerous enough where we do not need to go looking for risk. Most of us have seen enough or heard enough to know that it is healthy to be afraid."

I'm smiling reading your description of why inner city blacks are afraid of bugs. "While I was taught about bugs as a kid, the only bug we commonly saw was a cockroach and no one wanted to play with monstrous bugs." And you did laugh at (or at least teased) people like me; "Whites often catch all sorts of unheard of viruses and get bit and tore up by nature because you want to touch and see everything. Where, as blacks, I do not need to touch it; I can see it from here just fine thank you."

What, you asked me, do I think it is that causes my irrational estimation of safety. Is this perhaps an extension of my white privilege that gets me to thinking I don't have to be afraid? I would have to agree that it is partly my white privilege because I get to live in a safe place where forceful crime is rare. And another part of my privilege is life experience. I have never been physically hurt.

So, I turn the question back to you, Mr.-six-foot-three-size-fifteen-feet. Other than bugs, what are you afraid of? What aren't you afraid of?

A week later, I picked up a new letter. I folded the unopened envelope and put it in my pocket, thinking anew about how feeling safe could be a privilege.

I parked but had no burning work responsibilities that morning. The college is walking distance from the free Henry Vilas Zoo and fall warmth had returned as the world turned on its head. Orange leaves were no longer above me; they were now under foot. Often on beautiful days, I walk to the zoo between classes, as I did that day.

The zoo is a good spot for reflection. My favorite area is the carousel. At times, I have purchased a couple of the tokens and given them to kids who might not be able to afford the $1 tab. I feign sadness saying these are extra tokens and I'd hate to see them go to waste. Then I watch their smiles (and feel mine) as they go round and round.

The carousel was now closed for the season. Still I sat nearby.

Dear Judy,

What do I fear and what don't I fear, you ask. It's questions like that that, when I think about them, makes me realize how insane my life has left me.

First, what I am not afraid of. Death. Once I got caught slippin' and an enemy had the ups on me; put a double barrel one-shot to my forehead and told me to get on my knees. I looked him in the eye and told <u>him</u> he was a dead man. I refused. "Shoot me where I stand but I'll never bow to you." I was angry and offended that he would pull a gun on <u>me</u>. Didn't he know who I was? Had he lost his mind? He took a gold necklace I was wearing and then cocked the hammer. I gritted my teeth; my heart was beating wildly but I was ready to die. Even then, as a teen, I knew my life sucked. Secretly I had always wished I didn't do the things I done to squares or people who were afraid; that I had only done it to people like me or worse. I always figured one of these tough guys would end my misery. That's largely why I had no fear. Death seemed to be my only end.

And, yeah, I have had plenty of fear. Someone broke into the apartment and raped my mom. Fear. I held my son for the first time. Fear. He fell in the prison visiting room when he was about three. Fear. When he was eleven, the news said an eleven-year-old Kenosha boy was hit by a car; may be fatal. Fear. His mother's boyfriend had him in the car and someone shot at the boyfriend and knocked out the window. Fear. Being gassed for the first time in prison. Fear. Never getting out of prison. Fear.

It is funny to me the things that inner city kids are culturally afraid of: dogs, rodents, and other animals. A bat flying around the cell hall. Fear. Walking through a field once, I seen a snake. I was terrified and felt my soul leave my body.

Then there was this guy who has a spider, size of my thumb nail. He decides it would be funny to throw it on people. They are laughing as they let it crawl over one another. Now it's my turn. I'm very clear and direct. "I don't play like that; keep it away from me." He's testing me. He pretends to toss it and I don't budge. I let him know if he does I'm gonna kill the spider and put a foot in his ass in that order. He throws it. The spider gets whacked (sleeping with dolphins). The guy? He gets a foot in his ass. When I was asked why, I didn't want to say I was afraid of a itty bitty spider, so I played it cool. "My toes were cold."

I am remembering the time I came across a tarantula in a Kansas forest preserve (that is not an oxymoron, there are trees in Kansas). DarRen was right. I circled and circled it, examining. No sticks to prod it though. Happily I didn't get "bit or tore up" by nature.

. . . I feared my older brothers. I'd let things build up. Everything, inside me. The only way I knew how to deal with anger was to hit someone. There was no talking-it-through in our house. When I got into certain situations I'd become my older brothers. I'd act like them and talk like them. They were always in control (and seemed to have no fear). That was very attractive. So at times I'd be this bright sweet kid and other times I'd be this jerk.

But my brother, Vonn and me, we had each other's backs. No fear. That's when things were really good, when it was just me and him. Once we did fight. We somehow got on the topic of who was the better ball player. Admittedly he was but I always won because I would outwork him and use his energy. I went after every ball as if that ball would be the one that would win the game. I would verbally abuse him.

We were actually getting pretty heated in this argument so he says, "There is a park right there, mothafucka. Bet 20." I, of course, said, "Fuck 20 aggin (aggin is nigga spelled in reverse, from a Scarface song called "Comin agg.") bet what's in yo' pocket." He had about $200. I matched it.

I was a little worried because he is playing with more aggression; I had never seen him put forth that sort of energy. Suddenly, it is pouring, so I say, "Let's sit in the car and wait for the rain to stop." He is up one point. He says if we do that he wins. I say okay and we keep playing. The closer we get to sixteen, the more violent the game is becoming. My shirt is tore. I got a bruise on my cheek that is swollen up a little smaller than a golf ball. He claims it was a accident, he was going for the ball. "With your fist?" I was not sure but if it was a hit, I had to get my lick back. I swung a wild elbow a few plays later and bloody his nose. I got my point first and began celebrating. He said, "Win by two." I am pissed that he would pull that shit on me. I miss the shot. He gets it and scores, so we are tied.

Now I am angry and he knows he has lost. I am a much better player and more accurate shooting when I am angry. I score two easy ones in a row. He takes the money out of his pocket and throws it at me. I was shocked. He got in the car and left me standing there. My everything is wet. My shirt is tore. I am so pissed, steam is coming off me. I knew right then and there that when I caught him he would have no choice but to fight or just let me kick his ass.

I went home, changed, and got on my bike. The sun was out. I rode around looking for him and seen him. I started running toward him and chased him through his girlfriend's house. I hear people screaming and a guy yelling for us to stop. We found the one sport I could never beat him in. Track. That boy was fast. I chased him from 28th Street to 37th Avenue. I finally gave up. He had a advantage. Fear is a mothafucka. A person can do some real spectacular shit with fear on their side.

I was noticing that DarRen's letters were becoming longer and he was more vulnerable in his storytelling. What could I say about the older brothers always being in control? I thought of my grandfather, Gardner, who needed to be in charge at all times. I imagine white knuckles, hanging on. None of us can fully control anything. There are too many factors and I wonder why we try. It was very evident that DarRen had little he could control in prison. The system is set up to ensure that he knows that. But he could control what he told me. He could control the level of risk he was willing to take.

I thought back to the biggest conflict DarRen and I had had. I was helping out a friend, another person working with inmates. She asked that I write an incarcerated man who was having a very bad time and I agreed to do this, for her. When I told DarRen about it he raged, writing, *Don't you realize you keep me grounded and going? It makes a difference to have that support. It is nice when there are general groups or organizations who write prisoners. It's uplifting. But it is inspiring when you have a friend or someone special writing you. In here everything is shared to some degree. It's EXTREMELY important to have someone that is only there for me. No program or other agendas. Just one thing in my life that is about me. The real me, not my file, my rep or my past.*

At the time I had pondered this. Was I being bullied? Was I afraid? Should I be afraid? Should I accede to this? Did I want the responsibility for keeping another human "grounded and going?" Did I understand the significance of writing to another inmate?

Then I made the conscious choice to continue the journey DarRen and I were on: the journey DarRen, *my father* and I were on. I also knew that the "help" I was giving DarRen was two-way. How often in life do we get to authentically share stories and insights and frustrations or fears with another human being? At least in my world, it had been relatively rare and this conversation was extremely important to me as well. Would he hurt me? I mean, would he have hurt me when he was a teenager and I was this older white woman? I don't know about earlier times but I now felt confident that there was no danger. As our letter writing—our epistolary relationship—continued, I felt more and more that DarRen and I were genuinely connected. No fear. We were becoming family.

. . . As I grew, I remember when I noticed that my mother and others feared me. When they showed fear I liked it. Except my mom. I never done anything toward her. I was about eleven when I had had enough of it all and I went to war. I got those who got me. The bigger I got the more dangerous I became. I was not taking it anymore and that become clear to everyone. It was best to leave me be. Win or lose it was going to be serious. I never looked strong. Even now. But I've always had raw strength. When I went to war there were no rules. No cop'n pleas. If you were sleepin', that was your problem. If you were on the toilet takin' a shit, that was your problem. When I attacked, I went until someone stopped me. They had to learn I was no longer willing to accept any punishment. None! I had no problem shedding the blood of the guilty. Stick, bottle, brick, knife or gun. Made no difference. Before I was twelve, I'd seen, knew of or heard about double digit murders; less than twenty but way more than ten. Violence was my world.

We were taught to fear drugs in school. My reality was there was nothing wrong with the way we lived. Drugs fed us. Drugs kept us warm. Drugs was a source of jokes and pleasure. No fear.

As a fourteen-year-old boy fresh out of a bad situation, I shot a pistol. A .25 with a small jerk. It's pop and everything about it let me know it was power. It was a bully stopper. It was a rapist nightmare. No fear. I then got a .357 bulldog and a pair of Glock .45s and a Glock 9mm. I favored, as my tuck, the .380. I had a pocket in my boots and other places where you tuck it. You asked, "Where did I get a glock?" Is that a trick question? On the streets anything can be bought for the right price. This white guy—now I understand the potency of that—would show up ever so often with the trunk of his car laced with guns. Some days it may be SKs or AKs. Rifles of all kinds and of course hand guns .45s, 9s, .357s, .25s and so on. I got that gloc for $200 if I *remember correctly. I very rarely kept them long. Once they were dirty I would bend them with a hammer and toss them into the water (the lake).*

I had asked DarRen to paint "that Lake Michigan shoreline we shared growing up" in my initial letter, my response to his question of whether he could do a painting for me. I was realizing that, although we shared a proximity to the Lake Michigan shore, we did not share similar memories. Maybe that was why he painted a scene from Jamaica rather than "our" lake.

. . . There is fear and then there is panic. One night I was standing outside an apartment with about ten other people. I was leaning against—kind of sitting on a car—and everyone was around us passing a couple of joints in a circle. Puff, puff, pass. I leaned my head back, blew out the smoke. As I did I seen something move in the dark. As I tried to focus my eyes to see who or what it was, I seen a flash. Then another.

The guy standing directly in front of me, his head exploded. It was in slow motion. It took me a few seconds to realize what happened.

I looked for my brother. I panicked. I didn't see him. Everyone scattered. I got on the ground behind the car. I hollered for my brother. The shooting paused. I peeked my head out to see what was going on. I seen them reloading and moving toward the car. I ran. They began firing again. I ran into the hall of this apartment building. I'm out of sight but I'm stuck. The door is locked. Bullets knocked pieces of concrete from the wall. I remember I have a gun. Without looking I stuck my arm out and fired off several shots. I heard other guns being shot. I just froze, saving some bullets. Then just as suddenly as it started, it stopped. Tires squealed. Peeking out I seen no one. I eased out, looking for my brother. Three people were shot. Then I seen Vonn; he seen me and ran to me and told me, "Lie down. Don't

*move." I didn't know what was wrong with him. Turns out I had
blood all over me and pieces of slimy stuff.*

We realized it wasn't my blood; it was brain pieces.

*TwoLips' brain. We had grew up together. I had spent the
night at his house and took baths with him when I was a kid. We
ate Chuck, the goat, together. Death cut words. As sirens neared,
we just left him there. Two others were shot but they'd live. One
would end up walking with a limp and pissing in a zip lock bag
through a tube.*

Early on DarRen asked me what it might do to a person like me to
hear his story. He warned that I could never turn back. He was right.

The lions in the Henry Vilas Zoo roar. Imagine sitting in your
backyard in Madison, Wisconsin, and hearing a lion roar. Likely I
was the only person sitting in that nearly empty zoo with tears in her
eyes thinking about TwoLips, the little boy with lips he hadn't grown
into who loved taking care of a goat in a garage.

DarRen continued in that way I was learning he did. He would
tell me stories like this, without emotion. A defense? Maybe one
human cannot hold too much fear, too much pain, in his mind and
heart without separating story from feelings.

*. . . Today my fears are different. I'm more fearful of danger now
but still ready to respond. I fear the words of that judge coming
true. No matter how hard I try to pull people in closer, I always
seem to push them away. That "someday" is coming. In part,
the judge said, "Someday you'll die in a cold dark prison cell.
You'll have gone nowhere, accomplished nothing, no friends, no
family."*

*I don't think I could do what I've done in the past today. I'm
not sure I could stare down the barrel of a gun and have no fear.
I have a great appreciation for life that I didn't have back when.
At this point I still don't fear death but I'm in no hurry to get to
see the void. Of course, that can always change in a few days.
Some days I almost wish for it. If something happens and I am*

facing death, I would like to think that I'd take it on the chin like a champ.

I wrote a response to the story about TwoLips sitting there in the zoo. Seemed appropriate in some way. A place of cages. That DarRen was in a cage was never far from my mind as I wrote.

Dear DarRen,

Although I hated reading about TwoLips' death, I also thank you for telling me his story. Bittersweet. I was able to picture him taking care of Chuck, in Chuck's happier days (and TwoLips' happier days). I keep wondering if it is good for us to share these stories. Does it ease a burden for you in any way to tell them? Or does it just bring them back to life, back from the quiet compartment where you long locked them away? As I think about this, it is your choice. You have control. So we press on. I can only imagine your brother Vonn's relief when he realized you were not hurt.

Thank you too for more stories about Vonn. You wrote earlier that you and he shared good times at the Lake Michigan shore. My memories of that place were positive, which is why I had asked that you paint it for me. Now I see that we can have gone to the same place and experienced completely different things. That is something our differing life experiences have offered us. I cannot assume that shared experiences or shared places bring forth similar memories. So tell me more about Vonn and what memories you and he shared.

CHAPTER 10

Babyface Vonn the Donn

I was teaching my first on-line course that semester and discovered that the computer hardly ever cooled between responses to student comments and questions. The computer was hot when doorbell rang and I got up to answer.

There stood a handsome man, a small boy about three years old next to him. The sun highlighted their hair. And their shiny black suits. The man smilingly talked a minute about the beauty of the late fall day and the twinkle of the nearby water. I agreed, thinking I wanted to finish typing and head out into the sunshine too, to celebrate the beauty. Then he said, "I am here to talk about Doomsday," as he produced a pamphlet seemingly from nowhere.

I try hard to be open to people's differences and idiosyncrasies. I have a lot of them myself. But walking around on one of the year's most beautiful days talking about Doomsday was just too much. I said, "No. I'm not going to talk about that. But as you walk back, be sure to watch for the family of red foxes that has lived on the marshy side of the street this summer. They are the color of pumpkins and their tails are white tipped. You might catch a glimpse of them; be careful because they are cheerful tricksters." I addressed the comments to the small boy as I pondered my definition of child abuse.

The interruption pulled me away from the on-line class (work could wait), to DarRen's long letter that I discovered was about his relationship with his brother, Vonn—Babyface Vonn the Donn—a relationship I saw as a parallel with the one my father and his adored older brother, Weldon, had had. DarRen had written that Vonn was like a parent.

". . . Vonn was really smart and well spoken. This cat was cool for real; naturally smooth. If he had been bigger, he would not have been able to protect me the way I did him because he was a thinker and he had a conscience; he had an off switch. In some situations, thinking too long could work against you and those were everyday situations for us. Do what you are going to do and do it quick. My first time in County Jail had been for fighting in school. I creamed the security guard who had grabbed Vonn from behind. You could not do that to my brother when I was around."

I turned to DarRen's latest letter.

Dear Judy.

You asked before if Vonn was blood and I told you that he was there for as long as I can remember and we were forbidden to ask and make any distinctions. Those who were not by my mother was assumed to be my father's. Outside the house, I protected Vonn most of the time. He was two years older than me. Everyone always thought I was older because I was taller and bigger and for some reason, not talking much made me seem more mature. My facial hair started sprinkling in early but Vonn was a pretty boy and smooth. Even going into 8th grade, just shine; gloss from the light that was in him. One time we were going to the skating rink and he took my sister's make-up pencil and tried to color his moustache in. I never laughed so hard. He was trying to figure out if the girls knew. Even at nineteen, he had just a few strings of hair on his chin. I would often tease him that we should not have the window down in the car because the wind might blow them few hairs away.

Violence is not where me and Vonn started. We'd always been tight, but violence posed the question of how far will I go *to protect the one I love. Will I stand before the most evil person I have ever known and take whatever for or with this person? For us, it was never really a question. In school, around Sweetest Day and Valentine's Day, the school would sell carnations for like $1.00. Vonn always got a lot of that sort of stuff. They would deliver it to homeroom and one day they called my name. I was shocked. No name on the card, it simply said, "Stay Smooth." I know Vonn sent it though he denied it. (I didn't mind that Vonn got lots of attention; it bothered me that I didn't get it. I didn't like being different.)*

Sitting in the computer chair now ignoring the blue screen, I imagined an especially tall early teen boy, in the Kenosha hood, with two hearing aids, a slight speech impediment, and thick glasses. Was that the definition of a kid others were going to attempt to bully? Yes.

. . . When I first got both hearing aids in about 7th grade, I wore them to school. I was self-conscious and frustrated. I had always known that I was different but I did not know what made me different. I did not know that something was wrong with my hearing even though when there was a crowd and someone was talking or kickin' a rap, others would respond and I had not heard a word. At times I use to think that they were just messing with me. I was always being yelled at to turn the TV down and not sit so close to it. And then I guess subconsciously I learned to watch people's mouths when they talked and watch their actions to figure out what was really going on in school.

When I got the hearing aids, the world suddenly became a lot noisier, but interesting. I kept hearing this sound all day and could not figure out what it was until I witnessed the janitor sweeping with a push broom. I had never heard that before.

On the bus home, the kids were making fun of my new ears and Vonn wasn't on the bus. I don't use words to fight; I'll sit and let it build and then just start punchin'. I use to try to use words but I'd get mad and start stuttering and that just made it worse.

So I would give a warning and if they didn't listen, a fist to the
rib and let people laugh at the deaf boy kicking your ass.

DarRen was a gangly young man (6'1", 102 pounds, and size 15 feet
in middle school). We used to constantly tease my brother, when he
was in middle school, about being shaped like an "L." Feet so big for
his height that he sometimes tripped over them. Reading DarRen's
words, it sounded as if he was coordinated in his early height. As his
mom had said, he grew up fast. I ignored the flickering cursor and
continued reading DarRen's letter.

. . . Vonn used to buy five or six big boxes of butter pecan ice
cream. We would take these brownies and heat them up in the
oven. Hot brownies and cold ice cream. We would smoke and
watch movies. That was our thing. So every chance I have, I get
some ice cream. Butter pecan.

Me and Vonn always hustled to get money and we had this
neighbor that was white who would sit outside with a beer and
fly a kite. The first time I seen this it was like he was holding two
plastic handles with strings on them, not attached to anything.
So Vonn and I went over and asked what he was doing. He
pointed and then I seen it was a kite, high up in the sky, looping
and swooping. He asked us if we wanted to hold it and we did.

After that we wanted a kite. We went to the store. The kite
like he had was over $100. But there was one for $15. We were
collecting bottles and taking them to the store for five cents each.
We crossed the busy street to where all the white folks lived.
We put on our worst clothes—clothes that was meant only for
play or working in the garden—and went to wash windows, cut
grass, or rake leaves. Once we got $20 to clean out a basement.
Not this time though.

So there we sat, me and Vonn, huddled in the bathroom
counting our money so no one could see us. Our brother, Carl,
pushed the door open. "What are you doing?" We tried to hide
the money for fear he would take it but with all the coins that
was hard to do. He seen it so we told him we were counting it.

"For what."

"To buy a kite like the one Mike has."

"How much do you have?" We had enough but feared if we said $15, he would take it. So we showed him the $7 in change. We were sitting on the bills. He gave us $10 and said, "Bring me a bag of hot chips and a cream pop (soda pop)—about $2 worth of stuff. Me and Vonn joked about what sort of sick stuff he would want for the other $8. But we got our kite. Except it was so cheaply made that, before it got off the ground good, the plastic tore and the kite crashed.

DarRen and Vonn were just growing boys eating lots of cold ice cream and wanting to fly kites like other kids (well and smoking "out behind the barn" like my father was doing when he and his brothers stole cigarettes). *Ordinary kids*, I thought. What, or who, had triggered the violence that now surrounded this man? Struggles in middle school are pretty normal; people grow out of them (even commiserate sharing the memories of what an awkward time that is for so many).

. . . Me and Vonn talked about getting a tooth trimmed with silver. Me and him met this guy from New York and he had a tooth trimmed. It really did not stand out but as he talked, your eye would be drawn to it because you would see this flickering of light. We thought that was just the coolest thing that we had ever seen, next to Mike's kite. But this guy was way too slick for his own good. He ended up being sealed under somebody's porch with two bags of kitty litter. We did not do it, but it was the talk around of who did. The guy that did, after he put on the new porch, threw a backyard Bar-B-Que. I now wonder if he got some pleasure from having us walk on/over the guy. Kitty litter absorbs the smell while the body is rottin'. I do not know why he done that because he did not need it. That is for burying somebody in a shallow grave or something where there may

be people around, like in the projects. But under cement, the cement will lock in the smell.

It is funny what you learn in them streets. I look back now and think at the time I should have been learning about kites and shit like that I was learning how to hide a body.

My computer screen went to black, saving itself.

. . . When I first got to junior high school, after gym class, we were told to hit the showers. When I was there and guys began to strip naked, I quickly got up, leaving my clothes and books and when I got in the hall, I threw up. I told Vonn I was all freaked out that I had seen another guy's penis.

"Were you looking?" he asked.

"No. I was sitting on the bench; he was standing at his locker next to me and without warning he just dropped them."

Vonn told me it's like fighting. Before you had your first real fight, you were afraid. But you knew what had to be done and so you done it and found it wasn't so bad. And even if it was bad, you learned to pretend it wasn't. You can only be gay if you like men. If you do, that's cool; you're still My Ace. I might try to get you some pussy but it wouldn't change nothing because you never felt sexual attraction for men.

I knew then that I wasn't gay but I always got nervous and tense in there. But I done what he said. I went in there and done what needed to be done. Many talked and laughed. I used my hearing as a reason to take care of business and get out of there.

Like DarRen, I remember standing in a school line waiting to go into the group shower; I too was in 7th grade. The towel I had was school-issue and way too small to cover my nakedness. It was so very evident how different the girls' rounding female bodies were and mine was on the humdrum end. Like DarRen's experience, I was getting more information than I wanted. I didn't go into the hall and vomit, but I did take the world's fastest showers and got away from the big-breasted banter. Back to DarRen's letter.

... When we lived in Jamaica those months, we played marbles. Some of the kids didn't have marbles and we'd use rocks. When we got back to the states, me and Vonn collected cans and pop bottles to save up some money. I took a bunch of pictures—they didn't believe me that we had a library in our school—pictures of the gym, the park, and snow (someone else's snowman)—a bunch of stuff. We went to the Goodwill and bought shoes (sneakers mostly). There was these fake All Stars you could get for $1.00. We got a couple of big bags of marbles and two soccer balls. Some stuff we brought and the lady at the Goodwill gave us more when we told her why we needed the clothes. We washed them and sent them all over. About $25 worth.

Once I said, "I wish we was back on that island, but just us two." I remember clear as day Vonn said, "Man I ain't staying on no island that ain't got no girls." Girls lit up whenever Vonn came around. He said no girl could get with him that didn't like me too so girls would give me a kiss on the cheek. Girls most definitely must be on our island.

That led into 9th grade. I pretty much had said fuck school. It was a place to sell drugs, meet girls and be out of the house. I did the bare minimum.

Finally me and Vonn left Mom's apartment and moved into an abandoned building. We made it a home. We hooked the lights up with long orange extension cords and used space heaters. We brought furniture from the Goodwill.

We had a system. We would take turns hustling in the cold. There was a building on the corner that had a security lock and when the door was closed it could not be opened from the outside. The person outside would hit the door for however many bags the buyer was suppose to get. Whoever was inside would put that number in a tennis ball and drop it, so they could not complain that they did not get what they paid for. We had learned that hypes (crack heads) can be very foxy. "Take your stuff and leave the money on the ground by the door." Don't give it to us because then if this person was a undercover taking the ball, we would be an accomplice. But without that, all we had did was take money. I was a door man, not quite an elevator operator like your father in the Seattle hotel, but I provided service to the people that wanted that service.

One night a darkened car pulled up and a voice from inside said, "Give me two." I looked. It was Mom. I told Vonn; he paused and then said, "Fuck her." We made the sale.

Two boys. Protecting each other's backs. At the same ages, my sister and I were cruising Sheridan Road in mom's car and these young teens were living in an abandoned apartment building, surviving by selling drugs. Early 1990s—height of the crack epidemic. DarRen had written they were trying to save enough money to move to California where their uncle stayed, away from their Wisconsin lives. Their decisions seemed to be made based on an incomplete picture of possibilities. But what were their choices? They knew they wanted out; DarRen has said it many times. I could feel the courage and depth of the relationship between these brothers and how their focus was on shared survival.

. . . The family moved us to Green Bay thinking a new environment would do us good. Vonn and I did not feel the warmth of a community embracing us.

The one thing I hated most was when people would get around me and begin to use words and phrases that were attributed to the hood. "Wha'up homie?" At the time I felt like they were mocking me. Now I realize it was their way of trying to connect. I felt really isolated. In the mall they'd ask me, "Who do you play for?" Walking down the street, the police would stop me and ask, "Who are you? Where are you from? Where are you going?" They would stop Vonn's car. It had black tinted windows and a loud stereo which we quickly learned to keep turned down. Eventually they took the car and when we got it back, all of our stuff—stereo, speakers, CDs—was gone.

I was angry. I wanted to go home. Vonn said we needed to stay. They followed me in the stores. They took my job because money was missing. I may have eaten a lot and gave extra stuff to Vonn, but I didn't steal any money. I actually liked working. (My mom always said she could trust me around money and other things, but not food.)

I was not doing well in school and felt stupid for the first time. I had no clue what they were talking about. I have never been good at penmanship, grammar or spelling. I knew lots of words and understood what they meant, just could not spell for shit and really did not care much for a period. The teacher said that you had to use a period so the reader would know when to pause and take a breath and my reply was if you need me to tell you when to breathe then you got bigger problems that has nothing to do with grammar.

There I was, one and a half black kids in the school. The black was more white than white folks, but his skin was dark like my dad's. He asked me how I had gotten the waves in my hair. At the time I had what's known as a baldfade, very short on top and it gradually fade into neatly trimmed tapered ends. He not only sounded white, he smelled white. Not saying it was a bad smell, just different.

Lots of bad stuff happened in a short space of time that let me know I was not where I was suppose to be. We simply did not fit in. Vonn and me made the decision to go back to Kenosha. He was nineteen so he could rent us a place. We were gonna take our chances. We loaded up the car with our clothes. We stopped to gas up. I pumped, he paid. A patrol car passed by looking at me hard and watching very closely; even slowing down. Vonn came out; I told him. The cop came again.

Vonn said, "As soon as he turns the corner we're going." We did, only this time he pulled right behind us and flashed the lights. Vonn hit the pedal. We got lost, parked the car and ran on foot. I ran one way, he the other. I hit the corner and was in that tree for about four hours. Vonn got caught and was sent to the Brown County Jail. He sat there for two weeks and was then sent to the Kenosha County Jail. He was given the option to pay the fine or sit forty-five days. He only done something like thirty days and then Kenosha sent him to Lake County Jail. He was there for a couple weeks and they gave him a court date and let him go. It was winter.

I pulled into Kenosha and stopped by my girl's for some lovin'. I ended up staying in Kenosha. We were suppose to get together for a Christmas party. Vonn loved Christmas. I never asked him why. Even when we were really little he had a thing for Christmas. I called him and he said he was cool and that we would pontificate *later to set up everything for our Christmas party which led right into our New Year's Eve blowout. That boy had a way of gathering people. If he said it was a party, people would come. He told me that he had a Christmas tree already; a white one, like the one our granny used to put up.*

My girlfriend's B day is January 16. I had a feeling that day. A very bad feeling. I couldn't reach my mom so left Kenosha and went to Green Bay to check on her. She was fine so I stayed up there with another girl. I was in Green Bay when I got the call. I jumped on the highway and did about eighty-five the whole way. It was three in the morning.

I got to Lake County Hospital to find that Vonn was not there; he was shot in North Chicago so I had to basically go across town. When I got there he was out of surgery and they said that everything looked pretty good and that unless something unexpected happened he would be alright.

DarRen had written me about identifying someone who had been shot. People living on the edge often have multiple names and friends who will protect their identity. He said there was no way to know what name Vonn used when checking into the hospital, if any name was given at all. The family usually did not travel with identification of any sort. It was unlikely that anyone with him would have cooperated and given his name. He gave me an example, "I got pulled over in Chicago, out in the wild hundreds (where many of the murders are happening now). They asked my name and I gave them Eric ___. I did not have a license but did have his school ID with me (well, it looked like a school ID) and had his # by memory. I went to court and rather than pay the fine I sat forty days in Cook County Jail as Eric ___. Another friend was just recently released after doing ten years under a fake name. In Wisconsin, if you give a fake name and are convicted with that name, even if they know the name is fake, they will continue to use it."

. . . Vonn was 5'7", give or take an inch and about a buck sixty. Laying in that bed he looked like he was every bit of 240. I said, "That is not him." His face and body was swollen from the gunshots. He was in the hospital for five days and when the swelling went down some, he looked like Babyface again. When he woke up I was sleeping in the chair next to him. By this time my mother had made it to the hospital. He was talking and everything.

I was asking who had done this. Vonn told me, "Don't worry about that." I agreed to let it drop but he knew I wouldn't so he made me promise to wait until he was better. I said, "Okay." The police had been trying to get a statement from him. He would not tell anyone what had happened.

He asked me to go check on his girlfriend and to get his lucky hat. I got to her house; she was gone. I got the hat and headed back to the hospital.

When I got there Vonn was dead.

My sister said he just died.

"What the fuck you mean he just died!"

I think somehow Vonn knew he was dying and sent me away so he could go.

In any case, he is gone. He sent me to get that stupid hat. What happened to Devonn? We never learned the full story. Babyface Vonn the Donn was murdered by them damn vampires. He was shot eight times. He was 19. There was one person I was sure had something to do with it. When pressed, he said, "I can't tell you." Not, "I don't know anything", but, "I can't. . . "

Vonn's dog, Duke, never liked me. He was a huge Rottweiler mixed with something like St. Bernard. A very big dog. Lots of people were having celebrations of life parties in honor of Vonn. I was the opposite. I did not want to be anywhere that reminded me of him so I avoided the parties or left early. That dog was sitting beside me somewhere and someone snapped a picture. This guy was talking about how much he liked the dog and I gave it to him. A lot of that time is not very sharp. I cannot even tell you what that guy looked like. I was looking for trouble that night and even thought of killing myself. Several times I put the gun to my head but I just could not do that.

When I packed Vonn's stuff, all I kept was that stupid cap. I stuffed everything into two black garbage bags; I gave Mom the few pieces of furniture he had. I gave the clothes to a cousin; Vonn use to hate when I wore his socks because I'd stretch 'em out. I tried to pretend him passing didn't bother me. I never talked about it. My mom would try to talk and I'd shut it down. "He's dead. Let 'em stay that way," or something just as cruel.

Before you came along with your unending questions, Judy, I rarely thought of Vonn. I don't stop and reflect on the day he was murdered. I think that would only prolong the suffering.

But, being more confident and creative in how I approach and talk to women I learned from him. Enjoy every moment and make the most of every opportunity I learned from him. Fear doesn't stop us, it motivates us. I learned that too. So incorporating him (his life lessons) into me keeps him a part of me. I remember him that way.

After Vonn's death, I started drinking and stopped taking them pills for what they called mental illness. Why bother?

I turned off the computer and walked into the "Doomsday" sunshine. The attractive man and his son had been correct. It was a time to consider doom. I sensed I was feeling DarRen spiraling into the depressive side of his bi-polar personality. Increasingly, I was not sure what to write back. He did want to tell me the stories because, well, he did tell them. What did it cost him to bring up these memories?

CHAPTER 11

In the Cause of Science

arRen and I paused in our writing after he wrote about his brother's death. Fewer letters; shorter letters. It felt as though we needed to take a deep breath and allow ourselves to mourn. Had I tipped over the edge and asked too many questions? Had I reopened wounds?

DarRen sent links to a couple of songs that had been played at Vonn's funeral—songs about gansta deaths that happen in American cities where tragedies are reported as statistics rather than as names, in places like New Orlean's 9th Ward, Compton, Newport News, Gary or Chicago's southside. I watched the YouTube videos and read the lyrics. He seemed unsure whether to trust me further and I continued to be uncertain how to best respond to him. We were both struggling with what it was meaning to us to "be family."

In addition to the festering questions that lingered around Vonn and his death, I still had not faced the impact of my father's medical research in prisons so took advantage of the reflection time, the semester's end, and the proximity of one of my favorite places: the University of Wisconsin Memorial Library. Now that may not sound overly exciting, but I have this affection for books. Picture an aged building laced with 78.5 miles of shelving and over three million books. Winding staircases. Narrow passageways. Basement drawers of dusty books organized by Cutter rather than Dewey. Sounding better? A fine setting for a real world game of *Clue*. I recognize that the words clustered in those library books could probably be held on one sophisticated disk or drive today. But the opportunity to weave among the miles of books, smell them, reflect on the hands that had touched them, and then sit in the wire study cages with stacks of book-friends around, well, it just doesn't get much better.

Memorial Library offered insights on prison medical research, much of it done in the 50s, 60s, and 70s—the prime years of my father's education and research work.

As Director of International Clinical Research, I believe my father sought to heal his own woundedness as well as authentically wishing to help humankind. I think he was wounded by being one of the children *not* abused by his father. I think he was wounded by his crime and subsequent distancing from his family and his faith. And I think he was wounded by orchestrating medical tests on inmates, humans in situations he understood intimately.

He held to the essence of the physician's Hippocratic covenant: *First do no harm*, yet he lived the fundamental ethical conflict in human experimentation. In the unexpectedly soulful book, *Clinical Investigation for Medical Practitioners[1]*, my father and his colleague Brian wrote,

> *It is a matter of great importance to the human race as a whole that [medical] human experimentation be carried out. Without it, enormous advances in therapy which have occurred during the past thirty years could not have been achieved. . . [But] quite apart from any formal code of medical ethics, there is a broader question of human ethics. This implies that experimentation must have a worthy purpose; that unnecessary suffering is not inflicted on an experimental subject; that possible goals (and benefits) from an experiment must be weighed against possible detriment to those taking part.*

---

1 Gwinn, R.P. and Brian Lees (1965). *Clinical Investigation for Medical Practitioners*. Lake Bluff, IL., Lees Associates.

I now realize that when I was growing up, my dad hardly talked about his work, although sometimes he literally brought it home.

There were basement experiments: the mud dauber wasps enclosed above the washing machine. What in their secretions made mud stick so effectively, my father wondered (and might that discharge somehow close wounds in human skin)? All was good until the wasps escaped, creating an invasion in our house.

Then there were the caged white mice and their charts, precisely positioned on his pitted basement roll-top desk. I sat by him, on my stool, as he turned up small glass vials, inserted syringes and filled them to the precise cc level. He tapped to remove air pockets and injected whatever into the tiny mouse rumps. That experiment went wide of its mark when my cat ate the mice, without noticeable ill effects on the cat.

There were the soldiers, too. Young men in snappy khaki military dress who came to the house some Sunday afternoons. A soldier and my father would retreat to the knotty pine, third-floor guest bedroom for "military physical exams." I later read that military human radiation experiments were conducted at the University of Chicago during those years. Human subjects drank, inhaled or were injected with solutions of plutonium, polonium or uranium, or other radioactive substances. Results were used to establish the exposure standards thought essential for national security. During the Cold War, my father gave presentations on the effects of radiation.

In the library books I was scanning, I read horror stories about the greed and criminal irresponsibility of some researchers and pharmaceutical companies. Thalidomide babies born without limbs. Hasty and harmful effects from the early release of birth control pills. The immortal HeLa cells distributed from Henrietta Lacks without permission. The Tuskegee syphilis studies. In 1965, Congressional hearings were held on the abuses. I cringed reading that at one of the hearings it was recorded, ". . . pharmaceutical industry officials acknowledged they were using prisoners for testing because they were cheaper than chimpanzees."

And there were other books about major advances in heart surgery, the polio vaccine, nuclear medicine, and human kidney transplants that took place during the 50s, 60s and 70s. Even as I write, I hear my dad's voice saying that the greatest drug ever developed for human benefit was aspirin. He was in the thick of it all.

"Who goes first" is a prime ethical issue in human experimentation. There are whole books on this subject. Is one person's life more valuable than another's? I know my father struggled with this question professionally; he and his co-author, Brian, wrote about it. But what did it mean to him personally? In my mind's eye, my father had that investigator's spirit of adventure and nagging curiosity. He also had the privileged risk-taker's arrogance.

He went first in medical experiments as a student, prior to his incarceration. As requested by his defense attorney after the robbery he committed just prior to his wedding, my father wrote about those activities:

You asked me to relate something of my personal habits in as far as smoking, drinking, and the use of drugs is concerned. I do not know from what source you learned that I have used certain drugs, but I will be glad to comply with your request. Part of this account I must ask you to keep in strict confidence due to the obvious reasons.

As far as smoking and drinking are concerned, the answer is simple. . . I have been very moderate in the use of these because of the pride which I take in my physical fitness, because of my early training, and because of my limited income.

Regarding the use of drugs, six months ago that question would have been answered emphatically, "No." However, at the present time I must tell you of three drugs I have been using.

First, there was the male sex hormone, methyl testerone and testerone propionate, that I took along with eight other medical students as part of experimental work at the University of Minnesota. I took intramuscular injections of twenty-five milligrams of testerone propionate in sesame oil every other day for a period of four weeks.

Secondly, I used the stimulating effect of Benzedrine and Benzedrine Sulfate to help stay awake during the last few weeks when I was only sleeping every other night. I was provided with master keys [to the labs] making it readily obtainable. I began with the regular dosage of one half to one milligram, but later on and while driving to Seattle, I was taking as high as three to five milligrams every twenty-four hours. I might add that without the stimulation afforded by this powerful drug, it is doubtful if I could have gotten through the summer quarter.

The third drug I have used is the one that I require your confidence in connection with. As a result of my own carelessness while handling and working with certain bacteria, I acquired syphilis. You are familiar with my background and I do not have to emphasize the fact that there was not any history of sexual intercourse connected with the disease. If there were, I see no reason for denying it. The main thing is that I was terribly concerned over my impending marriage and the obvious complications. I had the insane idea to keep the entire episode a secret, and so after verifying my fears by running a Wassermann test on myself, I began treatment aimed at a radical cure. In connection with this, I took 0.6 grams of arsphenamine (Salvarsan) for three consecutive days, and followed this with 0.4 grams weekly thereafter. The symptoms of arsenic poisoning became so alarming that I dropped back to the weekly treatment. Among other things, I was having serious nightmares. Until the Sunday following my arrest, no one knew of my affliction, and at that time I confided in both my dad and my fiancée. I sincerely hope that no one ever finds out, not so much for my own sake because it is of little concern to me what people may think, but rather for those of my family and my fiancée's family, as well as for her sake in the eyes of the general public. As I'm sure you are aware, there is a hangover of stigma connected with syphilis.

After multiple days in the Memorial Library, I wrote DarRen about what I was piecing together.

Dear DarRen,

I continue to live in a small library cage. Our circumstances are similar these days except that I leave my cell for meals or a walk on the crisp sunny days. I wish you were able to do the same. Reading about the impacts of my father's work has brought me closer to him; that and my visit to Seattle talking with his sister and other relatives. I realize my father believed in the power and benefit of drugs, even though ironically he rarely prescribed medications for us as children. Interesting that both of our families were supported by drugs, even some overlap perhaps with my father's bennies and his later self-medication with alcohol. Physician, heal thyself.

I have learned that World War II military research fostered clinical exploration—my father's work (at the same pharmaceutical company where your aunt worked). So German doctors were executed for their wartime human experimentation and my father supported our family through a related field, not with the same inhumanity though. I am seeing the serendipity of my father's life path unfold along with what may well have created spiritual torment for him, doing medical research on the prisoners he had come to know as humans.

Could you ever see yourself being part of a medical experiment? If it would give you a sentence reduction, would you do it? Some of the experiments I read about were grisly. Here is a quote: "After World War II, prison experimental trials exploded: ranging from exotic blood tests to skin grafting to flash burn studies, malarial and venereal disease experiments. Viral hepatitis studies took place in New Jersey prisons. Polio and live cancer cell injections in Ohio. Mind-control experiments in Iowa. Syphilis and amoebic dysentery studies in Texas. Testicular irradiation in Oregon and Washington. Skin and radioactive isotope studies in Pennsylvania. Plutonium studies to establish radiation exposure tolerances in Chicago."

These experiments explain our annual family spring break trips to places like Joliet, Illinois; Jackson, Michigan; Detroit; and Iowa City. While the rest of the family was exploring state parks or museums, my father must have been visiting prison experiments in Statesville Prison (where your dad was locked up), Southern Michigan State Prison, Detroit House of Corrections, Anamosa State Men's Reformatory and the like.

And this quote shocked me: "In the early 1970s, the Black Muslims stepped in and basically stalled human experimentation in prisons. By then, however, three-quarters of all approved drugs in the U.S. had already gone through inmate testing." Three-quarters!

DarRen's answer was swift and very clear in the letter I read a few days later, again sitting in my library cage as snow began to stick on the nearby window ledge.

Judy,

I never felt as if the American rights and dream applied to me. I have great respect for those who serve in the Armed Forces, but tempting as it would be to relieve my own suffering, could I transfer it to another? I wonder if your dad ever considered this. Would I do the experiments like what your dad did? It would have to be one hell of a sentence reduction for me to even consider it. They couldn't give me enough money to let them inject me with anything. And $100 to cut a man's nuts off?!! That's some serious messed up bullshit. So your pops was truly a mad scientist.

I read more about prisoner research, books piling up in my study cage that was reserved for ten more days. Inmates were considered ideal for research projects, an author wrote, because they were cut off from family, friends and the general public. No viewing eyes. They were a stable population—especially lifers. Many were unschooled so they did not raise questions. Could these men consent freely if unable to understand medical terminology or the nature their risk? And they were poor. (Poverty and mental illness, more so than criminal behavior, continue to be the common links among those who are imprisoned.)

I thought back to my father's prison journal story about Jack, who lost the use of his legs and how that impacted my dad. I can only imagine his reactions to experiments on prisoners that left them hurt or disabled: the tension between wanting to help humankind through the medical experiments and the trauma to individuals affected by the studies. I thought about my father's siblings being abused by their father and the remorse he may have felt for not intervening. I read that researchers marched through the prisons in white lab coats and I remembered the prison doctor my father questioned and mocked as he asked about testing the men's urine. Did my father believe that, as a medical researcher, he could be the protector and provide more compassion than some other physicians who did not see incarceration or injustice in the same ways he did? Possibly. Possibly.

The reasons prisoners participated in these studies? Poignantly, they were given benefits like having a little money to fill their canteen bags, additional freedom, rides into town on clinic days, free physical exams, more frequent showers, hot meals, calmer and more secure surroundings, promises of cures, a way to step beyond prison routines and monotony, and occasionally pardons or a reduced sentence or at least a letter in their file from the warden. For many, it was simply a privilege to be singled out, to be important human beings and expiate their crimes by contributing to something larger. In an environment devoid of genuine, humane affection, one author wrote, "The volunteers had a place where they could be respectfully addressed and [physically] touched with kindness and concern."

Who might have been hurt by my father's studies? Who might have been killed? Who might he have turned away from? Did this wake him in the silence of the night?

I remembered my mother whispering as my father's coffin was lowered into Seattle soil, "He took three secrets to his grave." She never said more and took them to her grave as well. I will never know.

Dear DarRen:

My journey to understanding my father's choices is coming to an end. Thank you for helping me come to peace with his death-by-alcohol. Through you, I was able to see him as a boy and man in new ways as I walk beside you learning about your childhood experiences and challenges. Sometimes I don't get boys—the fighting and competing and all. But I now see ways you and my father were alike as boys. That has helped because I saw early on the ways you and he were alike as men. I believe my father was caught between the good he felt was possible from human experimentation and the evil he saw firsthand from those experiments on humans, especially incarcerated humans. I believe the balance tipped toward evil over time—maybe something specific happened and he was caught in the claws, unable to escape. So he drank and drank and eventually that killed him. A physician knows how to end a life.

Another thing I realized from my research (and it may be something my father saw more clearly than I), that the healthcare and access we have today is truly balanced on the backs of prisoners. We owe a debt. Gratefulness.

If you are willing, I want to hear more stories—not to better understand my father any longer. He is gone. He is buried. But to better understand you. As I have come to make sense of my father's journey, I am realizing that you and I have taken quite a journey as well. I have met your parents. I have seen the joy and despair in the paintings you have shared with me. I am able to see the patterns—the emotional swings from peace to fury—of your mental illnesses (and the effects of incarceration). I more fully understand the peace and ras'pect of your Rastafari beliefs—respectful, giving, loving, kind, humane beliefs.

What I have come to see through the complexity of our connection is simply this. You and I are family. We are kin. We share warm blood.

CHAPTER 12

What is a Prostate? Where is it? And Why do I Need to Have it Checked if I Don't Know What it is?

ronically I was sitting in the plush sea-green waiting area in my dentist's office, next in line for a routine six-month cleaning, as I opened a letter. DarRen hadn't paused long after I sent my insights about healthcare, and my request to continue the stories. Although he offered a counter to my new understanding of access to healthcare, he did so gently. And, in some stories, I saw his quirky humor that, again, reminded me of my father's attitude.

> *Dear Judy (or should I call you sis now that we are family and does this mean there are certain topics we can no longer discuss?).*
>
> *So you have figured out that access to healthcare and wellness has come about on the backs of inmates, mostly blacks. I guess I won't say "You are welcome" since I haven't and won't be personally involved in any medical testing. But my people were and are. Still, let's talk about my family's healthcare.*

My granny had the sugah. She'd gotten sick from her diabetes but she didn't like doctors. She didn't want to go to church and that meant something was really wrong. She couldn't get out of bed and still no one could convince her to go to the hospital. The family would wash her daily when she was still at home. My mom found a tack buried into her heel. Finally Granny relented and went to the hospital where they done an emergency transfer to a hospital in Milwaukee. We drove up there. I refused to leave her.

They cut off her heel, then her foot and then finally up to her knee. A few days after, she called to me. She often called me by her sons' names, but somehow I could tell who she meant by the tone of voice. I went to her. She told me to scratch her foot, where her toes were. I asked which foot and she told me. I said, "Granny, you ain't got no foot on that side." She started crying.

As a boy, when we would be taken to the dentist or to get glasses, we'd get state assistance. I'm laughin' now at the tricks that were used. But we got by. Once we almost got caught. K saved us. K was blessed with sexual charm dripping from her. I wasn't sure what sex was but she was it. As the doctor was asking questions about why did a different child use the same card as the other child, she jiggled her tits and wiggled her hips and he stopped asking questions.

Once I had a nice deep cut on my arm. Mom pinched it. She heated up the ice pick on the burner.

I said, "No."

She said, "Okay, turn your head."

She had C sit alongside me and grip me. I was burned and stitched up. The burning makes the scar smaller and seals the skin together. It hurts like a mothafucka! No other way to put it.

Once again, I am impressed with DarRen's mom and her raw savvy. She saw what needed doing and she did it. I don't even feel her flinch in these stories. Strong woman. I turned back to the hand-written pages as the receptionist told me it would be a few minutes more before the hygienist was ready for me.

. . . Not all injuries required burning or stitching. I was about nine, maybe ten. My mother had gone on a date and my cousin was spending the night. He and my brothers sat in the kitchen laughing and smokin' cigarettes. My cousin got on the phone and said he knew some girls. It was set they were leaving to go spend some time with these girls. I was not staying at the apartment; I begged and begged to go until I made it clear. "You go, I'm going!"

I rode on the handle bars of the dirt bike as we rode fast, jumping curbs and swerving between parked cars, a little too close. He went to jump a pothole. We went up and as we landed I went tumblin'. He ran me over. The sprocket cut open my knee and blood poured. They picked me up and carried me home. They claimed they could see my bone and made me lay down and propped it up. I got a few shots of Crown Royal, a few tokes from a joint; then they cleaned it up and wrapped it with a ace bandage. When my mom came home, they told her I was outside riding the bike and tried to jump a pothole and fell in. The cut was about three inches. The scar is about a inch wide and about two and a half inches long. Maybe it would have been a smaller scar, but burning and stitchin' were not my first choice.

Injuries were treated at home when it was necessary. Things like gunshot wounds are reported to the police, so that means if it is not serious you'd stay home.

J was shot. The bullet went through the other side so he was burned and stitched up. Sometimes we would dip next door to Zion, or if we were that way, we'd dip this way to K-town—usually they only looked within the state and county hospitals, although the Internet may have changed that now. There were a few nurses that were well paid to come for serious stuff, births and severe wounds that couldn't be burned and stitched.

One night C was beaten and cut pretty deep in several places: hand, arm and cheek. The cuts was like two pieces of meat flappin'. A John raped her. Her skin was pinched together, a needle was burned, an ice pick was set on the stove and she too was burned across the cuts and stitched up. About a month later she was back to work.

At times women would show up when they was about eight or nine months. They'd stop workin' and we'd take care of them until it was time. When P was pregnant she went into labor; went into the room and closed the door. There was a lot of hollering and screaming and about a half a day later we had a new baby brother. We weren't ever allowed to watch. I couldn't figure out what the hell they done in there but I do remember washing the towels and sheets after the fact. It was kind of a joke; no one wanted to get that towel. It wasn't until the fifth grade that I understood more. The mom get about six months off of work. Usually right away she was moved to another apartment or house. Later I realized that it was to break the bond with them. Not much I can say because, as I said, we didn't see much of that. Sometimes we never seen the woman; Pops just came home with a baby. A 6'0" black stork.

DarRen thinks I am often slow to understand what he tells me. That may be true because our worlds are separated by more than miles. But I got this point. Healthcare and access are great for some people. But not for everyone. It appears that, often, the poorest care comes to those whose families may have endured the most, which allows *me* to have state-of-the-art healthcare. My father may have authorized medical studies that were done on DarRen's extended family members. I also saw why DarRen and his granny and others would distrust doctors and the formal medical care. Generations of people were used and abused. Today, that generational mistrust might translate into losing a leg or a life, once a person did get systemic medical care, because it was too late. Well, and the financial cost. So people end up burning and stitching. Reading on, I saw the distrust play out in DarRen as he experienced prison healthcare. I remembered my father's dim assessment of the healthcare he saw while incarcerated.

. . . Everyone comes through Dodge Correctional when they are going to prison in Wisconsin. Everything is checked: eyes, ears—a complete physical. So I'm standing there. The doctor

WHAT IS A PROSTATE?

just finished sticking a Q-tip inside my penis and asked me if I'd like to have my prostate checked. I don't trust doctors—think I got that from my granny—and never blindly accept or agree with nothing they say. So me—not knowing what a prostate is— in my mind I'm going back to health class and nothing on the checklist of known body parts matches a prostate. I ask, "What is a prostate? Where is it? And why do I need to have it checked if I don't know what it is?" The doctor points to a diagram and for me that ended the discussion. There is no reason I could think of why this guy should be allowed to stick his finger up my ass.

So they moved a new guy in the cell with me about a week later. White M. I couldn't figure out why he call himself "white." That part was self-evident. But this dude was so fuckin' annoying. I understand that the urban world is comprised of all sorts of people and as a result they will have a common urban accent and vocabulary, but this guy would get around other white guys and sound like Axl Rose, from Guns and Roses. When the police are around he'd sound like a academic or an intellectual scholar of some sort. But in the cell with me, he'd sound like E40 (a rapper famous for his creation of urban words). I hated the fakeness. So they come to the cell and let him know that afternoon he'd be going to the doctor for his physical. He asked me, "What all do they check?"

I told him and asked if he ever had his prostate checked. Like me, he had no idea what it was. So I told him where it was and said that the doctor would only look and if it was swollen he could see it and if he didn't have it checked it could kill him. He asked again what was involved and I assured him he'd only look. "They may have to pull your cheeks open to get a good look."

He went and came back. He was no longer "white," but red from his neck to the top of his head. I asked him how it went and he shot me a look, then said, "I'll tell you as soon as I wash the gel off my ass." No further words were needed. The next day he asked to be moved to a different cell. At the time I thought it was pretty funny.

125

Growing up, I somehow assumed everyone had access to a doctor in their family like I did. What was healthcare like in a doctor's family? Well, it was free for one thing; physicians and dentists operated on a system of reciprocity. No charges for a doctor's family members. When it came time for school physical exams, my father would line us up, sitting on the kitchen counter, and gently hit our patellar tendons with the orange (burnt umber) reflex hammer, making our legs jump. We'd giggle and he'd declared us healthy, signing the medical forms. When I once challenged that, he said he watched us constantly and would know if anything was wrong medically. I remember my unpleasant surprise (not unlike DarRen's roommate) at having my first real physical exam at age seventeen. Do what?

DarRen offered one more prison healthcare story. Again his mischievous humor emerged, after he felt better, that is.

> . . . I had been behind the walls for five years when I was moved to the Resource Center—Wisconsin's secure mental health facility. They put me in a cell where an inmate had smear shit all over. I was naked. I stayed in the same spot for three days. I didn't drink, I didn't eat. I caught an infection. I was in and out of consciousness; I did not know what was going on. I hit a nurse who tried to give me an IV so they strapped me to a hospital bed. When I woke up I went absolutely nuts. I hate being restrained. I <u>cannot</u> be restrained. They thought I was psychotic and shot me up with something.
>
> I woke up in-population—among other inmates. I questioned if it all was a dream. I couldn't move. My body ached and finally B and this other guy called Big One came and asked if I was alright. "I think they are trying to kill me; I need help." They said I been in the room for days. I pulled the covers back. My leg was red. The sheet was green and pink. My leg was swollen so much the skin bust and it was oozing this greenish looking stuff and blood from splits. I had pissed myself. I felt hot and dizzy and dry. My lips and throat was like sand paper.
>
> Them brothers told the guards, "Get him to the hospital now or we about to tear this mothafucka up."

After the threat of getting me to the hospital or else, a PCT—I'll never forget this—said that, if I wanted to be seen by the nurse I had to walk to the nurse's station. They would not allow anyone to push me in a wheelchair. I had not eaten and was dehydrated and was passing out. When I stood, even if I didn't put pressure on that leg, just being upright caused this pain unlike any I'd known. My bones hurt. It was like hot lava shooting through my veins. My head was pounding. From Unit Six, the nurse station is about fifty feet down one long hallway, and uphill.

So I crawled.

I'd stop every so often. I was sweating. The funny thing is there are two security bubbles—one on either side of the hall. I couldn't believe no one helped me. I was sure that someone would have helped me. When I finally got to the nurse it seemed like a half-hour. He poked his head out the door and seen me sitting on the floor. He asked how I got there. I told him. He looked at my leg and said, "Oh shit. We have to get you to the hospital now. Oh my God. How long has it been like this?" He was talking to me at the same time he was dialing the phone.

I don't remember how I got to the hospital. I woke up there with them poking and prodding. I was vaguely aware of people in the room. I was in and out of consciousness. I woke up when the doctor came in. He said, "You have an infection and it is in your bloodstream and moving up your leg. If it makes it out of your leg, you'll be in real trouble. I think the best choice is to amputate your leg to keep the infection from spreading."

I told him, "I want to wait one more day. If I haven't gotten better tomorrow..." The next day my fever broke and the redness had not went up any more.

I hadn't eaten in days. I went to work, eatin' that is. The doc told me to eat all I wanted and I did. When I turned on the TV, one of the prison officers reported this new change. The institution was demanding I be sent back. I heard the Doc tell the prison people that I was not to be moved and if they tried...

I was drawin' pictures and give them to the nurses. They were hanging them in the break room. One of the prison officers *watching me in the hospital was a natural redhead and a free spirit. She was very talkative, slim with big breasts that she made sure were <u>always</u> up and out. She looked okay for a woman in her 50s who was a heavy smoker. I was flirting. "How about a sponge bath?"*

"This is a real hospital and that is the nurse's job."

Worth a try.

The prison began making it a hassle to keep me in the hospital. They sent four officers. They were telling the hospital I shouldn't be rewarded and that I was an escape risk and needed to be in a secure unit. The nurses told me that they were getting ten to fifteen calls each shift about having me sent back. The doctor stood firm and would not send me back until the infection was cleared. Each time the prison tried to move me, I'd be taken for blood work, X-rays or some other test they had already done a hundred times.

When the infection was gone, my leg was still badly swollen with pitting edema, but the Doc had to send me back. I had been in the hospital for about a week or so. Maybe two. I'm not really sure. I was getting some very good drugs. It could have been four days or two weeks.

I started writing a response to DarRen on the back of his letter—a response I would later type into a longer letter. I had completed a few lines when the dental assistant called my name.

DarRen,

I think the guard with her breasts pointing to the sky helped you recover, even without the sponge baths. Nice try though. If you are willing, tell me more about Wisconsin's secure mental health facility—the Resource Center. Why did they send you there? Your mom said you had had mental health challenges as a boy. What has that meant in your life? As always, don't answer if you don't want to. No pressure.

Chapter 13

Sometimes I Would Do a Long Line of Stupid

Dear Judy,

Yes, I will tell you more about the mental health challenges, as you put it, that I have and have had. Sometimes it come as anger; sometimes as depression. I do wish there was a way to control it. At times it is so sudden and the drop is so fast. It can be scary in the moment but I'm not against it. It feels like where I am suppose to be.

When I was younger the mental health stuff was new and a whole lot more frightening. I didn't know what it was when I had my very first experience. I was about nine. They had locked me in the hot box and I was playing this game. I'd throw the button I'd taken off my mother's old winter coat and then I'd look for it, to pass time.

The hot box? It was suppose to be a closet; a walk-in. It was about five feet long, maybe three feet wide, and seven or eight feet tall. There was a sliding door that folded in the middle so it would allow a little light in. The carpet was brown. Facing the back of the closet, to the right, there were large boxes with clothes in them. From time to time there would be mice in them boxes and usually

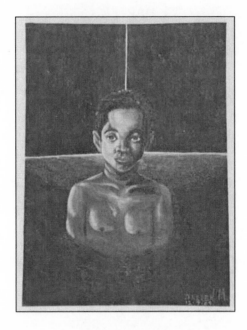

"Boy in Closet"

roaches; sometimes ants and spiders. I had a metal lunch box Vonn bought for me at the Goodwill that had a thermos and a plastic cup. We kept stuff to eat in it (usually crackers, Vienna sausages or spam and water) for the hours (sometimes days) in the hot box. To my left on the floor was a hole me and Vonn dug through the wall that connected to the small supply closet in the bathroom. Sometimes when I was locked in the hot box, he would get in the supply closet and pass in food and we would talk. Me and Vonn and a few others were put in the hot box. Me and Vonn the most. The reasons?! There was no predicting that. I use to hate being in the hot box but sometimes, after a while, it became nice because if I was locked in there I was safe.

I had the sense that DarRen and I were stepping off a cliff together. I knew a future question I would ask would be about the hot box, the abuse, and who it was that locked him, and sometimes Vonn, in that closet. Tread slowly, I told myself. Tread slowly. There is no turning back when such questions are asked—well, once such questions are answered. Timing was important. Early on I had shared stories of my childhood, but progressively I had nothing parallel to his experiences to share. I could only listen—actually, read.

Okay, I admit it. I plan and prepare well in advance of everything. Two of us were taking the group of students to Trinidad and Tobago for ten days—two Caribbean islands not too far from Jamaica. We wouldn't leave for just over a week, but I had the few clothes I planned to take laid out on the bed, ready to be packed. There are some fine perks to college teaching, I'm just sayin'. I was looking so forward to being warm in the Wisconsin January. More important was the clothing each of us was taking to donate where needed. Most of the suitcase space would go for those little T-shirts and shorts. I thought about how DarRen and Vonn had done the same thing when they had returned from Jamaica and gone to the Goodwill to get clothes and shoes to mail back. *I need to purchase some kids' shoes, too,* I thought. Instead of continuing my packing, I sat on the bed and read DarRen's words about his earliest mental illness experiences.

. . . On this day I heard in almost a whisper from behind me, "They are going to kill you." It seemed to echo or as if the same voice was on one side then the other, almost immediately. I jumped, afraid someone was in there with me. But I didn't know the voice. I called out, "Who's in here?" I felt around in the dark to see if someone was there. I thought it was a ghost.

Later, when I was freed from the abuse at about age eleven, I liked punching people and doing much worse because I felt in some ways I was suppose to and I liked that it was not me getting hurt. I still felt people were following me or sneaking up on me; I'd see them out of the corner of my eye. It was not a thought; I felt it. I was being watched. Sometimes when I woke up I would see people run from the room. There were times I was home alone and this happened so I knew I was not being screwed with. But that made no sense to me; who would believe that? People believed in aliens so I said that these shadows were little green men.

In an earlier letter, I remembered that DarRen had explained to me how at least some people in the black community felt about mental illness. He had written,

> *. . . In prison, I am being treated with medication for floating diagnoses of bi-polar psychosis and schizophrenia. Just yesterday, at med time, S said this,*
>
> *'Hey Rasta, you tak'n psychotropic meds?'*
>
> *'Yeah.'*
>
> *'Ah, man, Rastas don't take medication. You ain't like those weak ass niggas; your mind is too strong for that shit.'*
>
> *I explained to him that the question should not be do I take medication, but do I need the medication I take. This is a common idea; that mental health issues are not real in the black community unless a person seen it up close, meaning a family member. Something other than that is labeled a person is faking or a person is weak minded. If you have a strong mind you can overcome it. But blacks, we believe can overcome any and everything."*

With this letter, I was feeling anew the depth of what DarRen confronted and confronts regularly. I was feeling the ease of my life experiences in a world where medical care was and is accessible and valued. And, yes, stigma around mental health issues continues.

> *. . . One day, I was sitting up in our bedroom. My sister kept going to the bathroom; this was in the middle of the night. She just kept going and I saw her because I always left the bedroom door cracked to see if anyone was coming. She went downstairs. "She's going to let him in," I thought.*
>
> *I crept downstairs and peeked around the corner. She was in the silverware drawer. I went to get my knife and when I came back, I grabbed her. She screamed. I·held the knife in front of her and told her to tell me who she was working for. My mother came and eventually we were able to end the situation.*

I was building and linkin' random things. I seen two kids; they were eating cherry pop tarts. I thought that was odd. I don't know why it just seemed out of place although many kids were eating them. Like a half hour later, I seen the same two kids and again they were eating pop tarts. I tried to make sense of it. They were assassins and they were going to kill me and this would be on repeat, "Kill you, kill you." These would be the voices. The more story I fed in, the stronger it got. They were hired by one of my brothers or by so and so who I did this or that or the other to. These pop tarts were cameras.

Was this the guy from the mall? It IS him; I recognize him, so they must have followed me. They know where I live. I must protect the family.

When these episodes happened, I'd be afraid and angry. Over the next several days I could not sleep. I could not eat. I would not drink anything in the house. I'd feel like I'd been poisoned. I'd ride my bike across town, stopping and peaking around the corner to see if they were following me, to get to McDonalds where I'd fill up three two-liter water bottles to keep in my backpack. I was confused and at the same time it made sense. I was afraid and yet afraid of nothing; not one then the other, at the same time I was both.

After the episodes, there was also a lot of shame and guilt. I didn't know what was wrong with me. I then became what I now know was depressed. Often for a few months. I did not feel safe in that house and from what I have learned since then, I blamed everything on the mental illness but that was only part of it. Emotions and personality as well as environment; are all components of that explosion. During these times, Vonn was my counter weight. He knew how to balance me back out.

So many times, as I read DarRen's stories, I asked myself, where were the adults? Again the question now. Then I thought about the mandated one-on-one meetings we did with the first-year college students (that had just been completed for this semester) and realized I <u>am</u> one of the adults who should be intervening in situations like those he faced as a boy. Had I ever intervened? Minimally, a few times, but not anything like the sort of interruption that would have been needed to get early care for a young adult in DarRen's situation.

I noticed the weak winter sun warm on my shoulder as I sat on the edge of the bed, letter in my hands. How many of the students I work with have faced what DarRen encountered?

. . . As I got older this cycle went on. I'd get really paranoid and do something stupid or a long line of stupid. Alcohol was not really my thing. I'm in love with Mary Jane. She's my main thing. She makes me feel alright. She makes my heart sing—hopefully you are familiar with that song by Rick James.

But I did both—alcohol and marijuana—especially closer to the time I got locked up. One or the other, I was fine. But when I mixed the two. Not good. I would usually have a psychotic episode. During those times I could not figure out what was wrong. I <u>knew</u> I had been poisoned. This was not me. I didn't understand what I did to call all of this down on me. It was hard times. I could not really hold a thought. Just as soon as I thought it, it was gone, with the exception of being in danger. But there are times when I would obsess about other things or people. So between my thoughts and those voices I would often be placed in a situation where I had little time to think. My father always told me, "Strike first, strike hard, strike fast, never show mercy, never show fear."

My roots are tough. My situation forced me to decide to be tough inside our world. If you aren't tough, you better act like you are, out in them streets especially. If you're not, even on the playground, you have to be either rough or tough or be okay with being picked on and beat up every day. So, I thought if the voices are here to kill me, then let's go!

My mental illness escalated when we moved to Green Bay for my new-chance-to-make-it. I had had this really strange headache for weeks. It was like pressure but on the inside, not like an ordinary headache. It felt deeper. I told them my brain hurt. I had no other way of describing it and during those times, the voices would boil over and mix with all sorts of other stuff.

At a local club, one night, I jumped from 0 to 60 quickly. Friends were unable to restrain me. The police were called and we fought in the yard. Thankfully they did not shoot me. They too were unable to restrain me. More cops were called. They sprayed me and cuffed me. They kept me in the Green Bay Mental Health Center for more than a day this time. They believed something was wrong. Both times I told them that I had been drinking and getting high and someone gave me something. I had not but it was the only thing that made sense—that I had been drugged. I couldn't be crazy. My mind had never been so clear. I felt right. I had it all figured out.

The doctors took blood and urine samples. Nothing was in my system except twenty-six mgs of herb. The note on the side said that this was such a small amount that it was likely that I was in the area where someone else was smoking. No alcohol. Nothing.

It went from there. My mom refused commitment after they tied me to a bed and I reacted with this flood of unpleasant memories. I cannot be restrained. They took us to court and tried to get me committed. The court said I was so young that if they put me in an institution it could do more harm than good so they agreed that for ninety days I would be on this sort of probation (a Consent Decree to do outpatient treatment), waiving the battery charges. I had to go to AODA counseling even though the test came back confirming I had no alcohol or drugs in my system. They got my records from Kenosha where they had diagnosed schizophrenia. They put me on Cogentin and Haldol. When I explained the smells and the creatures, they said this was not typical of schizophrenics. My mom said, "Well he never said he was that; you said he was that."

They upped the medication.

I've always wondered how I was around all of these experts and professionals and NO ONE seemed to notice I was struggling to the degree that I was. And then Vonn was killed and I started drinking and stopped them pills. Nothing mattered.

Dear DarRen,

You are filling in the missing pieces for me. I can tell by the look of your handwriting that this is difficult for you. Some of your words SCREAM at me. And, frankly, this is difficult for me too as I see you are hurting. I focus on the reality that you are not screaming at me, but at the demons who have so many times climbed into your psyche; maybe this writing allows a few of them to leave you alone. I was ignorant about the mental illness terminology you were sending along so I stopped to look up the terms and then tried to make sense of what they mean to you and how they are expressed in your letters—your actions.

I don't always know what to say back to you. I am uninformed. So I just lean in and hope I am expressing compassion. Am I afraid of your mental illness? A bit I will admit. That is different than being afraid of you. I do not feel that. I truly wish we could be having these conversations face to face (maybe the prison won't deny us visitation in the spring) so I could see your body language and hear the tone of your voice as you tell the stories. I think I would know more then. But even though it has been a very long time since we have seen each other, I reflect back to seeing you in the three years of weekly meetings we were part of and think I can "read" the emotions in your words. Strangely, these current written conversations are more real than what we experienced as we sat talking in the group. Still, I am unsure. Know that I am trying. (You may respond, "Yes, very trying!")

Anyway, here it is. The question we have—no, I have—so long avoided. Why are you in prison? Is it related to your mental health challenges? Why do you have a 100-year sentence with no possibility of early parole? I have learned it is a complete lack of prison etiquette for me to ask this. But ask it I am. I will send you a postcard from Trinidad next week and remember that I am gone for ten days.

I wonder if Trinidad will look like Jamaica did to you when you were a boy and felt so safe there.

CHAPTER 14

Head High, Hustle Hard

The day before the ten of us were scheduled to leave for Trinidad, I picked up one more letter. I was running final errands, getting PeptoBismol and Cipro as recommended by the travel nurse where I had gotten yellow fever and typhoid vaccines. The envelope from DarRen was thin and I paused to read it, sitting there in the post office parking lot. One page. I could tell immediately, as I unfolded the paper, that this was an angry letter. I knew that DarRen was frustrated by many things going on in his life at that time and the holidays are already the most difficult time to be incarcerated since the music and the TV and the visitation (and even talk among C.O.s—corrections officers—I expect) is all about being with family. If you do not have family who can make the trip to the prison (a six-hour trip for DarRen's mom), you know no one will be coming to visit.

Again this year.

> Judy,
>   So you are leaving town.
>   Which do you think hurts more, getting shot or stabbed? There is so much you don't understand, don't know. Do you understand anything?! You have to keep in mind I come from a

very large family and inside this very small area we were known for being dangerous so as one of the babies, I am the fourteenth child, I had my own sort of privilege. I would do those things I done and people really did not want to do anything to me. At that time my ego told me it was because I was such a bad ass. But as I look back that may have played some factor but I am willing to bet that no one wanted to mess with my father's son or any of that family. So I did not have any regard, plus this was the nature of the streets. We have a saying, "The Game is cold, but it's fair." One of my favorite rappers said, "You have to take the bitta wit da sweet, when you gamblin nigga..." And that sums it up. I will get you today, you'll chalk that up as they "charge it to the game." You know like charge it to your VISA. And then tomorrow you will get me. That is why we put so much on being on point, or being alert, because I can't get mad at you. You doing what you do. I was suppose to be aware of this and be on square and not let you bump me like that. Plus you know in the streets who the lames and suckas are and who the killers are. When you dealing with a killer he has no regard who your family is because with him, it is do or die and neither matters much.

I did develop a death wish which meant I would rob people that the police would call Mister. But once again, I had done two things without intending to. I showed that when it came to the streets, I was a natural. I was alert and I had no issues with pullin' that trigga' and I had no regards for nothing. If you crossed me, I was comin'. Whatever you got, you betta have it with you when I get there because I'm comin' and I'mma bring mine. Now I also, because of this, placed myself in the view of some very serious people who were true killas and they had a team of killas with them and knowing that I was with them made it very difficult. I was more in danger of being killed by the people we worked for than the streets because anything that makes threats to their business must go. So, had they felt my antics were getting' out of hand, they could have killed me without regard. I once heard the rumor that it was why they killed Vonn because they were afraid that because we were trying to leave for Cali we may have been a threat to them and working with them other people. These were the kind of people that once I went over to a house and on the table was about eight or nine kilos's of unrocked dope. If this is what is being shown, imagine what was hidden. In a room there were about ten large black garbage bags filled with money, mostly twenties, fifties and hundreds. These are the sort of people I was around. They shoot.

I would shoot and not ask why. They loved that about me. I told myself that they must have been bad people and done something wrong. I know these people here and they are good people. These people would not have this done to you if you had not done somethin' to deserve this. So take what you got comin' and stop cryin'.

IT IS AMAZING HOW LOST I WAS. I did not have a clue what I was doing. I am paying for that now though. AT MY CORE, I'M NOT VIOLENT. Then I dealt with things by placing the most distance I could between me and the threat, which sometimes meant violence. Action was my expression. I didn't sit around and think of ways to hurt people. I had no desire to hurt anyone. At my core, I'm alone and afraid and don't know how to deal or express. I had no tools to address the secret thoughts or feelings that were a whirlwind inside me. Now I still feel that way, I just deal with it better than I did.

Did I mention my abandonment issues? Do you even care about that?

Well, have a good time in Trinidad.

By the way, the answer to which hurts more is getting stabbed. Getting shot is loud and explosive. It burns more than hurt. But being stabbed is a very sharp and searing pain. Now you know. I hope you have a good trip.

This wasn't the first angry, pointed letter I had received in the time we had corresponded. Early on, I had responded in kind, with frustrated anger. I was slowly figuring out that that did no good. Still, this letter hurt. Well, I have my own life to live and am doing it.

But sometimes I get really pissed at this man. Is it some sort of personality disorder in me that I stick with this? And yet, I have to again ask myself, who would I be if I had been sentenced (at age 17) to spend the next 100 years incarcerated? At this point, DarRen has spent more than half of his life in maximum security prisons. I don't know who I would be.

I should have left this letter in the mailbox so there would have been other letters surrounding it when I finally read it after returning from Trinidad, to soften his bluster.

CHAPTER 15

I Understand that Some of this Behavior Is Caused by Factors Well Beyond Your Control, However. . .

rinidad pulsed with heat and music. There were dreadlocks everywhere and so many people who looked like DarRen. I could easily imagine him there, free and contributing to that world. I've never been to Jamaica, but imagine that country would also feel like his natural home. I had sent the promised postcard, with a photo on the front not unlike the early painting DarRen had done for me. Mountains and a river. No distant woman in a white dress in the valley, however.

I returned home and slept for many hours before resuming my regular routine, which included checking for letters. There was one in the box. A fat letter, many pages. I sensed that I was going to hear about the case that put him where he was, in prison for life. I took the letter home to read carefully, sitting snuggled up by the gas heater in my living room. Coming back from a hot island with excellent food and sandy beaches and riveting calypso, reggae, soca, steel drum and rap music, made re-entry a trial. It was getting dark; I turned on a lamp. Reading the letter, with a cat who had missed me badly curled on my lap, I quickly saw that DarRen had made no reference to his earlier angry explanation of the world he grew up in—the hoods of Kenosha, Waukegan and Zion. That was forgotten. Or maybe by expressing his frustrations, he had laid them to rest.

Judy,

You want to know why I'm locked up? I will tell you although I don't talk about it much. I've painted it: the demons. But not so many words.

After Vonn was killed, my mind was unraveling. A buddy and I went everywhere and done everything (well almost) together. At one point, he said, "Man, I had no idea yo ass was nuts."

I was paranoid and thought the people who killed Vonn were after me. When I left Kenosha to go back to Green Bay with my mom, I stopped taking the medications for what they called childhood/adolescent schizophrenia: Cogentin and Haldol. And I stopped taking Ritalin for ADHD. I began doing odd stuff like taking the long route to school, making extra turns and parking to see if I was being followed. I sank into depression. Everything was wrong. Smiling was not high on my list.

I was around people in Green Bay that was afraid of my skin and the image or idea of me. I saw women clutch their purses in the mall or move to avoid sharing the space. In my mind they were more of a threat to me than I was to them. If they misplace something and claimed I stole it, I would go to jail. If I took a walk, I could be referred to as a potential burglar scouting out places or people. I hated being in Green Bay. I was not welcome. I was different. They never let me forget it.

This paranoia spread into other areas of my life. My mom would try to enforce curfews on me and often I rebelled. At times I would be angry for no real reason. I couldn't explain it. I attacked two guys at school basically because I believed they were trying to corner me in a small hallway. I much rather play

offense than defense. The psychologist put me back on Cogentin
and Haldon again. Within a matter of weeks things went back
to as close to normal as I had been for a while.

But once again I felt better and I went off the medication and
around the beginning of March I was back in the thick of it.

How many people are there in the same situation that DarRen was in?
I know that the U.S. has pretty much abandoned mental healthcare
for people who have no resources, turned it over to "criminal justice."
(Jails or prisons are often the last resort, the places that cannot refuse
to take in people with mental illnesses. Of course, most prison staff
do not have the education needed to handle mental health issues
other than controlling with physical coercion or drugs.) Could the
crime DarRen committed have been tempered, or avoided, if he had
received treatment and counseling? It is a legitimate question. At
some point, I will ask him what would have worked for him, what
sort of help would he have responded to.

. . . Being off medication, the things I was doing just made
matters worse. I went to buy some of Mary Jane flowers from the
friend of a girl I went to school with. We met in a parking lot of a
nearby apartment building. It turns out that the girl had set me
up and I was robbed at gun point. Yes, in Green Bay. Who knew?

I attempted to grab the gun which was a rifle of some kind
and it went off. I ran and about two blocks later there was a large
group of people—mostly teenagers—in the parking lot of a pool
hall. That was the largest group of blacks I had seen since I had
been in that city. I went over and stood with the group thinking
that if they, meaning the robbers, were still following me they
probably would not chase me in a large group like that. This is
where I met my co-defendant. I did not know the people standing
there. But I introduced myself and was invited to a party for my
co-defendant's girlfriend on the 22 of March. I agreed to go but
had no intention of doing so. On the 22, my girlfriend at the time
said she wanted to go to her friend's birthday party and better

yet she wanted me to go with her. I went, but soon after it was clear that was not a good choice.

A couple of people in the apartment were classmates of mine. For some reason they thought it was funny to play on my paranoia. They began spreading the rumor that the people who robbed me were in the parking lot and they had a gun. The girls would run from window to window and claim that these people were aiming the gun at them. A few people left the apartment and ran back in saying that they were being chased by the people.

This went on for hours. I hadn't seen anybody but I knew they were out there and that they were there to kill me. There was only one way out of this apartment and I had gotten to the point I said, "I am going to go. I am not going to hide in a tiny apartment." I grabbed the only weapon available—a knife—and went outside with the other twenty or so people from the apartment. As fate would have it, there was a man out there sitting in his truck. We approached him and I quickly seen that this was not the guy. As we walked off another guy said, "Let's steal the truck." I said, "Good idea, I need to get the hell out of here."

He went back toward the truck. My co-defendant's girlfriend told my co-defendant that the man in the truck was the man that had slapped her. We went back to the truck. My co-defendant asked the victim why he had slapped his pregnant girlfriend. I cut in and told him to get out of the truck and then I punched him in the face and reached for the door handle.

My co-defendant pushed me aside and stabbed the victim twice in the neck, right side, right above the collar bone. Because of our heights and the height of the truck I did not see where he stabbed. In fact it was not until he pulled his arm out of the window that I seen the knife. He turned and raised his arm with the knife in it and as he did I got spots of blood on my shirt.

I looked back toward the victim. His face. He was frowning as if the words he spoke were bitter.

I seen him lean forward in the truck, reaching for something. I reacted with these things in my head. "I can't let him think I fear him." Then I was thinking of what was said earlier. "He was a [gang] rival and he had a gun." I grabbed the knife I had picked up and stabbed at him. He was still reaching for something. A gun? Just as I was reaching for the door handle the truck pulled off. Because of my limited hearing, I often respond to what I see, the facial expression or body language to support the "words" or replace them. I don't know what he said; I couldn't hear him. He made an angry face and then reached for something. He could have grimaced from pain or asked for help. I simply don't know.

I shiver and pull my chair closer to the gas burner. Much as I care about DarRen as an adult, I do not know how to put myself in his place as he describes these events. I cannot imagine his teenage paranoia. I cannot imagine the girls trying to get him to escalate. I cannot imagine picking up a knife or deciding to steal a truck. I do not know how to take this walk into the crime with him. The one thing I can connect with is the fear. And I think his fear was greatly heightened both by paranoia and by life experience. I wonder if he would agree with me.

. . . March 23, 1994. I had just woken up from a restless night. I was leaving town that day at 10:30. But something was wrong. I got up and put on pants and looked out of the window, the house was surrounded by the police and they had their guns drawn. I went into the living room thinking I was about to be charged with reckless endangerment or assault. They asked my name and I told them. I started to put on my shoes but they stopped me and walked me out in hand cuffs. I could feel the cool concrete through my socks. That was the last day I was physically free. A cool grey March day.

It was the last day of the victim's life.

Later, at my trial, they had crime scene photos and I learned that the truck was a floor stick. He was reaching for the stick to put the car in gear. I also learned in court that I had stabbed him in the left shoulder but I wasn't aiming for any body part;

I just stabbed at him. He died because the wound in his neck cut the top of lung; the artery in his neck was severed and that bled into his lung; basically he drowned. The hospital was very close; approximately 100 feet away. He drove away toward the hospital. He seemed fine. I didn't know he was stabbed in the neck.

I believe the victim had been drinking. But that did not matter at all. His name was Johnny Fish. He was Native American, a college student and Desert Storm vet. He had been fighting with his girlfriend; he dropped her off. He was leaving; he was halfway out of the drive and came back. I've always wondered why would he back up.

Sprinkle drugs, alcohol and mental health issues on top and I had one fucked up cocktail. When I left the scene, I didn't know that Mr. Fish was dead.

My case was big news and my judge said that it was going to be a warning to all gang members.

In Green Bay, I was not in any gang.

My co-defendant did not get away. At the time, he never knew that I stabbed the victim. After he stabbed him, he turned and ran off. So when he told the police it was all me, all he could do was account for them two stab wounds. They charged him with party to a crime; they gave him a deal for thirty years on a reduced charge.

The court did consider my crimes of recent vintage in Green Bay. But Lake County refused to send my records because the State of Wisconsin would not share information with Illinois about why they wanted my file. This seemed to anger Wisconsin; they kept bringing it up: "We have no idea what he has been involved in down there." They did not know about my childhood but they knew of my battles with mental illness. I was so drugged up on antipsychotics (10 mg of Haldol two times daily) that it was not me the judge was looking at. No one questioned whether I could hear all that was going on. The need to punish outweighed everything else. The District Attorney asked for my Parole Eligibility Date to be in fifty-two years. But the judge

"Night Watchman"

was hell bent on me paying with my life. He said, "I understand that some of this behavior is caused by factors well beyond your control, however..."

I got sentenced February 5, 1995. The judge gave me Wisconsin's version of the death penalty. It's called Life. Ironic because the judge told me, "The journey you started when you joined the street gang as a youth will end when you die in a cold, dark prison cell someday. There will be no family, there will be no friends. You'll have gone nowhere. There will be nobody, it will be nothing. If the prison guards in that prison are kind enough to give you a piece of paper and a stamp, I suggest you write to your gang friends and you tell them what the gang did for you and tell them what the gang will do for them. Maybe in that you can add something to this world."

He set my parole eligibility date at 2095. I was seventeen years old.

I was a bad guy and I've done <u>a lot</u> of bad things. I have to consider that is why I'm sitting here in prison. I've hurt a lot of people and the emotions I've left them with are like ghosts in the night. Although I'm not the same guy now, I have to accept that in many ways I am the same guy. I can't shed my past. I have to accept that I was not always a victim but also a victimizer.

After Mr. Fish was stabbed, I can't remember what I felt. I suppose fear. Shock. I had no plans to do anything that extreme to this man. I did not realize that anyone else was going to hurt him to this degree. So when I seen the blood on the knife I was shocked. Then, fear because I seen him reaching. But after that I was numb.

The people I had hurt I felt they had it coming. They were not unjustly hurt—well at least the ones I've seriously injured. With Mr. Fish, I felt like I was in fog; some kind of bubble. Reality set in. I needed to get out of there. The burning of my shirt with the blood spots was not my idea. But once it was said, I thought it was good and burned half of the shirt, saving the part I had painted. Again I was reacting; I don't remember feeling anything. That next morning the police came to the house and placed me under arrest for PTAC—1st degree intentional homicide. That's when I knew that Mr. Fish had passed away. At that moment I was angry and I was sad. Unfortunately, then, I was not in a space where I could truly appreciate the loss of life and the taking of life. I didn't get it then but I get it now. Not only for my role with Mr. Fish but with every one touched by any of my actions over the years.

March 23 is the day the victim in my case was murdered. I have no ritual. I think about him every day. It's kinda hard not to. If I could, I'd like to cleanse the earth of that blood. On the spot where he was killed, burn a small fire and throw some incense on it. Fire purifies (spiritual). The Imperial Fire. It's an atonement of sorts. Which brung me to this realization. When

"Eagle Wolf"

we have hurt some people; we must balance that out. A selfless act of kindness for another? What do you think?

What does it feel like to have contributed to the death of another? There is a sadness. Recently I've begun to think more about what does his family feel. Did he suffer? Was he afraid? Did he know he was dying? Did he have time to pray or speak with his God? A couple of cells down from me is a family member of his. I've always wanted to express an apology to the family but now I'm not sure what to say or how to say it. I will not be able to atone until I can, one, make a grand gesture in his name and, two, save a life. What can be said after that? I have found myself repeatedly wanting to tell someone about the stories and then. . . well, who do I trust that much?

I laid the letter on my lap and turned off the light. The flicker from the gas flame reflected a scattered pattern on the walls and windows. Several years ago, a survivor named Jackie (not a victim, she says) and I wrote her story about the two boys who shot her execution style and left her for dead. She survived and, over time, has both forgiven the boys and come to love them. And they her. How different this felt realizing the victim, Mr. Fish, did not survive. Can forgiveness happen here too? Can Mr. Fish's family forgive over time? Can DarRen's family forgive? Can DarRen forgive himself? It is clear that he seeks atonement. As I sat near the flame, I wondered to myself if part of that reparation comes from publicly telling the story so others will learn. Taking that piece of paper and stamp and adding something to this world, in Mr. Fish's name.

Dear DarRen:

Thank you for your trust, for telling me about Mr. Fish. I do believe we need to balance it out when we have hurt someone. A selfless act of kindness, a grand gesture in his name. Save another life. Maybe a day will come when family will burn sacred sweet grass on the spot where blood was spilled, to smudge and purify. It might bring some healing for all. I don't know. It feels to me like telling the story is honoring him; his life.

There is so so much anger, DarRen. So much anger. Why? Where did all the anger come from within you that allowed you to hurt other people? The abuse? Are you ready to talk about the abuse?

CHAPTER 16

I Just Hope My Soil
Doesn't Soil You

Once these stories started, the deluge was unstoppable. Violence, abuse, sex, anger. I still think of these collectively as the abuse letters. Sometimes I would read around the edges of them; picking them up from the mailbox but opening them slowly or reading a page and then putting the rest down for a while. For much of a year, DarRen and I had talked around this. Before the abuse letters, I had not understood that Mr. Fish's death was not the final passageway to traversing the maze—to understanding the tangle of DarRen's violence. Much preceded that event.

> *Judy,*
>
> *The things I'm telling you now are the hardest part. I've looked down the extremely large hole of a gun and into the eyes of a man who wanted to kill me. And I dared him. But telling you that I was once a victim is terrifying to me. The telling of these stories terrifies because it breaks Rule #1, Protect the Family: What happens in this house stays in this house. I fear that some parts of my story are so dark I am not sure I want to be judged by them. Is it really good for others to know everything? How much*

to reveal and to who? And once you know, you cannot unknow. I like to rip the Band-Aid off; I don't like to pull it one hair at a time. I just hope my soil doesn't soil you. These fragmented stories will help you see how I became who I was at seventeen years old in them thirty seconds, that contributed to the loss of a life and damage to many others.

As these letters arrived in sequence, I regularly paused to read about boyhood trauma and abuse in an oddly comforting book by Richard Gartner, *Beyond Betrayal: Taking Charge of Your Life After Boyhood Sexual Abuse.* I had to know that people were seeking to understand and amend the sorts of things DarRen had experienced. I went to the place I go to understand—written words. Gartner's words told me that admitting victimhood could feel like confessing to not being a man. I know that men are always supposed to be powerful and in control (something I saw in my father and something I now see as cruelty to males, but that is a separate topic). Was the need for a man to be powerful even more the case in the neighborhoods DarRen had described and lived in where strength equated to survival, literally. Above all else, protect the family. Man-up.

Through his painting and our writing, I had also realized that DarRen has an eidetic memory—the ability to recall images, sounds, smells with extreme precision. I believe the clarity of his visual childhood memories.

...I was three. Here is what I remember. Coming into our apartment, the steps was very steep, almost vertical. The kitchen was to the right and Mom's bedroom to the left. The curtains were yellow ochre and too long; they touched the brownish shag carpet even after Mom had tucked and pinned them up. I remember liking how the carpet felt to lay on in front of the TV, which was in the living room corner next to the window. The dresser in the bedroom was long and black; shiny like it had been polished. It was right in front of you as you went into the

room. *The bed was to the left and the closet to the right. It had no closet door. There were other rooms but I cannot say for sure where they were or what they looked like. I do not remember my own room. Funny, huh.*

My mom was boiling rice; she was going to make tuna fish, eggs, rice and cheese. It is a favorite dish of mine. I had helped her open the tuna cans while the rice was cooking. Then I picked up my father's gun from the dresser and was playing with it. My mother seen me and took it from me. She tried to hide it in the closet, on that shelf up top. I pulled out the bottom dresser drawer, climbed up, and from there I was able to use a clothes hanger to get the gun. I remember laughing when it hit the floor. I thought it was a game.

"Don't play with that, it isn't a toy."

She reached in to take the gun. It went off.

I do not remember the bang but I remember the flash from the muzzle. I remember being instantly afraid. Up to that point, everything was black and white. She fell backward on the bed and slid down to the floor and then I remember red, spreading. For some reason I thought it was this red bedspread she had. I would not touch the thing under her because I was convinced that it was the blanket. I tried to wake her but she would not wake. The red was all over me. I do not remember anyone else being around. I was crying.

My next memory was being at my granny's house. While my mother was in the hospital, we stayed with Granny, her mom. The bullet went in Momma's stomach and ricocheted off her spine leaving her paralyzed from the chest down. She was in a body cast. Much later she told me the cast was like being in prison. The doctors told her she'd never walk again.

"Bullshit!" She shook her head, "No."

It took two years before she was walking again. She overcame much of that and end up with partial paralysis in her leg.

But, I was the-boy-that-shot-Momma. My brothers pointed out that I knew better. It began with the brothers' comments telling me, "Momma might die because of you. It should have been you that got shot." I see most of my problems in life stem from that injury—the shooting. I took her youth from her; maybe that's why I lost mine. I feared that my mother did not love me; that she hated me for ruining her life.

Why did DarRen's family need to blame someone for the accident, I wondered. Their refrain was, "Protect the family." The possibility of losing Momma threatened the whole family. DarRen had taught me that there are different kinds of threats. Looking into the barrel of a gun is one and DarRen and the family could do that unflinchingly. But a threat to the family was another kind of survival risk. In a family where "things weren't talked through," they may not have had the skills to deal with this sort of challenge to their core. The children I know are generally taught not to color outside the lines, but it felt to me as though everything this family was doing was outside the lines, secret. When that is the case, how do you deal with a threat to family stability? When the *red* is spreading outside the lines and is getting all over you?

. . . At first "the punishment" was all physical and, in some odd way, it was good to be punished. That is until things began to change. The abuse became more vicious and the sexual stuff started. It was no longer redemption. I did think the in-house punishments were normal at the time until I visited other people's houses and seen that there were no locks on the closet doors and things like that.

The reason for the tortures? That is like you asking me what are the reasons that water is wet. I have no idea.

At first they were stealing my food. We'd have to sit on the floor to eat in any space you could get in because there was so many of us at Granny's house. Newspapers were spread out on the floor. The older boys would take my chicken, pork chop, cake or whatever. There were a few times they took it all and I'd get in trouble for asking for more—for being greedy. Later I'd hide cans of chili in the basement so if things were not good I could at least feed me and Vonn. My great-granny had those little tomatoes in her garden and I use to steal them and eat them raw or sometimes I would dice them up and put in a bowl with a few splashes of white vinegar and some black pepper and some of her very hot hot sauce. And there was a bush in the back yard that had these red berries on it. I ate a bunch of them once but got really sick.

One day I seen my uncle reach in the dog food bag and eat it. "Go ahead, taste it," he told me. I did; it wasn't bad. That came in handy until Granny caught me in the middle of the night eatin' out of the bag. They locked it up.

From age three until around eleven, I was the focal point of mass abuse—verbal, emotional, physical and sexual. I was the-boy-who-hurt-Momma and this was my punishment. I felt so guilty although I didn't have that word at the time; I accepted it. When I was called, I went. What I was told to do, I did. Usually without complaint.

DarRen later explained to me that, although sexual abuse among men is probably just as high as among women, it isn't talked about because somehow it calls a man's sexuality into question in a different way. Talking with men in prison, he realized that many men are victims of abuse. His story was not unique, not unique among black or white men. He recognized how his past affects so many areas of his life today. *"I remember two quotes from an Oprah show about abuse. 'It killed who she could have become' and 'Forgiveness is giving up the hope that the past could have been any different.' And then Jaycee Dugard told Diane Sawyer, 'Telling my story will free me; it was not my shame, it was his.'"* I think of how DarRen could have benefitted (could still benefit) from counseling around the abuses and trauma. But that is not available to him inside a maximum security prison. People incarcerated for life are not first in line for any programming in the prisons, at least in Wisconsin. "It may be true that keeping secrets killed who I could have become," DarRen reflected.

. . . And shame? It's shameful. It shouldn't be but it is. I remember moments where I could have and should have said something. My granny would have shot them. She kept a shot gun by her bed. She was from the South and knew how to handle it. She loved me. And that's where it gets tricky. If I had said something, would there have been help for me? Would that have saved Vonn? So giving up hope it could have been different is difficult.

Naming and describing traumatic experiences gives power, I read. Boys with confidants learn to put emotional experiences into words, so they can include the abuse in their life story and gain mastery over it. The experience makes sense in some way. It allows steering around the emotional triggers, when they are understood. Maybe the power comes from the act of being vulnerable (the trust) before another human; of stepping beyond the cool pose to raw humanity. DarRen's deluge continued.

. . . Carl pushed me down the stairs. He had this rubber spider and it looked real. I hated that thing—I hate spiders. He had a remote control car and it was moving toward me. I kept backing up. "You pussy." The car got stuck or something and stopped working. He got up, picked up the car, did something and the wheels spun. He had the spider in his hand and shook it toward me. I was standing at the top of the stairs and I moved. "Don't run from me." He pushed me in my chest and I went tumbling down the stairs. The next thing I remember the doctor was working in my mouth. My teeth went through my tongue; I got stitches. I didn't tell anyone that I was pushed.

"This is your punishment for what you done to Momma."

They had me standing on objects. A bowl. We had a metal dog bowl. They'd flip it over and I'd stand on that until my feet would hurt. I was tied in the basement to some pipes in the ceiling with a phone cord. Under my feet was a white bucket that once held laundry soap; it now had no lid and was filled with water. I had to stand, without my shoes, on the rim. If I spilled any water on my socks or on the floor, I was beaten with an electric extension cord.

And then we'd start all over.

I was kicked into a wall and thought that some of the dry wall got inside my head. You should have seen me trying to get it out to stop the sound.

I have no idea when my back was damaged. Was it when I was hung with my feet and hands bound together so that my back looked like an O or when I was tied over the couch?

To get a sense of being tied to the couch, take a chair with no wheels. Stand with your back to the chair as if you were about to sit down bending at the knees back straight and rest your neck on the back of the chair, hands behind your back. The only part of your body touching anything would be your neck.

The telephone wire was usually the rope of choice. We had many of them. They would get shorts in them and rather than throw them out they were used for clothing lines and for binding me (us). On the couch, the line was tied around my neck and went around the couch, well actually under not around, and came out the front. I cannot remember why or how but something prevented me from closing my legs. The rope went between my legs and tied both my hands. From there I am not sure what else Carl done. If I moved my feet, it pulled and tightened on my neck. When my legs got tired and I felt like I could no longer hold the position, my body would sag and the weight would pull the rope so I would be choking myself. I have often wondered if that is how my toes got to be so long. I have two very long big toes.

Humor is such a fascinating thing. It is used to make us laugh. And it can be used to keep us from sobbing. Yes, those were the same offensive long toes that would stretch out Vonn's socks, making him yell at his brother.

. . . I was tied like that over a couch and remember being there so long that my body went beyond the shaking and muscle quivers

to physically going numb. I thought that I was dying a little piece at a time.

I often had no clue what I had done wrong in the immediate moment. I know you like to ask how I felt. I do not remember feeling, emotion-wise. I was too busy trying to figure out a way to stay that way and not die. Thinking about this, I just realized something that I never remembered before. There were people who passed by me, tied like that and they barely acknowledged me. In the beginning, it was a group thing and in the later years it was mostly one—by far the worst of all of them all—Carl.

I had to keep returning to the abuse book. Often as not, I'd read a page from DarRen and then go back to Gartner's writing to try to make sense of what I was learning. DarRen said he had no memories of feeling anything. Reading, I learned the concept of dissociation: disconnecting feelings from unpleasant memories. Detaching facts, one from another. Even separating from the memories totally. The trauma can be frozen in time and space. I realized several things. For one, DarRen had experienced trauma like that humans may face in a war zone. And I came to understand the real courage it was taking him to tell me these stories. He was saying words—well—writing words, that had not been said for a very long time. If ever.

. . . There were times with my brothers where things were almost normal. There were times when we played and teased one another.

Once we had to travel down south to visit a dead uncle I had never met before. Funeral love—the time when the whole family got together. The women were in the basement of the church, preparing the meal to be served after the funeral. The kids were sent to go play outside. Somehow we ended up on the stairs in front of the church and there was the casket. A brother said that the body was not in there yet and each was daring another to go up there and open it. Finally two of them did and before it snapped open we all took off running.

Now we were seeing who was scared to go up and look at it. So we are about at it and someone said, "I bet you won't touch it" and, going to show my heart, I reached my little hand up there to touch him. I was more than a little afraid. As I almost touched him, my brother reached over the top of me. "Move you pussy; he dead. He can't do nothin'." He thumped him on the forehead. The body sat straight up. I tried to run but my legs stopped working. Everyone screamed. When the dust settled, I found out that I had pissed on myself but I was not alone so there was no teasing. The body had some sort of spasm. My uncles had to come and pull the body out and break its back in order to flatten him back out so he could lie down and rest. My mom and aunts found this particularly funny and so did my granny because it seems that was his thing—scaring people. He had one more left in him.

Maybe humor is about sanity. Or perhaps it is a way of taking control over things that color outside the lines, like a dead body sitting up. Or a group of older brothers torturing the younger ones. Maybe it is a form of escape.

. . . In my right eyebrow there is a tiny scar from a brother who came home from football practice when I was about four. He gave me a knife after taking his shoe and sock off and told me to shave that down. I didn't know what I was suppose to do. He snapped, "Bitch, I said shave it down." So I scraped his foot with the knife. He slapped me. I fell and hit my face on an end table. Blood started squirting everywhere.

More weird shit. I'd be told to stand somewhere for a really long time. Sometimes I'd have to hold a glass of water. I couldn't switch hands or rest it or use my other hand to support my arm. When my arm started to shake, they'd laugh and threaten me. I'd beg to put it down or rest and then usually Carl would say if I did I'd have to do something else as my punishment. Not knowing what was next, but I couldn't hold the glass any longer,

I'd put it down. As soon as I set it down, "All you had was thirty second left."

At first I thought cryin' anger them. They acted like it did. Whatever they were doing when I cried, they'd do more, longer or harder. <u>Nothing was ever over</u>. <u>Nothing was ever good enough</u>.

You know, I had never thought of it as torture. Sometimes I even forget to call it abuse. I often think of it, as they said, my punishment.

But then the sexual punishments began.

I went back to my calming and distracting academic insights. Men believe they must not be penetrated, violated, subdued or forced into submission, I read. If this happens, manhood may feel threatened. I thought about the man who held a gun to DarRen's head and his response, "Shoot me, but I will not bow to you." Or his words when trapped, "I'd taunt them. 'I dare you. Fuck death, I hate life. Reach bitch! Reach!'" I thought about the prostate exam and his response, "There is no reason I could think of why this guy should be allowed to stick his finger up my ass." I thought about the mental health center restraining DarRen and his statement, "I went absolutely nuts. I hate being restrained. I <u>cannot</u> be restrained." And I read that incest is perhaps the most psychologically catastrophic form of sexual betrayal. It can have even more far-reaching consequences. . . . This is especially likely when incest occurs regularly, often for years.

. . . Carl woke me up one night and pulled me into the bathroom. I rubbed my eyes. He shut the door. He said, "I want you to wash this off." I looked.

He had his penis out. I was scared. It was pointing at me. I had never seen an erect penis and I backed away but the bathroom was small. I started crying. He held it in his hand and moved closer. I looked at the floor. He told me I had to, because it was my punishment. If I didn't, Mom wouldn't forgive me or love me anymore. I kept looking at the floor. I didn't know what was going to happen but it did not feel right. I felt disgusted. I had no knowledge of sex. But I knew on some level this was wrong.

He pushed my head back and told me to open my mouth.

"I don't want to."

He said, "Okay, you chose. You can open your mouth or take your shorts off and turn around."

I opened my mouth and closed my eyes. He pushed it in and for a long time he just held it there and very suddenly he started pumpin' it in and out. I felt like I was choking. I couldn't breathe. I was pressed against the sink. I couldn't move. I put my hands up and tried to push his body back but he kept going. I felt something hot and wet in my mouth and I thought it was blood. Pretty soon it was over. He never said a word. Just left. I spit in the toilet, rinsed my mouth and brushed my teeth five or six times. I don't know why but I couldn't leave the bathroom. I was there until morning. I slept in the tub.

Once it began, nearly every night I'd be woken up and would have to do this. One day I felt it squirting in my mouth and he snatched it out suddenly and in one motion he slapped me so hard I hit the wall first and then fell in the tub. My head was ringing. I felt hot and fuzzy and seen spots for a while. My neck hurt and my face was tight; it was swelling up. I laid there and cried. I didn't understand what I done wrong. I spent the night in the tub again.

I watched Carl. People moved when he came. Rarely people denied him what he wanted. If I slept during breakfast, that usually meant I would not get food. Carl could over-sleep and food would be there when he woke up. When I slept I would wake up every ten or fifteen minutes to do a security check. Carl did not sleep balled up; he would be sprawled out. He was a sound sleeper and he slept like a king with the arrogance that no one would dare touch him. He was the definition of power at that time.

Why didn't I reach out for help? As a kid, I was really shy. I would shrink away from the crowds at home. I never said anything and any marks on me was not unusual because we were rough boys, so unless they had super powers, there is no way they could have known with the certainty I imagine it would take for anyone to step in. I think my granny knew something was wrong in our house. She would always ask but I was terrified to say a word. I wanted to tell but what if she didn't believe me? This was not something that was done in the living room or discussed at the table during dinner. Carl never told me not to tell anyone. So why not tell? To be honest, I do not know what a person could have done for me. I wanted to be loyal to my family and I knew that he was very dangerous. I was more afraid of Carl than anything or anyone else. So had someone asked me, I would have likely lied.

DarRen was telling me that nothing could have been done to save him from the abuse. He would have lied out of fear. What does that mean for the DarRens in this world—the abused children? I read that one in four children is abused. I am disgusted by this. I hate this fact. Would other children like DarRen lie about the abuse? Well, if some percent lies and hides the abuse, that only makes the statistic worse, doesn't it. How was DarRen able to go to school? To be involved in sports or even the locker room where the boy next to him dropped his shorts and DarRen fled to the hallway to vomit. Constant pain and no one to talk to or vent with. Well, no one except his brother, Vonn.

. . . I was terrified of my brothers and didn't know to face them. Carl was a big guy, about 5'10" or so and a wide powerful body. We had a weight bench in the house. He worked out every day and played sports. He was a lineman in football.

Another of the sick games—if Vonn was protecting me or me him, Carl would make us choose who got it by rolling the dice and sometimes the dice would decide what would be done. When I got older many kids played craps but I would never touch dice. Neither would Vonn except with my granny when we played them board games that she loved, like Trouble *and* Sorry.

Sometimes when Vonn got it too from another brother, we would lock ourselves in the bathroom. We'd take a knife and jam it in the door frame. Because of how close the door was to the toilet, we could sit on the floor and use our legs against the toilet to keep it shut. I use to wonder how many times I had to do that before my punishment was done. Vonn said, "We can cut his thing off and stick it in him." I said, "And sew it shut." We thought that was funny.

I learned to recognize when one of them brothers was sexual. If I was to be punished sexually, I could tell before it started. There was a vibe in the air and once I identified who was the punisher of the day, I'd become whatever it was that softened this person. I tried to be nice to him. I'd sit by him. I'd give him some of my food. Because it was easier and less painful to do whatever to keep my clothes on. Taking the offensive usually kept my backside intact. I'd give oral. As sick as it sounds, it became a game to get it over with as soon as possible with the least amount of damage.

For me it was what it was and each time, because I survived, I said to myself, "Well, that wasn't that bad." One of the hard things is how easily I embraced it and how I had gotten to a point that I preferred certain things over others. If I was to be beaten or something like that, I had learned how to manipulate them to lessen the situation by getting what I preferred, if it must be. That was a sort of victory for me.

There were times when I got erections during my punishments and that memory is tough. All sorts of questions—one of the main, though not the only one—is, does this mean I'm gay. There are things that I like about men but I don't have any sexual attraction to them. That was the deciding factor. It was confusing because I liked girls. Shame, guilt and sadness ruled those days.

I read that a victim of sexual abuse may blame himself for the whole episode if he experienced any pleasure or desire during the molestation, not understanding that stimulating nerve endings is an involuntary response to what was happening. And DarRen's fear of being gay in neighborhoods where that was not okay? Although sexual orientation is virtually never a conscious choice, fear of gays was close by. DarRen had written, "My mother didn't want any of her kids to be a sissy or fag. It was her way of making us tough to survive the world as it presented itself to us. In our neighborhood during that time homosexuals were beaten up and chased off the block. I heard from my Jamaican uncle, 'Dem nuh walk a'bout de yard like dem a true cockwielder. . . mash down de batty bwoi.'"

. . . I was six, seven, eight, nine, ten, eleven. They were fourteen to eighteen. At times my comfort (being gentle) was not on the to-do list. Away from them it was a lot easier for me to relax and when I was at Granny's overnight she would always keep me by her. I would sleep in her room. Best sleep I ever got. "Smile," she would say, "That's the weapon of a Jamaican prince." My grannies would give words of encouragement. They would talk about how much of a gentleman I was. How smart. How I could be anything I wanted to be.

Then Mom came home from rehab. I thought it was over. I ran to her and hugged her tight and kissed her. She was in a wheelchair and others hugged her and I tried to hug her again. She used her arm to very lightly nudge me back and hugged the older boys.

In the same way I once turned to my stuffed lion to soothe the little girl I was, I was now turning to Gartner's book. At times just the smooth, cool feel of the cover brought relief since I knew I had someplace to turn. I didn't consider myself to be as naïve as DarRen thought I was or as out of touch. But these stories were the stuff of nightmares.

"Evil, AKA Carl"

. . . After Momma came home from rehab, everything did stop for a while. Then Halloween came.

Granny's house was pretty big—three rooms on the first floor. Four on the second, plus the basement and the attic. We went room to room in our costumes, trick or treating. When I got to the room Carl was in, he had his penis out and hard. He tried to pull me in. I snatched away and ran.

We played games in the living room. My granny loved to play games. We ate candy and played. Tic Tac Toe with the bean bags. Hungry Hungry Hippo. Trouble. Connect Four and Sorry. She loved Sorry. When Granny landed on your space in Sorry, she would thump your piece clear across the room and you'd have to go get it. To be partially fair, you could do the same to her, you just had to go get the piece when all the laughing stopped.

165

We were playin'. I looked up and seen Carl staring at me. He looked at me with such hate. I was so afraid, I peed on myself. I got in trouble for that and Granny took my candy and gave it to my brothers and sister to split up. That night I couldn't sleep. I knew he was coming and he did. He was so angry. I was terrified. He grabbed me and ripped off my underwear and pushed me back. We were in the upstairs living room. He grabbed my arm and spun me around. I was face down. My face in the cushion. Feet on the floor. He was on me. I felt he was naked. His penis bumped between my legs. I struggled to get away. I tried to scream. I wasn't really sure what was about to happen but I knew I didn't want it to happen. He gripped my head and pointed it into the cushion and pressed it down. I felt something wet being poured over my backside and it dripped down my leg. I felt something pressing at my backside. It wasn't that bad at first. Just pressure. And then I felt a very sharp stinging like pain. He huffed and puffed loudly. Soon it was over. He spun me around, gripped my face in his hand, squashing it. "Don't you ever run from me again." And he spat on my face. When he let me go, my legs gave out. I laid there and cried. My back and back side throbbed. I tried to stand up and it seemed like everything hurt: my neck, arms, stomach, back, my side, my legs. Everything. I wanted to take a bath. I felt something running down my leg and somehow I knew that this was different than before. I went to the bathroom. I stuck my hand in my pants and felt my backside. It was wet and sticky. When I pulled my hand out, I had blood on my fingers. I was horrified. The floor was white and as the water ran into the tub, I noticed red spots. I got into the tub and the water turned pink.

Dear DarRen,

I am listening, reading. I am here. I have few words of response right now, but I am hearing every syllable you are telling me. I am not afraid that your soil is soiling me.

CHAPTER 17

Granny Was the Best She Could Be Through Trouble and Sorrow

Who do you talk with if you are a big masculine guy? Well, maybe you tell a 5'3" woman like me, a caring woman who cannot look you in the eyes as you talk because the prison system believes she is a security risk and won't allow you to meet face to face. Maybe you tell because you know the story needs telling and doing so may help others facing similar... what? Incidents? Traumas? I don't know what words to use. DarRen's story continued.

... My father went to prison again and when he got out, he and several of my brothers and me went to Jamaica for part of a year.

I liked that I had been on a plane and others hadn't. When the plane landed in Jamaica, it was hot and when we got off the plane the smell was very strong. We were greeted by strangers as if we'd always been known. The drive was long and bumpy. We finally got to this very small town that had about ten or fifteen settlements. I do not know what else to call them. On ours there was a larger wood house with wood roofs. It looked like bamboo but bigger. There was mud or clay in between the cracks. Out back were several more one room houses, an outhouse and a bath house that no one ever used because it was easier to go to one of the bays or beaches nearby. In Jamaica, my father's family were farmers and so there was work to be done. But as a city boy I'd never done any real work. Out there, in the hot Jamaican sun, carrying the bags as the elders lop-n-top and sang these songs that seem to put you in this trance and pulled strength from my body I didn't know was there. I loved every bit of it. After I worked with them I was no longer "De fresh watah yankee bwoi" though I was still half-caste. I ate good. I slept whole nights. I was hugged and kissed. We sang. We laughed. We danced, not randomly but every day. I stopped having nightmares. The bed wetting stopped.

I played on palm trees and the vine trees—don't know the names of them. But we would run, jump, grab a hold and swing out and let go and drop about fifteen feet in the water. Then we'd run up and do it again. We played with banana leaves, which I didn't know were that big. They made great fans. Here's the trick. Take coconuts and get them from a tree in the shade. We'd take a rock and crack a hole in it and drink the milk. It's kind of bitter but it's nice and cool on a hot day. Sometimes we didn't go home for lunch; we'd take the boat out on the sea—a long walk—but a real adventure. We'd take the net and throw it in the water. About a half hour or so later we'd have fish. Cut it and gut it right there. We would sometimes cook it on a stick over fire. Other times we would take and make a hole in the sand first, put some rocks in the bottom and make a fire and cover the hole with banana leaves. Then we would go fishing and by the time we got back the fire would be either burnt out or near burnt out. Take the white stuff out of the inside of the coconut; we'd clean and gut the fish and stuff 'em and put them in the hole. By then the fire would be out and just set it on them hot rocks, cover it with the leaves and take a nap or go play and it would cook. We would take the fish, cut it up and mix it with the coconut and this green fruit (kinda bitter), or plain. Pretty good. I don't remember seeing a clock or a watch. Life was easy. We done our chores and we were free to go and do as we pleased. And we did; I loved their word sound and they loved mine. Funny how we wanted to trade spaces. Or so they thought.

For me, Jamaica is a reality/fantasy of a better time; a place to call home, which is why I painted that water and them mountains for you, Judy. We climbed to that cliff in the painting.

Having recently been immersed in the sunshine and song and smells of Trinidad and Tobago, I could imagine the relief of going to such a place, especially when that also involved being around family members who hugged and fawned over these half-caste boys who were blossoming more daily.

. . . But then we had to come back to the states. Mom was happy to see us. When my older brothers hugged me. I froze. I didn't know how to take that. Seeing them made it all came back.

It wasn't long before it all started again. This time things were a little different; there were lots of beatings and weird posings— standing or kneeling in difficult and often dangerous positions. Me and Vonn were close before but we grew even closer during our time on the island. They started in on me. Vonn stood in between us and told them to leave me alone. This sealed my connection with him. But then things got really bad. The bindings got longer. The beatings were unpredictable and they would sometimes result in a loss of consciousness, bleeding from somewhere and swollen this or that. One day, being told to give oral, if it was over too fast, the hot box—locked in that closet. The next day, if it took too long, hot box.

In school one day, a teacher asked me what I had in my pants. I didn't tell her it was tissue to stop the bleeding. She took me to the principal's office. I feared being discovered. I panicked and grabbed a glass candy dish off the secretary's desk and threw it. I was suspended. They no longer cared about my pants. I used Aloe Vera to help myself heal and tissue to cushion sitting on them hard ass chairs for eight hours. Sometimes if I was caught off guard there would be bleeding; likely some tearing. I wondered how other teachers could not notice this bulge, but they didn't. The schools said I was a problem child. In my photos, I barely smiled.

Sometimes I forget, reading these stories, that DarRen was a little boy when most of this was happening. A child playing board games with his gramma. He has suggested, and it may well be the case, that at least some measure of his mental illness came from these years of trauma. Paranoia, his doctors said. Imagine lying in bed night after night with the door ajar so you could hear your abuser coming to get you. Imagine your punishment being determined by a dice roll. Imagine being tortured while others walk past, unconcerned. Childhood/adolescent schizophrenia his doctors said. Imagine tearing holes in the walls trying to get to the voices in the dark and seeing people and creatures slithering away—some real.

. . . One day Carl grabbed Vonn. I knew Carl's knee was sore so I kicked him there as hard as I could. He dropped Vonn. I tried to get away. Carl fell as I ran but turned to chase me. He grabbed my foot. Vonn hit him with something. I kicked him. He kicked Vonn, who flew across the room, hit the stove and broke his arm. I ran to the bathroom and grabbed the knife we used to lock the door by jamming it in the frame. Carl spun around so his feet were toward me. Each time I approached, he kicked at me. Vonn ran out the back door. I ran out the front.

We ran to my granny's house. She took Vonn to the hospital. We told them we were jumped by unknown kids. Two days later, I had another tangle with that brother. I got hurt pretty bad.

Sex, drugs and violence was my teens, and of course jail. Some really bad stuff has happened and I've done just as bad or worse. As I've gotten older I learned that this was not about punishing me. These people were just sick pervs. I'm sure (almost sure) that everyone in the house suffered some form of abuse.

My cousin, P, and her unborn baby was killed. Then my cousin, N, was killed by a serial killer. C, the sister of a friend of mine two apartments down, was shot and killed. T was shot and killed by Vice Lords (a rival gang). M was also killed by Vice Lords. This was all in that one summer.

What do you mean what do I do with image of someone being shot in the head? I saw TwoLips and others shot in the head and I even seen one shoot himself. When these things are presented as normal to you, they are not as upsetting as you may think. It was not until I began to fully realize that these things were wrong, and I mean really wrong, that the stress really set in. They were hard at the time but they are harder now and I think that's the reason I seem to cry so easy. They sit in my head, undisturbed until I see or hear or smell something that reminds me and then I have to deal with them again. I was not told that these things were not normal and that I was being traumatized. It was just life, so I dealt with it as best I could.

I began to understand death and how you could kill someone and it was clear. I seen it. These people were not my family and they were trying to kill me. My granny told me to always go after what I want and to defend what's mine with my life. She was talking about something else. But the words mixed with this new understanding.

Go after what you want, Granny had said. DarRen did that in large measure; he stepped beyond the physical abuse and emotional trauma the best he could, just as we all do the best we can. He fought back, but in doing so, resorted to extreme measures, seeking to take control over his own life. Over his and Vonn's lives.

. . . I decided the punishment was over for Vonn and me. Anger kicked in when I learned what sexual abuse was and about homosexuals.

I was eleven years old.

"RIP 2PAC"

Between the murders and my increasing size, I came to truly understand what it means to kill and what really could cause death. Tupac once said, "Get my weight up with my hate and pay 'em back when I'm bigger." I had the words before me and a basic concept from Granny, "Go after what you want." I knew it now. I realized in the deepest part of myself that what they were doing to me was wrong and could lead to death. I also knew that no one else was going to save me.

I became really aggressive. When you crossed me I could be extremely violent. I would not stop until someone pulled me off. My goal was to make it stop. If they were going to kill me then one of them was coming with me. Years of violence and forced sex led me to sex, violence and drugs. It became clear to them that if they approached me with their penis they could lose it. I remember a conversation between my uncles. They were laughing about Jim Brown reportedly biting off the finger tip of an opponent during a football game and when the reporters asked him why he bit off the man's finger, Jim Brown said, "Everything inside

172

the mask belongs to me; everything outside the mask belongs to him." Everything in my mouth belonged to me...

My emotional scars and personality flaws are still there. I had a girlfriend when I was sixteen and she was about thirty. She had no idea I was so young. I had a pretty nice car and I had no problem getting into local taverns around Waukegan and Kenosha. In any case, I was at her apartment. We (me, her and her son who was like five) had spent the day at Six Flags. I had fallen asleep playing with her son on the bed, watching Barney or something.

I felt someone moving my arm; I then felt something tight being tied to my arm and I began punching with my free hand and kicking and thrashing around trying to get free. When I realized that I was not being attacked, I looked and she was on the floor. I had kicked her in the side after I had punched her in the face. She was bleeding. She had tied my hand to the head board of the bed.

I was so angry that I could not fully appreciate what had just happened. I went and got in my car. I inhaled some Mary Jane flowers. I sat there for about fifteen minutes before I went back in. I felt horrible. She was pregnant and separated from her husband because he beat her. When I had slept with women before—not in the sexual sense—just sleeping, I had never had any problems. There were (and are) times when I had nightmares and I would just get up and go for a walk and have me a smoke and everything would be fine.

She asked what the hell was wrong with me and I could not tell her that I had been physically and sexually abused and a lot of it had to do with me being tied up or tied down. I just told her I have issues with being tied up and I just reacted. I gave her some money and I left. She tried to tell me that she understood but I could not look at her anymore without feeling guilt. Plus a part of me felt so exposed. I felt as if she knew.

Do I have lasting effects? Another one of your questions! Pause for my laughter. Yes but nothing overly serious. I have many bones that creak and pop: a wrist that clicks—more my right than left which I'm sure has come from being tied up and handcuffed and struggling so many times, a back that pops, knees that crackle, head injuries, and if I roll my neck from one side to the other it sounds like sand in my skull. I'm hoping that any rips or tears I may have are not noticeable to a layman. There are scars all over my body—most visually small—but I remember each one. Certain sounds and smells are bad. (Milk. Carl drank a lot of milk and smelled like it; I used to think people could smell him on me.) Jason Lyric is a really good movie. But I can never watch the beginning. The first time I did, I cried. Ever since then, if it ever comes on, I skip the beginning—the sounds of a boy crying as he is being raped.

Bugs. I hate bugs; remembering being in that hot box and having them crawl on me. Being tied up is an issue as well. Having my face touched—things were done to my face, having stuff smashed in it, stuff smeared on it, being grabbed by my jaw like some sort of animal. When I gained control over my body, I stopped people from touching any way <u>they</u> wanted to. I have deep insecurities and trust issues. But, hey, everything works.

I think of the number of times DarRen has written that he is not sure he can trust me. He says he is an action man. The way he builds trust in someone is through seeing what their actions are. I think of Vonn who stood up for his brother against the most frightening and violent person either had ever known. Action. Trust.

. . . I'm thinking back to the day my girlfriend told me she was pregnant with our son. She did not know that I had been told that I could not have children. I always said it was a football accident but that was not the cause. I had an injury from one of my punishments. I sat all day in school with my penis swollen and bleeding. When football practice came, as soon as we took the field, I told my friend to tackle me. I used that as my chance to see the nurse. They wanted to call the hospital. I refused but they called anyway. I took off. When I got home, my mom took

me to the hospital in Waukegan. I did not get then why she done that, but she was taking me across state line because she must have known that the police could not get the records.

Two doctors, at different times, told me I could not have children so when my girlfriend told me she was pregnant, that was proof that she was unfaithful. I have always thought what if I had known that was my child she was carrying on that day she told me, would it have been a life-changing event? That memory, for some reason, is in black and white. Almost all my memories are in color. (I first saw my son after I was incarcerated.)

I got diminished hearing, waning eye sight. I have trust and abandonment issues. I'm suspicious of nearly everyone. As far as being told someone loves me, well, those brothers told me they loved me. I can tell you, them words don't mean shit. And as a side dish, I'm in this stinkin' cell.

But I won. Most of them are dead. I'm still standing. Before all that has happened happened, I was a baby born to parents who I'm told loved me. Grandparents and brothers and sisters claimed to have showered me with love and affection. So though I do not recall those days, my core/center is love and affection. Some part of me must have kept it on file. I have a handsome son and grandbabies, and a better relationship with my mom. And my granny? She was there for me the best she could be, through trouble and sorrow.

Dear DarRen,

I'm sending you a Christmas gift from the Department of Corrections approved inmate property vendor. A scarf. It is prison-gray (Is that a color?). But think of it as a hug from me. And a thank you for telling me these stories of the soil, as you called it. I understand many things better now. I see why trust is a big deal, as we have discussed. And I see how some of my actions have felt like attempts to control you. I didn't understand. I am also thinking that I cannot imagine a worse environment for you than prison is: a place with chains and belts and punishments and dark cells and bugs and restricted access to food. You wrote that your homeboys admired the fact that you have heart. I agree with that in a different context. I admire the fact that you have maintained heart. And humor. And sanity.

CHAPTER **18**

Journey Home

F amily members had arrived—no sleighs, few bells. The Christmas
tree was unfurled. Others in my family don't deeply care about
this part of the Christmas shimmer. For me, it's not so much about
the presents or even the spiritual message; more pagan, actually. It is
the promise of warming lights in the darkness. It is the smell, sap and
softness of a white pine or Fraser fir. The tradition is to unpack the
decorations and put the ornament my son made in first grade from
a toilet paper roll at the tree top, even though those cylinders weren't
designed to last and the ornament is now worn and unglamorous.
The cats always share my joy as they drink water from the tree stand
and imagine they are wild woodland creatures, red in tooth and claw.

The turkey had browned and was perfect with grilled pineapples
arranged along the edges of the large turkey platter I inherited from
my parents. Sweet potatoes mounded with marshmallow. Green
beans with almond slivers. None of my mother's lost wedding
silverware, but still a family (albeit it small) gathering.

The letters describing DarRen's abuse had stopped; enough of the
story was told. It was as if we had called a truce for the time being. A
storytelling truce, although he described it differently.

Dear Judy,

I understand your need for time to think about these stories. The reality for me is that around every bend there is a new problem, so I need to make peace with what I can and move on. I do not have enough hands to carry all of that baggage and I'm running out of closet space to tuck this shit away. Your life is very easy, so for you, who is clearly far more adjusted and well put together, it cost very little to explore your pains and pangs in life. For me, there are very deep and dark traumas. There are nightmares, sleepless nights, abandonment, mistrust and a fleet of shit. There is no warm sand and easy days to wash it all away. No soft warm bed, no comfort of having someone nearby if you need them. You have many people who can be there in that moment if the exploration of them pains gets to be too much. I have only me and a belief—hope—that this unseen spirit I call Jah will not allow it to go too far.

Your support is great, but in digging into some of these issues as we touched on the past, some very raw emotions came up and I truly felt alone in those times. Your kind words that had no physical touch with them were not enough. You have not seen my darkness. I cannot afford to go there and if I am there I MUST get away fast. I will do what you will not do; I think what you cannot imagine. So this abuse and rolling memories of Vonn days are very tough for me. Think about how rocky and tense things got as I was writing about those things. There were situational things, but underneath there was more. Okay, was not planning to go there, but there we have it.

Sometimes I get down, especially when I realize how much destruction I've left in my wake. I am looking to heal the wounds and Jah tells me, in helping, I am helped.

The family gathering had been just the right length. There is something equally cleansing about the end of that seasonal celebration when the ornaments are packed away on the closet shelf and the new year begins. Classes would start in a few weeks. My birthday was coming.

I wanted to be alone to think and try to make sense of all I had read. Greedily I wanted to go back to the warm Trinidadian retreat and just be in the sun. But, of course, that wasn't practical. Instead, I decided to drive the path from my girlhood home to the long-ago site of the family's summer cabin. A journey home. Along that roadway lay a geographical link between DarRen's and my lives.

First, I drove to the suburban Chicago village of my youth. Then and now, I love the ancient oaks and elms, enveloping branches touching over residential roads. This suburban community could have been one of those DarRen's family drove through to see the flickering Christmas lights of what his mom called the white peoples' houses where concern for the electric bill was nonexistent.

Tidy. That is a word that describes Chicago's North Shore. Orderly. Controlled. Beautiful in terms of color, pattern, and design. Details are attended to. After a lunch together, my brother and I drove past the three-story Colonial house we grew up in. Built in the 1920s, it has been remodeled since we played in the stairwells, nooks and crannies. It looked pristine. We shared some laughing memories, then went our separate ways.

DarRen had given me some addresses of the places where his family stories had taken place. From his descriptions, I realized he had family or connections spread out along that nearly 300-mile path I was following. I wound north along Lake Michigan, as my sister and I used to do. Wilmette, Kenilworth, Winnetka, Glencoe... and then North Chicago, where my father had spent half of his career in medical research.

I drove to the front security gate of the pharmaceutical company to ask if they had a library or archive area open to the public where I could read about the medical research my father had been involved with. I won't describe the look I got—the idea that an outsider would even ask such a question—and simply say I was told, "No."

I was on a self-imposed budget for this weeklong trip, but hated the sameness of the motels with numbers like 6 or 8. So I looked for an old motel in Waukegan/Zion and spotted one just off to the side of an overpass. It looked like the Mom-and-Pop motels from the days when people drove Route 66, listened to Johnny Cash, and wore poodle skirts—well, the women, that is. I parked. The Middle Eastern couple who owned or managed the place looked at me questioningly when I asked for a room; an inexplicable glance passed between them. I asked if they had wireless Internet connection in the room. A bit of a smile and then they called their son—a ten-year-old—who said he would help me connect to their router. They carefully positioned me in room number one, next to their living quarters. I smelled curry.

After the 10 p.m. news, I turned off the lights to sleep. But there was much activity in the parking lot, so I peered out. A van pulled up. Many women got out and went into the rooms down the way from mine. Shortly, men pulled up, one going into each room. Flatbackers. I even knew the term. I slept restlessly until finally, about 3 a.m., I heard the women collectively get back in the van and depart.

What did I feel? Slightly more aware of the world that DarRen had grown up in that had not intersected with mine until he and I began sharing our stories. I felt grateful to the Middle Eastern family who cared for me in their own way. I felt sad that they had to make a living doing something that was surely a violation of their (probably) Islamic beliefs. But again I recognized that people do what they have to do to survive and sometimes that hurts themselves and even hurts others. Any answers I could offer to this cruelty and this met need would be simple and superficial, so I'll offer none.

Early the next morning, I drove back to the icy lakefront, exposed by leafless trees, and on north toward Kenosha. I was very aware as I drove that DarRen and Vonn and their brothers had taken this very road—these roads—many times. This was his territory. I remembered his stories of getting chocolate milk and donuts and sitting by Lake Michigan. I remembered the story of the drive from North Chicago to Waukegan hospitals when Vonn was shot. I remembered the chilling stories of physical and sexual abuse as I drove past some of the home addresses DarRen had written down for me in Kenosha. His grannies' homes. The apartments his family had lived in. When he sent me the Kenosha addresses, DarRen also described his neighborhood.

... From that school moving toward the park (and the bridge where the little girl and I sat) and beyond in that direction was middle class. From that school, moving in the other direction was not middle class. If it was, it was lower middle class. It was the poorest part of town back then: 18th to 14th, 68th to 69th; boxed in a very poor area in comparison to everything else. Across from K.C.C. was a factory that covered about four blocks one way and about five blocks another way. It was torn down and is an empty lot now. They fixed some of them houses over there but it's still hood. When we moved from that area to across town, we had been considered as stepping up. Someways we did. Others we didn't. The gangs were worse over there and the drugs; more people by the park were in one, sometimes two family homes. The other side of town were four family buildings. From 38th to 36th and part of 35th—both two blocks on 37th and 36th—were these four family apartments. More people in a smaller space, more guns, more drugs, more gangs, more problems.

A huge factory that once provided jobs and a reasonable wage in the neighborhood. Gone.

I drove past the places where the hideous abuses had happened. Those buildings had to be haunted. My stomach turned. How can such things happen? As was true with my own father's stories of his siblings' abuse, where were the older siblings who might have intervened—could have intervened? But in DarRen's experience, unlike my father's, the older children were not spared from involvement in the abuse; they were the abusers.

I watched children coming out of the elementary school DarRen attended across the street from one of the addresses; the place where he once ran his bike into a wall while intending to demonstrate his bike-riding skills—the school where the teacher asked him what that was in his pants and, when it came time for him to confess, he broke the candy dish so no one would ask more questions. Another suspension.

Children were coming out of that school. Many of them. Bright faces. Playful. How many were being abused in the same way? What percent. Ten? Twenty? More?

The second night on the road, I stayed in Kenosha. Whether it was because of the previous night's lack of sleep or just being in Kenosha, I was afraid. I double locked the door. I was afraid of a ghost even though I knew the abusive Carl was dead and that those who supported him were dead. And yet the unaccountable disquiet remained.

My girlhood world had been all safe and cozy and well fed. It was the world where little girls frowned as they got their pigtails pulled and little boys were the stuff of snips and snails and puppy dog tails. What is real? What about right and wrong? Why does so much go to so few who are then unwilling to share? How will we be judged by history for stories like DarRen's (and mine)?

My journey continued north to Green Bay, where I spent two days in the library, just as I had done in Seattle looking up information on my father's crime, only this time it was DarRen's crime. I wanted to see the local Green Bay perspective. (My academic training taught me to triangulate information—to look at the same subject from different perspectives, which I was reflexively doing.) There were pages of information on DarRen's crime. Newspaper articles and headlines. Pictures. I read and read and finally returned to my hotel and wrote down the fury I was feeling. Furies, actually. This is an excerpt from my journal that night.

I have spent the day in the downtown Green Bay library nauseatingly going through microfilm from the Green Bay Press Gazette. *I copied 27 or 28 or 29 pages from the papers—the number differed each of the three times I counted them, so just paid for 29 pages. The inability to count may be a symptom.*

I then drove past many different addresses in Green Bay— the site of the killing with the hospital next door that could not save the victim because of the depth of his injuries. The family apartment. The apartment DarRen went to after the stabbing.

Newspaper headlines on DarRen's crime

And the site of the famous big-ass burger that was "nearly as good as DarRen could cook." (It was torn down.)

It takes a lot for me to build to fury. But fury is what I am feeling right now. I hardly know where to start; so many things are setting my teeth on edge.

The first fury is with the massive social services systems that are supposed to be in place in this civilized country to stop the kinds of abuse that DarRen experienced. Where were they? Why didn't they intervene? Why did the system break down in event after event and city after city and school after school and juvenile justice system after juvenile justice system?

Fury two: Where in the hell were the adults whose job it was to protect this child and the other children around him?

Fury three: Race and economics. This man is African-American and African-Caribbean. I see prejudice written all over this story. Four hundred years of slavery that has burned its message of struggle on the face of a major segment of this country's population. An extended and intertwined family unit that was into drugs and prostitution and likely more as a way to make a living—to survive in a world that discounts the skills and insights and energies they could bring to legal economic systems. Why have they had to resort to these underground economies that both hurt others and hurt themselves? Families deliberately broken apart so that even that sustenance was denied.

Fury four: The disconnect between the judicial system and state-of-the-art scientific knowledge. Why isn't neurocriminology (the constraints on free will that emerge from a mix of known biological and sociological factors) part of our legal system? Medical groups issue clinical-practice guidelines to physicians, for example. Why aren't the findings from brain research used to help offer compassion to those steeped in violence, criminal behavior and anti-social acts?[2]

Fury five: The parochial judge who could not see the victim in the delinquent and who sought to change a whole systemic problem by punishing one individual. Not only is this deeply wrong at a humanitarian level, but to my mind, it is criminal. (Is there any connection between punishment and deterrence of crime?)

Fury six: Drugs, the impact of the war on drugs (especially crack), on DarRen and the entire family unit where hard drug use was a source of amusement and teasing among children and adults alike.

Fury seven: The media that portrays violence, sex and drugs as positives, as exciting. Violent TV, movies, music and video games all aimed at revving up kids—males in particular—to drift toward acts of viciousness.

Fury eight: Our narrow societal stance that links the norms and ideals of mankind to violence.

Fury nine: The cruelty and insensitivity of the girls who played on DarRen's mental illness and heightened his paranoia. And he stabbed a human being out of reckless panicky fear.

---

2   See Adrian Raine, *The Anatomy of Violence: The Biological Roots of Crime* (2013). Pantheon Books: New York.

Fury ten: The Green Bay Press Gazette *that ran front-page articles on gang violence after the stabbing, stirring the community toward terror over this issue. No one explored DarRen's story or the fact that he wasn't in a gang in Green Bay. No one examined his role in this event. No one cared about his family and what they were going through. No one even interviewed them—or if they did, that information was not put in the papers (well, and what would they have said if interviewed?).*

Fury eleven: The media, again, with their obscene coverage of the OJ Simpson trial, which was going on at the same time as DarRen's trial and sentencing. "Violent black men. . . "

Fury twelve: And this should be earlier on the list: the abusers. The siblings who hurt DarRen and others. Why?

Fury thirteen: DarRen's knowledge of his own mental health issues that he could have tried to control as he was moving toward adulthood.

Fury fourteen: The whole prison system that focuses too much of its energy on punishment over rehabilitation: a system that we, the public, allow to lock up people with mental illnesses rather than treating them. A system that, in my final estimation, is even more about power more than it is about punishment.

Fury fifteen: The family's move to the ultra-conservative Fox Valley area with troubled kids, putting them in line to conflict with the community and systems. Why couldn't DarRen and Vonn have stayed in Jamaica? Where was any recognition of their assets—artistic talent, heart? There was no one to foster this. No one who had the strength or knowledge of how to nurture these talents.

And finally, feeling sapped, I drove on to Door County. It was winter quiet in this resort area where my family had spent many summers in the house we collectively built (no longer ours). Cedar branches hunched under the weight of the snow. The winter ferry to Washington Island ran sporadically, smashing through the ice. I took it across Death Door Straights and stayed in a bright, beautiful place, overlooking Lake Michigan. I walked (pulling my scarf tightly around my neck) and thought and wrote and walked more. I wrote and walked and walked and wrote. A poem.

Today I saw
an out-of-season newborn rabbit that'd been
chewed in half.

Cotton fur.
Silken ears,
  like clipped wings.
Head and heart intact.

A life, bit.

The secret, they say, is to do a
life bit
with integrity.

How?

Teacher with textured mind,
Teacher with rainbow heart—
  who stares into predatory eyes
  and smiles —

How do you do your life bit?
How do I do mine?

CHAPTER 19

So That Is a Robin

I had driven back to Madison slowly, taking back roads. Mounds of snow pushed aside in parking lots, waiting for the thaw. Winter has its own kind of beauty. I struggle to see it each year. Best of all, the spring semester was coming. Even though school began in earnest in February, it still offered the promise of new beginnings. It felt good to be back to the solid base of home and routines after my week of travels, the Christmas family visits and the Trinidad adventure.

At the post office, letters—DarRen's response to poem and my questions about his life in prison.

Dear Judy,

So you think I'm a rabbit? Cut a 6'4" rabbit in half and you have two 3'2" rabbits—still nearly as tall as you and your sister, together! Okay, not quite that bad—I'm only 6'3".

Ironically, prison may have saved me. If I hadn't gone to prison, I think I may have taken my own life a long time ago but as long as I'm alive, I've got a chance to change things. That which is meant for you will not pass you by. If I give up or give in, they win. They are the courts, the witnesses that refused to tell the truth, my brothers, the system. Who knows, they still may win. It may be the divine plan for me.

I was trained for prison. As kids, we visited my father, brothers and uncles in Wisconsin prisons. It could have went another way but I didn't learn my lessons early on. I've been incarcerated since I was seventeen and I figure, Jah willing, I have about fifty years of life left in me. Fifty more years in prison! For years I've felt my life had a purpose. I didn't know what that was and I've questioned Jah, "Why would you let those things happen to me? What happened to protecting your children?" Still, Jah light shines in me despite them hitting me with the best of their worst.

As I entered prison, my father told me "Strike first, strike hard, strike fast, never show mercy, never show fear." After my trial, I was taken to Dodge Correctional Institution for processing, like every Wisconsin prisoner. Pulling up, there was the fence with all its wire and razor. Once inside they took my property away.

"There are pictures of my son in that bag. He was just born and I want them pictures back."

"You'll get it back; we have to check it first."

They took the chains off me.

"Sit down." A lady who never looked up asked all sorts of questions. "Name?" "Race?" "Gang?"

"No gang." She checked a box.

"Tattoos?"

"Yeah."

"Describe them."

"I have my mom's name with a heart and wings on my chest."

"Show me."

She looked, then went to the earlier box about gangs, scratched out "No" and checked the "Yes" box. There went my fresh start.

After we left there, we went into a basement. "Step into the shower stalls and strip."

"I need a cup for my hearing aids."

"You deaf?"

I just stared at him. "Show me your hands, spread your fingers, arms over your head. Take your finger and fold down your ear. Now the other. Open your mouth—tongue up, tongue

*down. Let me see your gums. Flip down your bottom lip. Now
your top. Lift your penis, now your sack. Spin around."*

*When I spun around and was facing him again, he seemed
angry. I waited for what was next. He motioned for me to spin
around again. As I did and faced him again, from his neck to his
scalp his face was red. When people are angry, they don't speak
clearly so I cannot follow the shape of their mouths. I pointed to
the cup and my ears because it was clear he wanted something
from me. I just didn't know what. He looked at the cup on the
floor and at me. He laughed, picked up the cup and gave me my
other ears. I put them in.*

"Can you hear me now?"

"Yes."

"Turn around and bend over."

"Why?"

"Because I said so."

"I'm sorry but I can't do that." He asked me why.

I stammered, "I just can't."

He leaned in closer. "How old are you?"

"Eighteen."

"First time in?"

"Yeah."

"Is there a problem; do you need to see a doctor?"

"No."

"Well, I need to see."

*I persisted, "Is there another way where I don't have to bend
over?"*

*He grumbled, "Arms in the air over your head, squat and
cough. But you better find a way to get past your issue otherwise
refusing could land you in the hole."*

I thought, "Hole?"

*That first night they took me to Unit Seventeen, a basement
cell. I was not easy sleeping in the room with strangers; I had
been beaten badly in the shithole Brown County Jail when
guards intentionally put me in with Native American prisoners,
twice. The news of Mr. Fish's death was in all the newspapers.*

After a week, we were watching the first video about prison lovin' and tattoos. I hear a whisper, "Nephew." I did not turn around or anything. I heard it again, I still did not answer. Then I heard, "DarRen D'Wayne." No one calls me that. I turned and seen my uncle smiling at me. I always liked him—he named me and my twin, who died as a baby—so not a problem. He pointed to the cigarettes—squares to your father, Judy—I had sticking out of my bag and said, "Send me a pack." You know, thinking back to when your father paid the kitchen worker with packs of cigarettes for extra food, today that would be a major offense, meaning time in the hole. I wonder what would have happened, if anything, if your father had been caught? Or was that another way his status allowed him to have a unique prison experience. Anyway, my uncle and I did not get caught.

I get sent to Unit 9. The guy ask me for my name and number. I said, "DarRen Morris 920-555-0507."

"What the hell is that?"

"My number," I say. He shook his head and put me in cell 1. It was the first time he had smiled. He was coming off as the mean one before that.

In the cell, all the stories about prison flooded my mind. My roommate stood up. I had never seen a man that big. Very mean lookin'.

"What's your name?"

"Psycho."

He was in for 2nd degree homicide. Someone tried to steal his car and when he went out to defend his property, the guy hit him with some sort of board and Psych, as we called him, hit the guy back. Psych figured he was knocked out so picked him up and laid him on the curb side. Psych called for help. The guy never woke up. He was in a coma; he died a year later. Psych was a gentle childlike giant. He was playful and liked to wrestle. He had a lot of respect for me because I was not afraid of him. I was terrified. But I could not let him know I was afraid.

My next roommate was a young white guy from Milwaukee. He was only there for two days. The first night, just like had been done for me, I offered him a few cakes and such as he had just got there and did not have his stuff yet. After I gave it to him, he said, "You one cool ass nigga." I could tell in his mind he meant no harm because it was clear from how he acted that he was very much a part of the urban world either in reality or through music. I let him know I was not a fan of that word and would appreciate it he did not call me that. (I say the same thing to blacks.) He apologized and we moved on. Next day he said something very similar and I restated my position. "Whatever dude, I ain't nevah met no nigga that was ashamed of being a nigga."

Then he had a accident getting off the top bunk. The stool slipped and he hit his head on the sink, well, actually his face hit the sink. He was bleeding a lot. They took him to get him fixed up and asked me what happened. "Don't know." Two days later, he refused to come back in the cell with me so they took him to the hole for refusing to lock in. They took me too.

Later I was moved from Waupun to the North Cell Hall of Green Bay Correctional Institution. It was January, 1995. As we walked in, it was wild like in the movies. Green Bay prison was known as Gladiator School. It was nothing like the small little quiet place we just left in Waupun. Big. Loud. Boom boxes blared. There was a popular song out that use to be one of my favorites 'til they changed my image. It was called, "I wanna sex you up" by Color Me Badd. The prisoners were singing this to us. The officer with us was laughin'. Paper was set on fire and thrown at us, floating from the tiers like fiery angels. Guys were making comments as we walked in. "I get the tall yellow bone; he looks like he likes it rough." Me and my buddy are the same height. I looked at him and said, "Good luck."

I went to court in February, 1995, and got sentenced. That judge choose to exercise his discretion as he set my parole eligibility date. When he said 2095, all I heard was '95. I replayed it in my head. My public defender said, "Don't worry, we will appeal it." It clicked this chump did not say 1995, he said 2095. So that's 30, 40, wait, 100 years. I turned and I saw all of the cameras flashing. My mother was crying. Everyone with me was crying. And I wanted to cry to, but I couldn't. I knew I had to hold it in. I had to do something and the only thing I could think of was to throw up a gang sign. I do not know why but I did. Deflection maybe?

They took me in a side hallway. It was long and narrow; all white. At the end of the hallway was a holding cell. I replayed everything over and over in my mind. I felt like they were taking me to the electric chair. It looked like that the way the light came in. Everything got blurry and my legs went out. I fainted. When I came to I was on my back and they were all kneelin' over me trying to give me water and telling me to be still. I was trying to figure out what had happened. They took me back to the joint and put me in observation/suicide watch for the night.

The next day they put me back in the cell. People were calling my name and they were threatenin' to beat up the guards. "Man, dem honkeys ottah order fo' given' shorty all that damn time." I had no fight in me. I slept in all my clothes for two days. I was getting drugs sent to the cell by people I did not know. I did not want them. I gave them to my cellmate but he was a health nut so he flushed them.

On the third day, my cellmate said, "Times up with all that soft shit. They gave it to you now you got to do it. That's all to it." He kept talkin' and I embraced the logic in what he was sayin'. I got up, brushed my teeth and as I brushed I became violently angry. My face got hot. I felt as if my blood was on fire. I said, "100 years," out loud.

I turned and I saw the judge standin' there smiling at me. When it was over, he had 21 staples and over 100 stitches, I think it was 117. I fractured his skull and his eye socket, which I did not know was possible. I broke his left leg and his right arm in two places. I do not even remember the incident, just the report stating I beat my roommate.

It was maybe a year from the incident that I was laying in my bunk one night listening to music when I remembered how my roommate had to absorb my pain in the most violent way. To this day I regret doing that. It was what I knew how to do.

They put me in to see the shrink and put me back on medication. The delusions did not stop. Back then they had this part in the Department of Corrections rules, if you were mentally ill and your mental illness was a factor, they would not punish you as harshly. Well, so much for rules. I am not sure how long I was in the hole. I was so doped up. They had double doors in one seg unit and if I was yellin' or acting out, they would close that second door. Once it was closed, complete silence and I could not see anything. It was hot, I mean hot to the point where the walls would be sweatin'. There was no set time limit to be in there. Sometimes they would forget about me. All meals were served on a brown napkin like the kind you see in most schools. No eating utensils but it didn't matter because I would be so hungry that before they had fed the guy next door I had eatin' mine all. One scoop of eggs and a half orange every morning. A very dry sandwich with one thin slice of deli meat and a few white crackers with a carrot or fruit for lunch and dinner. My real mental challenge was because I had only me in there and that was not a fun roommate. It was like being in the hotbox all over again.

When my mom came to see me, I barely remembered it, patchy memories. She complained and soon after they lowered the medication dose and let me out of the hole. They put me in a single cell and gave me a fan and loaner TV. It was the summer.

For a while, I was not a nice guy. I was frequently bullying people. I would go to a person's space and ask what they had to eat and my thing was you can either give me something to eat or I can come in and take it all and I usually made no secret about what I was doing and I did not discriminate. I especially liked the so called tough guys. I was a lot more muscular then; I worked out nearly all day from the time I woke up until I went to sleep. Not only did I fight but I fought well and often. I was mean. I was drawn into the gangs. I was growin' but I was still under a spell so to speak.

I met this guy who says, "I will pay you to be my security. If a dude start something I will pay you extra to smash him for me. If a dude don't pay me, I will pay you to go get the money or smash him for me." This was on top of a standard fee of $30.00 of canteen every week. I said, "Cool as long as you aren't start'n stuff and I wasn't fightin' sissys or fightin' over sissys. Cool."

One day we were on the rec field and I told him I missed my son and wished I had spent more time with his mom. He glared, "Fuck dem streets. Your life is in here now. Thinking about streets ain't gon' do nothing but drive you crazy." It made sense so I dived deeper into prison politics. But there was moments where I hated my life. I wanted more for myself. I tried to live two lives. I took parenting class and completed my high school equivalency degree.

One of my roommates had a visit from his son and daughter (two and seven). His ex-landlord brung them. His son hadn't seen him since he was eight months old. Now dial back two weeks, my roommate said with pride, "Junior is such a demon." I asked gently (because he could be touchy), and based on my new parenting ideas, "Do you think referring to him that way could cause him to live up to the title?" He admitted it was probably wrong.

His son, on the visit, can't sit still and is throwing things, hitting and trying to bully his older sister. This guy couldn't get his son's attention or find a way to calm him. The officers told him if he could not control his child they would terminate the visit. He tried to explain the situation and finally elected to end the visit after he became so overwhelmed that he cried. He then came back to the cell and cried again. I got him drunk. He cried some more. I was a little shocked to see this taking place but I told him that he couldn't allow himself to see one situation as the entire picture. Between sobs he said, "My son doesn't know me." I wonder how the situation could have been improved by compassion.

After some prison visitors, the C.O. will do a strip search. When we are searched, we have to present every part of our body for visual inspection. I always wonder if there are telltale signs of what I've been through—the abuse. I usually block the event out and just go through the motions. Recently when I turned *around after a C.O. visually inspected the bottom of my feet and my ass, he had a kind of smirk on his face. I wanted to ask about scars but said nothing. It stayed with me. When I came back to the cell, I didn't go right back to writing. I couldn't. I was alone. In that space, I was that boy locked in the closet again. Knowing my roommate, had he seen me crying, he would have reached to comfort. History shows I would have lashed out at any male who approached. I was very emotional and balling like a baby. I was not thinking and I fear me when I'm not able to think. My instincts come from a bad foundation. I can and have over reacted. It's been a very long time since I've felt anything close to that.*

Dear DarRen,

Every time I read one of your letters, I am filled with questions. Are you pleased that I am not asking every friggin' one of them? I expect there is some relief in that. Now I'm simply listening; listening and trying to figure things out. You know, when I first visited prison as a way to learn more about my father's incarceration in order to write his story, I had no idea where the journey was going to lead. Of course, I couldn't have predicted you (how could I?). Your story has radicalized me. The reading, the visits to your family and to Kenosha and Green Bay, the memories I have of visiting you in person last year, all of this has changed me. I do not look at the world with the same eyes. I see the need for prison reform at nearly every turn, whether the topic is four-year-old kindergarten, healthy diet, or the price of healthcare (in part, ironically, for an aging prison population). There are problems prison will not fix. Early on you hoped your soil would not soil me. It hasn't. But it has removed the cloak I was previously allowed to wear, unchallenged. And you were right when you said there is no going back. Never.

Dear Judy,

I wonder how changed you are. Growing up, my mother said there was kids who had "no home training" and that had done them a disservice. I have seen many of them. They usually go from one extreme or the other. Either they lick the boot so often and so hard they take the color out of the leather or they are in seg, because they cannot handle having the freedom. How does one move beyond their upbringing? I wonder. I too struggle with changin'.

In prison, I met this guy named G-man—a smooth player. At least that's how it seemed. I talked to him and turns out he wasn't a player. He was a very sharp dude and positive and he told me about this group called self-help. The lady who ran the group grabbed and hugged me. I melted. I realized that I had to try to change. Was that what I need all along? Someone to reach out for me and just hug me. Of course not; I am a man, right?

But I couldn't change yet. The political ties I had wasn't letting go. I had to create a situation where I had enough power behind me that would give me a platform to stand on, to keep them from trying to hurt me. I pulled it off. I stood my ground with the gang I was branching out from. This division led to lots of violence within the prison. Several people got injured, but not too seriously and this led to my transfer back to Waupun. It was different and I couldn't adjust. I had several lapses in my mental stability. I was sent to the Resource Center—the state's secure mental health facility.

People say you can't make friends in prison. But I met P at the Resource Center, where we had a little more freedom. He is 6'7" and I'm 6'3" and we use to play one on one in basketball every day for three and four hours. He beat me more than I beat him. He's good; more like a ballet dancer. I'm a center and I play closer to the basket and use power and aggression. Playing him I got better at guarding. And I toughened him up. We bonded. That's rare for me. He went home several years ago; sent me a photo (no letter), $50 and a pair of gym shoes.

Then another, a odd little guy, but I use talk with him. When I met him some white guys were using him and making jokes, that he didn't seem to get, about his half black side. He was slow. I was pissed off. I lifted my wing, he slid in and rather than have an issue with me, they stopped picking on him. He had a sex case. His family said he couldn't come home because of what he had done to his niece that sent him to prison. I was sitting outside in the courtyard as I always did at the Resource Center. There was a loud noise that snatched me from my dream. The door came flying open. He had kicked it. As he ranted and raved, I handed him a cigarette (he never had any). Quickly he calmed down, but began to cry. He told me he didn't mean to hurt his niece. He thought it was okay because his mom done it to him and now she wouldn't let him come to her home.

That day he hung himself. The guards rushed in to save him. We heard yelling and a lot of rumbling. I remember smiling thinking he was putting up a good fight. One of the things the guards do is they will place a knee or forearm across your throat or neck to pin you to the floor. He died from a crushed wind pipe that they claimed was from him hanging himself. But I heard the fumbling. So they fought a dead body? They kept shouting, "Stop resisting." I don't believe their story.

A guy that use to be next door reminded me of my boyhood friend who had cerebral palsy. Right away I liked him; he was honest. It's hard for me sometimes to understand people's reasons for wanting to be around me. Is it genuine or is this some sort of trick or game? So we'd talk and kick it. He had an issue with his spine that caused him to lean to one side. On his right hand he was missing two fingers (pinky and ring). He twisted them off with his other hand. They said he died in his sleep from a blood clot. Except when I was working in the kitchen that day; he came through the line. He called me Mo (MOrris). "Mo, I'm next." Somehow I knew what he meant. I told him, "Don't do that. Hang with me for a little while longer. Tomorrow is always better."

"Nawl Mo, I've had it. You've been a good friend. Hope it works out on your case, but I have to go."

The next day he didn't stand for count. He had taken a handful of pills, put on his headphones, and drifted to some other place. I was sad to see him go. He had a lot of pain from his physical injuries and he was sad. No way out of prison. So he left on his own terms. I could relax around him; never had to watch him or worry about him harming me.

There are many kids, grown boys and men who are like him and me, in prison.

And then there are other kinds of guys. One was my roommate for a day. He done this little space-out thing; it's his gimmie. He's a pervert to the highest degree and that mental illness game gets him lots of female attention. He moved in the cell and we were watching TV and out of the corner of my eye I seen him rubbing himself through his clothes. I said, "There's only two things I'm afraid of and that's God and a hard dick. I can't whup God." He got the message and told the police to move him. He wasn't a friend.

Dear DarRen,

Good that "the police" moved the guy with the gimmie or he might have lost it. Clearly you were serious and he got that. Do the guards ever advocate for changes for you all? They must be able to see, better than anyone, what would improve the system and change the recidivism rate, which I recently read is 70% in California (highest in the country).

Dear Judy,

Could the guards step in? In theory, I suppose. But they collectively remain silent. Wrongdoings are covered up and that razor wire is their protection. The public doesn't see the nastiness. In here the guards reign supreme with unchecked power. It's unthinkable to most of the so-called civilized world that the police would do these things. Think back to the medical experiments your dad was involved in. The public did not see the unchecked power then either until there were Congressional hearings.

There's no question that there are differences in the guards. I've seen some that were not police, just uniformed people collecting a check. Some are indifferent; don't care one way or the other; some treat us as humans and as men. There are even some that I can say a few words to and have almost normal conversations. But it is also true that the teased, the bullied, the racist, the unaware, the miserable, and the powerless work in the prison system and treat us as if we're filth underneath their shoes. They are often connecting with urban people they have no real experience with; people who may be economically poor, low-educated, racially different, and/or mentally ill.

At times staff say and do things that sets off one inmate and I've heard officers say, "Finally, some action." They spray a guy with gas. Then with helmets and all sorts of protective gear, seven adults, usually all men (although recently they've begun allowing women on these teams and they are often more brutal than the men) go into the cell and subdue the out-of-control inmate. I've seen male corrections officers (C.O.s) treat women C.O.s in a way that if it was proven outside of here, the DOC could be sued for sexual harassment and some of them might even go to jail. To the untrained eye and ear you'll think that this is necessary (sometimes it is) and humane. But if you listen to the tape beyond the officers screaming "stop resisting" you'll repeatedly hear the men scream in pain. If you look you'll see the sneaky tactics: the short jabs to the back or head or face; the well placed knee to your nuts. They've found a new toy now: shocking people with these stun-guns and tasers, often after the prisoner is secured. They had me subdued once, handcuffed behind my back, and then they tased me. Anyone who picks on the weak, the defenseless, the restrained. . . Magga dawgs.

One time when I was in seg, the guards were bored and wanted to create excitement for that shift. I was no danger to them; locked behind a solid steel door. I was not a threat to myself. I remember feeling like an animal. I seen a program on TV once and they were having a contest of cows I think it was. The man grabbed the animal's mouth, pulled it open and stuck his fingers in the mouth and then proceeded to check that animal. I was like that cow. I was attacked by the guards who said I was being disruptive and threatening. I was not. I have no qualms about admitting when I have done wrong or do something that would cause a reaction but this was not one of those times.

There was an officer, a young female, twenty-two or so. She liked me, not in a sexual or relationship way; just thought I was okay. So she'd talk with me. She was new and when they are new like that, the other guards tell them all of the worst about us. We are charming and funny and the devil at the same time. She seen through this but she told me they were mad that she talked with me and that made her want to talk more.

They said they got a kite from an anonymous source saying I was going to kill myself, so they came and took me to the fish tank (observation cell). They refused to allow me to comply with the strip search. I was cuffed to a door and, using a knife that any rapist would dream of, they sliced off all my clothes with one swoop. The white shirt (officer) ordered this young woman to conduct a search of my naked body. Feet shackled, hands cuffed and tethered to the door, I tried to resist. They pulled and pushed until my body gave in. I couldn't believe she went along with this. I was trying to see her face but her hair blocked my view.

A single tear landed on my arm as she reached and pulled up my testicles. When they finished doing what they had to do, they threw me in the cell. She mouthed the words, "I'm sorry." I was so angry that they done that to her.

Then I was moved to Columbia Correctional Institution and I met wonderful people, like you, Judy. In a restorative justice program I met victim survivors. These women changed my life. For the first time I learned how crime impacted the victims. With this new soft compassionate heart, I wept for days over what I've done in my lifetime; what damage I've left behind me.

Restorative justice made me think of all the wrong I've ever done. That list is pretty long. I had never thought how will it hurt this person or this community if I steal or hit; shoot, slash, or stab. I done so much in my young life that I may very well have to give my life to atone in other ways. It's easier for me to forgive others than it is for me to forgive myself. I've forgiven most of the people who I believed have wronged me and the ones I haven't been able to forgive yet, I've made peace in the sense that if I see them there will not be a problem. Because I still suffer from some of the effects it's hard to forgive but it's my goal to be free from that completely.

Prison is designed to strip a person of power and voice. Just to be heard and embraced, not judged or laughed at, is what I wish for. Prison causes self-reflection, but the physical and soul mirrors in this place can be a bit dingy. I am trying to find a way to deal with this madness as best as I can. Prison won't stop me from transforming; just as what they done hasn't destroyed me. Jah says, "Nothing can touch you unless you allow it." Putting this into action, I accept who I am. I can admit at least to myself the reality of what I've endured and that I'm damaged by it. I also see Jah working on me, in me. Last night I wished I could have laid back and watch the soccer game with my baby granddaughter on my chest until she fell asleep.

Dear DarRen,

One thing I especially liked about your time in the Resource Center was the relative freedom. I remember you once wrote that you could sit outside and see a lake in the distance. You could sit in the grass (and sneeze). You were in a place where you could allow the natural world to touch you. That feels healing to me. Guess what I saw today? The first robin with its brown wings and red chest, walking around looking for worms or bugs. I cherish the early opening of spring. The first hints. The earthy smells (well, rotting leaves, but still earthy and promising). The chirps of thawing birds. Okay, whatever the trigger, I love the first hints of spring. What do you cherish?

Dear Judy,

So that is a robin—dark sienna and cadmium red I am thinking. Me and S has been watching a robin the past few days do exactly what you described, walk and cock his head and then peck at the ground. We had been wondering what sort of bird that was.

There's things I've never experienced; I've never been out of prison as an adult. I've never held a turtle or a frog or anything like that. I didn't know that brown bird with the red chest was a robin. I've never tasted a raw blueberry or a raspberry. I've never planted a tree and want to do that someday. I've never been kayaking or camping. I didn't get to go to prom but I'm probably not the only one.

Anyway, you asked what I cherish. I try not to cherish anything because nothing is really mine. On any given day these people can come and take anything they chose. Can you imagine someone going through your underwear drawer and throwing everything on the floor? Snatch the sheets off the bed, open your food and leave it, touch your toothbrush. The lack of respect for our space is very frustrating. Some do it as a punishment. You know, it isn't their job to punish us. Prison itself is the punishment. They shouldn't be standing on our necks. I do have a letter and that drawing my son sent me when he was like nine years old. He made a list of things he wants us to do if I ever get out. I have a few photos of him the day he was born. I cherish those things (and thank you for keeping the copies so these are never completely destroyed).

The cell becomes home; where your things are but that doesn't mean I think of this as my room. I tell all that move in, "I don't sleep a lot. I'm generally up doing something." Most start

"K, Full Belly, Sleepin"

out saying it's fine but when they see how extreme it is, things change. I'm not suppose to but I often sleep with one hearing aid in. My latest roommate said, "You're a very light sleeper. You seem to react every time I move." He assumes I'm reacting to him but that's how I sleep. Tossing and turning and waking up every few minutes. And when I'm able to stay asleep long enough to dream, the dreams are usually not so good.

When there are other noises or people talking I can't really distinguish words or sound. I'll hear a sound and know that it is a sound being made or someone is talking, but can't understand the words. But I've gotten use to that and under certain situations I can put it together from the shape the mouth is making and the sound. Once I get use to a person's voice, I learn the sounds. As I was writing yesterday, a face popped up in the cell windrow and it was a guy that was sleepin' on the floor in here not long ago (not enough bunks for everyone). I thought he said, "I'm movin' in." Later the officer said, "I see your in the Easter spirit."

203

Confused? Why? Long story short it was not mandatory that this guy move in here. They were about to put him somewhere else. He didn't want to go there. They said if he found someone, they'll let him go there. I was being asked if he could move in but that is one of the draw backs to my hearing. I did not catch that inflection in the voice that made it a question. So, now as I write this, he's on the floor, snoring.

In the cell, there is common space: sink, toilet, floor and desk. Nearly everyone adheres to the communal rules. When using the sink or toilet, leave it as you found it, clean. And always a courtesy flush for when flushing is essential. Nothing is private. My own body is not private. The toilet is positioned so no matter if I take a piss or shit, I'm looked upon.

These Columbia cells are pretty big, about six by nine feet for two men. The cells in Waupun and Green Bay are tiny. Let's start with the door. The door is a solid electronic sliding door and it is alizarian crimson or cadmium red deep. There is a 2" by 4" speaker of sorts; just drilled holes to talk in and out of the cell. Halfway down the door there is a slot about 3" x 14" that is locked from the outside that they open for mail or for feeding if you are being punished.

In the desk are my personal and state clothes. Under it, all of my painting supplies in a box. I have an 11" by 14" diagram of the human body above the desk so I can look at the bone structure for my paintings. I cherish my painting.

There are two lockers on top of each other. They are about 6'6"—a few inches taller than me—they are about three feet wide and about four feet deep and they have one shelf in them. Mine is the top locker; I keep my typewriter on top when I am not typing. My locker is full and not the most organized space, but that is partly by design. On my bottom shelf is legal work, miscellaneous papers, notes from books I have read, letters and photos, mostly in an album. On the top shelf, my Rasta and art books. I have folders for all of the paperwork in my locker. But when I take them out of the folders it looks like much more

"Artist in his studio"

work to search through which keeps most officers and nosey roommates out of it.

On the other side of the lockers are upper and lower shelves for the TV or whatever. The back wall has bunk beds that extend from one wall to the other. The top bunk has a shelf at the foot of the bed which is loaded with more books. I keep all of my pencils and ink pens up there with a small pad of paper, for ideas.

I've learned how to maximize small spaces. I'm very simple. When I'm painting or writing I don't want to be bothered. One cellmate pointed out, "You're always doing one or the other." That's true.

I cherish music. Along the wall I have my radio, a black wooden table radio (Sangean WR-1). I have an antenna sprawled across the wall trying to capture a fraction of reception; that is no easy task. There are little pieces of tape all over the wall.

I cherish my spirituality. That cannot be taken away. I have a black and white photo of Haile Selassie I. We are only suppose to have 8" by 10", but I have used my connections in the underworld and I have had that one made into 11" x 14".

Yeah, and food. In prison there are few comforts. Food is the one small freedom that is left. The limit to spend is $75 every two weeks on canteen. Canteen has three functions in here. The meals *suck and therefore you're forced, if you can, to get something. You are depressed and want comfort food. And there is the social status, for some people, of having a big canteen bag. What do I like on canteen? I love to eat. I don't get fat for two reasons which are: I have a great metabolism and I can't afford it. In recent years (since I was stopped from smoking) I've developed a sweet tooth. I love cakes and soft candy: Starburst and Now & Laters. Iced Honey Buns, Fudge Brownies, Vanilla wafers, Sweet Obsession Chocolates, both dark and milk chocolate with peanuts. I'm also hooked on sunflower seeds, salted peanuts and mixed nuts. And those fruit cups (fruit cocktail). I like to get Ramen noodles and beef and cheese sticks—they're cheap and fill the spot in a pinch. I got a dish I mix up with tuna, mackerel, cheese and rice. Hot chili, with beans, beef summer sausage, and a few chili peppers are also very good. I try to keep a jar of peanut butter and jelly for when finances will not allow these other dishes. I got a box of Cap'n Crunch yesterday. I'd never had it before but it was my brother, Vonn's, favorite. I ate the whole box and my only regret is that there wasn't any more.*

And today, there was joy. We had a plum for lunch or rather with lunch. It has been a very long time since we have had a plum.

Dear DarRen,

A plum? I'm just saying, that sounds awfully healthy next to the canteen choices. Have you ever craved a Brussels sprout? (I had to look up the spelling.) Of late, I've been buying them by the bag full. But my real love is dark chocolate, so we have that in common. We will have to have chocolates and maybe a sunflower seed or six and a glass of Merlot when I'm allowed to visit you; we should be hearing from the warden any day now. Perhaps I'll beat you at chess.

CHAPTER 20

When You Know Better, You Do Better

Spring is about awakening and hope. I was in a March funk. Trying to force cheerfulness, I told a student I was pleased to see the colorful crocus that lined the walkway to the college library with their pastel colors and translucent petals.

She replied, "Oh, I hate them; their chirping wakes me up every morning." As a teacher, it is supposed to be my job to gently explain. But I just didn't.

The funk? DarRen and I were again denied the right to have prison visits. A cursory form letter came from the warden. Was it about a few phone calls that violated rules or was it just prison politics? I would never know, but I was still deemed someone who had demonstrated a willingness to violate regulations in a maximum security prison—a security risk. "Reapply in six months." DarRen and I decided to seek advice from a lawyer on how to break this cycle. He contended that the system only responds to force.

The Wisconsin Department of Corrections supports maintaining relationships as part of prisoner rehabilitation. So as distraction, we talked about community values, relationships and what a young man's fancy turns to in spring.

Dear Judy,

Hood women? The sistas in the hood are not delicate little flowers; no crocuses in the group. Just as the men have attitudes and positions, they too have theirs. What I've seen is that they will put up with a lot—some even expect it. If a man cannot handle himself with a strong woman then he cannot protect her and provide for the family in them mean streets. Both women and men want love, safety and security but they have unstable foundations so the house is unsteady.

When a sista sees me with a white woman, I get this lip smackin, eye rollin, hand on the hip, neck poppin response and then the I-hate-speech: "I hate when educated bruthas. . . " or "I hate to see a fine ass brutha with..." This even comes from women who have friends of all colors and who believe that the sista(er) hood of women is bigger than color.

As a boy in the presence of elders, the "Yes, Sir," "No, Ma'am," "Yes, please," and "Thank you" were automatic. You could not hurt an old lady, a kid or someone's mother on our block. If you did, you were safer with the police. (At that time I didn't see the contradiction in hustlin and all that.) But the point is there was a sense of ras'pect and responsibility to our people and to our neighborhoods. Growing up, I loved the hood and being around my people and our culture. At the same time I didn't love the life I was living or the off balanced ways of thinking.

I think that blackness should not be scripted and a person should be free to live his or her own truth. I don't knock brothas or sistas who dig the vanilla flavor. If you like AC/DC and hate P-funk, that's cool. If your style is more Common than Lil Wayne, I can dig it. BUT, I strongly disagree with shedding the weight of black responsibility; not lifting that burden is wrong (in my opinion). I look at the brothas that surround me in prison and I see what we have been reduced to and what our sistas are being subjected to. Much of it is because we are about self. We no longer feel guilty for or responsible to one another. In this, "I have to get mine, screw everyone else world," we have lost our shame. When I think of the greats before us, F. Douglass,

B.T. Washington, King, Malcolm and Garvey, can you imagine if they said, "I'm going to advance me, be who I am, and shed responsibility of furthering the race or the fear of shaming it?" When I meet 17-year-old boys, I feel that I've failed them. I'd rather see us function as a tribe and be accountable for action as it affects the whole. I demand that we be more than niggas, gangstas and thugs and that our women be more than bitches and hoes.

Today, in the hood, dating is gone; no time for courting and getting to know a person. It's all is about pleasure and joy right now. That strips away the moral fibers. Marriage is not strictly enforced as it once was. Relationships are, but there is this ownership aspect. Men chasing away potential suitors and the women askin', "Why you all up on my man?" Everyday banter. Relationships are generally based on fun or safety. Often both. Someone I can enjoy the moment with and someone who will protect me when I need protecting.

Parents in the hood want the same things all parents want, however the same opportunities are not always available and, living poor, all sorts of things rise up and attack the family. There are many single mothers and they are constantly on duty. No down time. Add to that the stresses and worries of urban life.

Boys want to be a man that women find attractive. We become what our mother seems to respond to or exhibits to us. Sometimes you have mothers who are not rough and do not have tough boyfriends or husbands. To the boy, society tells him that's a punk. He wants momma to know "<u>he a real man</u>." So my point is it starts with the girls and the boys. She must be taught how to be a woman and a lady. He must learn to be a man and a gentleman and the two need to learn age appropriate ways to interact.

My great-grandfather tried to teach us to be gentlemen. He was a preacher in church and a civil rights activist. At home, he did not talk much but between those long silences, he would say things like, "When you out with a woman, always be a gentleman. Open the door. Pull out her chair. If you walkin', you get between her and the traffic." If you did not ask any questions there would be another long pause and then he would answer what you should have asked, "In case a car jumps the curb you can protect her. Always protect your woman."

Great-Granny tried to teach us values too. Ever so often she would get a few of us over to the house to help her bake various kinds of cookies and muffins. We had to wrap them in plastic and put a ribbon on them—banana yellow, blueberry blue. She'd take us to the hospital and we would visit with the sick. She would ask the nurses which patients had not gotten visits and such. One lady would shout and call my great-granny "nigger" and "coon" and the likes. Great-Granny would reply, "I heard you, but now you've said that, how you?" Her Southern roots were showin'. She'd offer to pray with her. I hated that lady and told Granny this. "Ren, a child of God does not hate. The lady is dying."

And she did; she died. In my great-granny's spare room. Great-Granny said nobody should be alone when they dying. She brung that lady to her house. No pay or nothing just because she wanted this lady to feel love.

Most of the men in my family had football bodies—stout and powerful. Many of the other guys who were being chased by the women were all stout too. So when I looked at what others seemed to think was handsome or sexy, it didn't fit me. I didn't have big muscles and I wasn't a smooth talker. Being skinny is not sexy per se. Where I grew up, it was a sign of poverty and struggle/hardships. If a man has a woman and he's still skinny it means she's neglecting him and other women will see this and will try to swoop in and steal him away if he a good man. As the sayin' goes, The way to a man's heart is through his stomach. I have aunts who will not allow their man to eat another woman's cookin' especially if she's single.

Sometimes I would read DarRen's words and wonder if our friendship was going to survive actual face-to-face visits, if they ever came. Could we even communicate with each other beyond the written word where there was time to slow down and consider the meaning of language? Sometimes I had to pause to look up words in the online *Urban Dictionary*. We continued to talk about being family to each other. And the interactions between us—and between his family and me—were family-like. They were caring and sensitive and dependable. After talking to some family and friends about civil rights lawyers in the area, I had made an appointment with an attorney to talk about the repeated denials for visitation at the prison. We had decided to move forward toward playing chess and sharing chocolates in person.

Dear DarRen,

Thinking back to the values I was taught. Being slim was a sign of health and prosperity for women and men. Exactly the opposite of what you described. My father made sure we ate well and adhered to the nutritional beliefs of the time. No more than three egg yolks a week. No burned meat and cut off all fat. Two colors of vegetables with every dinner. Vitamins once a day practically since birth. (Thinking back, it seems counter-intuitive that he was so focused on healthy eating and living for us, yet drank himself to death. I have to believe alcoholism is a disease and that he had little control over that aspect of his life.) The values of your and my childhood communities differed. And, at the same time, they are paradoxically similar in the big picture as we seek to protect the children, find joy, and hear the wisdom of the elders.

An imperative I was taught early was never to talk with strangers. Only after I was formally introduced to someone could I interact with them. Well, young love intervened. You see, I had this crush on Doug. We hadn't been "introduced". I finagled and schemed with my sister to throw a surprise sixteenth birthday party for me. I asked her to invite Doug to be my date. He was this guy who had just moved out to the suburbs from downtown Chicago. Long hair and a motorcycle. Not only was he not the norm for the neighborhood, but my parents hated him and that seemed to close the deal in his favor for me.

The surprise party was organized. Food was ready to go; music was selected and cued up. People came, secreted in our basement in preparation for the party. Doug actually arrived. I got home from some pre-planned event, went to the basement where I was delightfully surprised when people jumped up yelling, "Happy Birthday." I never understood why I was surprised when I had been part of making every party decision, maybe surprised that we had pulled it off.

As the night wore on only the broken crackers, the stiff-edged cheese slices, and a parsley sprig or two were left on the platters. The music continued, lights dimmed, and Doug and I entwined to music that carries memories for me to this day. He called the next morning and we went for a walk along the Lake Michigan shore, holding hands and talking and talking and talking more. Over time, we fell in love and were together for more than two years. First love. Puppy love. The great dramas were countered by the tenderness of so many firsts. He finally went away to college in New Mexico as my parents sighed their relief.

And you? Who were the early women in your life?

Judy.

Each year I meet that bright-eyed toothless girl from my childhood in a different form to teach me a new lesson. Though I did not have perfect male role models, the women were really great—my grandmothers, my mother, my aunties, teachers and girlfriends. The women in my family, however, would not let a boy sit around them when they were talkin' because that was the making of a sissy. These women were all strong—mostly faithful, loyal and stood by their men right or wrong. What I feared was that my mother did not love me, that she hated me for ruining her life with the shooting. I carried that with me. I usually distrusted the affections and doubted the attentions of the girls/women I dealt with. I still have pieces of that with me too. On some level I felt as if I did not deserve their attention. Still, those women loved me.

I thought I was an average looking 3rd grader, but the girls didn't. Well, the girls I liked didn't see my cuteness. I've always had a thing for older girls/women and it first started (as far as I remember) when I was in 4th grade. I've always been tall and what I called a moustache came in then. C, a classmate, was assigned to be my helper in reading and math. She was very pretty, smart and lived across the street from me. On the block, when no one was around, she seemed to like me. But in school she avoided me until my brother Vonn came around. Everyone loved Vonn.

By the time I was in the 6th grade, I was 5'11" with a real moustache. The girls my age thought I was funny lookin' and strange. The girls who were like me, not part of the in-crowd, often assumed I was stupid because I didn't really say a lot.

By junior high, I was too smart to be with the so-called cool kids/pre-thugs. Too rough for the nerds. Too nuts for the jocks. Too shy for the social clubs. I just didn't/don't fit in. But as my name became known in the streets, girls who didn't talk with me earlier suddenly liked me, saw me as handsome and charming. Some really wanted to be around because of who my family was. They often would start stuff just so they could say, "I'm going to get Ren. Say that when he comes." I didn't like that because they didn't really like me. One girl, K, was the first black girl with red hair I ever met. She was very pretty and honor roll. She looked like a young version of the actress that played "Sunshine" in the Richard Pryor movie JoJo Dancer. In any case she flirted with me and began spending time with me. It became clear that she had no interest in me, just what I represented. She was upper middle class and I was this brute that even the seniors didn't want to tangle with. She had a boyfriend at another school but she liked how people would be nice to her even when she was a bitch because they did not want to piss me off. When I realized

"Awesome"

"Free"

"Unknown FaceBook
Woman"

"Jamaican Model"

"Island Gyal"

"That Quick Glimpse"

this, I learned that the only unattractive women were the mean ones and ones that were wrapped up in stupid stuff.

I didn't want to be the way I was and thought women from other worlds were my window into something/someone different. I learned how to use who I was as a way to connect because at that time it was all I had. Being admired by a woman was a place of joy and pleasure and I wanted to stay there. The only thing I had self-confidence in was my ability to bring joy into a woman's life one way or another. I am a pleaser. I want to please. I have always liked pleasing girls or women. I don't feel smart—though I do know some things, I don't know enough. But I do know how to make a woman feel good and it's my gift to those who give me emotional joy, happiness and love.

215

Because I had so many flaws and issues, women did not seem to look at me as a long term guy. So I wanted the time that we had to be special. Plus it felt good to me and I liked to feel good. Sex for me is like therapy. Strange but true. I know sex. It's the one thing about me that I have no insecurities about. So it builds my confidence when it's low. When I'm sad it makes me happy; when I'm angry it calms me and then I can think clearly and process what's bothering me. If it's my woman that I'm feeling disconnected from, it helps me reconnect and see that things are fine.

Needless to say, I have since learned that women are more than sexual conquests. The male body is very stupid; it will respond to most anything from a physical standpoint. I continue to work on how to be a loving caring partner. I am confident in what I bring to a relationship. However, I'm not very confident in my ability to maintain a long term relationship. I have many issues that add to an already tough situation and most women eventually get fed up and leave and because of this, I've developed an insecurity about relationships.

Relationships continue to be important in prison; we are human after all. It is at times funny. Women do all sorts of stuff and we appreciate it; it's a good feeling to know that a woman cares enough to dress a certain way to attract you or do other little things to get your attention. But usually women go too far and do not realize how simple we men are. It is in our nature (for the most part, there are some exceptions to the rule) to be attracted to women so dressing modestly will not change our level of excitement very much because, after all, women are women. Now add to that being isolated from women here in prison, other than those who are, too often, mean spirited and hateful so they will not be perceived as weak. They are not attractive. Most prisoners do not get visits and when we see a fresh faced, eager looking woman, it inspires the peacock effect. The chest goes out. The stomach is pulled in. It does something really wonderful to the soul to be seen and treated as a person; a man.

CHAPTER 21

Jah Lion:
Peace, Love, Ras'pect

Dear DarRen.

Or should I write, Romeo? (Teasing you.) Are you able to see flowers from your cell window? I know you have seen a robin and there is that solitary oak tree you painted (without bars separating you visually). Okay, a hard question coming. I believe that you are a badass flirt and that women of all colors and sizes and ages do flock around you. I believe that you know sex. But, here is the question, how have you moved yourself beyond the abuse and the abusers in your life? How have you—as I wrote in the poem on a life bit(ten)—kept your head and heart intact? You seem to have a clarity in your life; the ability to focus on what is important. I can imagine that you might have moved toward violence in relationships as a result of what was done to you. But I don't hear that in your stories. I have not seen it in the interactions we had so long ago.

Dear Judy,

You know, you have been through many things too and you are pretty well put together, so why do you assume that the same isn't true for me? Although I'm not the same guy I was, I have to accept that in many ways I am the same guy. I can't completely shed my past. I have to, as you say, accept it and as my friend and family you have to accept that I was not always a victim but also a victimizer. My view of the world and relationships to it is very narrow. My life has been physical. I connect with what I see, what I can touch. I flirt with life as I know it. I have not been blessed to see and experience as many modes of life as you have so I disagree that I have a clarity that you don't; I am very limited in how I see, react and interact. A good thing about the Restorative Justice program I was part of was that they gave me the information and space to deal with my issues. I was not told what to think or how I should be feeling; I was allowed to be and get it on my own terms.

Part of what has allowed me to grow in head and heart has been spiritual. Some talk about prison-as-monastery. I wouldn't go that far, but clarifying beliefs is one of the rights we do have in prison (First Amendment); it is something that cannot be taken away.

Growing up in the hood, church was on the fringes of life; not as strong as it once was. My momma said, as a girl, she was forced to go and as a result spent her time resenting being in church and never learned anything. So she told us, "If you wanna go, go. If not, you don't have to." So we didn't unless my granny called and said a special day was coming up and we had to be there. Granny's word was law. Sometimes if I knew food would be there, I'd show up but I'd wait until about 1:30 or 2:00 when the preaching had finally gotten entertaining and the choir had started and the joint would be rockin', plus there was about an hour left, then it was time to eat. I could almost always eat.

When I was first incarcerated, I remember my granny saying, "God will never leave you or forsake you." I needed someone. How was I going to do ten years and then a life sentence where I have to do one hundred years before I can see parole? How was I to survive?

Dear DarRen,

If we someday get to sit and talk, there is going to be a lot of food. Every time I visit. Have you realized—I bet you have—that you have been hungry most of your life?

I've wondered what it cost my father to leave the severe, strict religion of his youth. While prison started you on a more structured (your own structure) path toward faith, prison appeared to have completely severed the last residue of formal religion for my father, including connections to his family (other than with his brother, Wel). My father once explained his beliefs in a higher power to me, in what now seem like scientific terms. He said something like:

"There was this guy, Mr. Flatlander, whose world was totally defined by length and width. He saw, could understand and lived happily in his two dimensions. He envisioned God as being something similar to himself, but more than he could comprehend. He worshiped that something.

Then there was Mr. Hillander, whose world was totally defined by length, width and height. He saw, could understand and lived happily in his three dimensions. He envisioned God as being something similar to himself, but more than he could comprehend. He worshiped that something. He could only communicate with Mr. Flatlander in terms he could understand: length and width.

There was Mr. ?? whose world was totally defined by length, width, height and ?? He saw, could understand and lived happily in his four dimensions. He envisioned God as being something similar to himself, but more than he could comprehend. He worshiped that something. And he could only communicate with Mr. Flatlander and Mr. Hillander in terms they could understand.

And it continues.

Dear Judy,

I guess when the physical world provides you with what you want and need (or at least you can see how it could), you might not need a belief in Jah or your god. But I wonder if your daddy didn't have that powerful family and a well-connected father, would he have been so willing to forsake Jah? For me, I need to believe there is something somewhere that is on my side and that somehow this unseen being will let me have a day of rest and joy. I need to trust HIM to be fighting for me. The Kebra Nagast tells how Jah is in all things so Mr. Flatlander is not far off.

When I was first incarcerated at age seventeen, I was impressed with this guy named Y. Short dude, real serious and confident. Smart. Everyone respected him; most called him Mr. Y. I had talked to him a few times before I went to court and got all this time. It was because of him I wanted to be a Muslim. Well it turns out the reason he came to me in the first place was because he knew my daddy from Waupun prison. He said, "I do not know what they done to you as a kid or how they done it, but they ain't here, brother. The way you are going, you are in for a long trip the bad way."

He started talking about the Koran and Allah and none of it made much sense to me, but because I was with him, these dudes were coming up and shaking my hand. One day a guy tried to hug me and I squared up. Mr. Y stepped in; they were about to get me. Back then all Muslims moved as one so if I would have hit him, not good. Mr. Y worked with me for about a year. I came to enjoy the brotherhood and how they seem to defy the authority. But one day they discovered I was smoking— yeah, smoking—and they made a issue about that. "You got to stop that; that is against Allah. I thought to myself, my granny *smoke, almost everyone in my family smoke. It's natural; it heals, not kills. How could God be against his creation? Marijuana is not man-made."*

That was the first thing, but I said, "Okay, if I am going to do this I need to do it right."

Then they said that I needed to learn Arabic. They said God smiles and bless prayers that are in Arabic. I asked, "What, God can't speak English?" It was all so technical; your prayer could only be this way. You had to dress, act and be this way; talk this way.

Next it was my name. I needed to pick a Muslim name.

Then, they told me that Muslims sit down to pee. That was not going to happen. Women and kids sit down to pee. The last straw was when Mr. Y got into a fight with another guy over whose girlfriend this sissy was. "You sweatin me about smoking and you layin with a he/she?"

That pretty much killed Islam for me. A lot of stuff was not fit'n with me. Islam had an answer for everything. Christianity also had its charms but there were aspects of both that felt wrong to me. One of the main was how every image of Jesus was this blond hair, blue eye'd Euro lookin brother. I was not feelin' a connection with God. But I began to read all sorts of stuff and finally the day came when Jah shined his light on me. I began my path into Rastafarianism.

My momma's mom is a Christian. I told her, "I am a Rastafarian now."

"What's that and do you believe in God, the Bible and Jesus?"

Once she heard my stance on that she was okay. The Bible was her guide. She didn't care so much for the title, but she even said in her own way that my dreads were okay. "They ain't half bad but you'd look much better if you made them neater." I do pin my dreads back when my mom visits. She says I'm too handsome to have "'that stuff' on your head." It hurts because I love my dreads and I love how I look and how I feel with them. I can't imagine <u>them without me</u>.

"Jah heals all pain"

My father's mom was a blend of everything: Shango and Catholic. One of my uncles was a Dread Rasta. My granny told me, after my brother Vonn was killed, to accept the calling in my life. She's been telling me since I was a kid that Jah marked me and that I've got a calling to do something big. Her Jamaican prince. I'd always dismissed the words, as good as they felt, like things grandmothers say. I was too chicken to ask Vonn if she said it to him too when we were kids. I just didn't want to know.

So Vonn was dead and she was telling me to grow my dreads and accept my revelation. I thought I was way too cool, way too handsome for dreadlocks. At least once a year, every year, she told me this.

October, 1997, I had a dream. I was leaving prison, walkin' with this box in my hand and I could feel it getting heavy. People were lined up saying goodbye and wishing me luck. My locks was swinging. My granny told me that this was Jah talking with me and my soul pleading with me to listen. The dream was so powerful, I woke up sad to see the bars. It wasn't true. As I sat

222

there in the dark, tears in my eyes, looking at the moonlight seeping in through a crack in the outside window, I lit a cigarette and hung my head. The guard came by to do his round. He stopped at the cell.

"How you doing?"

"Fine."

He proceeded to tell me some very raunchy jokes, a much needed change of mood. Each round he stopped. We talked. Eventually he asked how much time I had. He said, "Don't worry. You will not be here that long; you'll be out long before you get old. I'm not sure why, I just don't feel that with you."

Fast forward to October 2004. I was in Waupun, Green House, cell three. The same exact dream. The same intensity. When I woke up I knew I was going to grow some locks. I didn't know how and I decided that if I was going to do this I wanted to know what it all meant. My granny told me to pray for Jah to shape my dreads and attach his spirit to them. I purchased Kebra Nagast, the Rastafarian Bible, Promised Key, A Way of Life and the Holy Piby. I never got the Holy Piby because it was out of stock. In any case, I began reading.

I met two Rastas, a Haitian and a Jamaican. They taught me to pray each time I smoked herb and to listen to the voice of Jah. Be patient. Every rec period, people flocked to "our" corner to listen to these guys. The administration noticed and split us up. My granny warned when I embrace Jah, if I really and truly embrace his love, bad things would come my way. The vampires (evil people) would see and feel the change and hate me for it. The devil will try to pull me back.

I was moved to a different prison. Three days later, I dreamed my baby sister was at one end of the hall where we grew up and I was on the other. She was glowing, the most beautiful light I'd ever seen. I was floating toward her and, without warning, something reached up and grabbed her. It was ripping her body to pieces. Blood flew. The sounds that thing made terrified me. I was stuck with fear; I couldn't move. As I woke up I seen a clear face and a real voice. "Talk to him."

"Him" was a guy on the unit. I didn't know him but I knew I had to talk with him. So I got ready for breakfast. As the doors open I went up to him. "I need to talk with you." He is short. I forgot how I look to others. He backed up and prepared, it seemed, to fight. I said, "No, not like that." He seemed to relax and said, "If we are going to talk it has to be today because God has told me I'm moving."

We went to the library. He told me he was a Christian and blessed as a vessel (a talking piece) for God. He sat at the table and reached for my hands. I snatched my hands back and stood up, fire in my eyes. He said, "No, no, I'm no homo." He then explained it was about completing the circuit of energy. So taking up the most masculine pose I could I reluctantly let him grab my hands. He prayed for a long while. Then when he finished he said, "God says first, don't worry your sister will be okay. Second, your wife will be back soon. And, third, God says he knows you love him but you don't trust in Him."

I was completely freaked out. I was in a single cell. I hadn't said anything about my sister. Wife, I don't have a wife; within the week I got a letter from M, the closest I've been to a wife. M told me in her letter she was checking on me because she had a dream I called out to her and she thought I was in serious trouble. (As soon as we left the library that day, they moved him to another unit).

I was confused. Why God sent me a Christian messenger; was I on the wrong path? I smoked and prayed for clarity and guidance. Then I got a letter from a friend, "Whappin di wi Rastamon?" Basically what's going on Rastaman. It was the first time anyone had called me Rastaman. I came to understand in that moment I was a Rastaman. Rasta say, "Blessed is he/ she that is called by my name." The name is Ras Tafari. Ras means duke or leader. Tafari means to be feared (in the sense of highly respected). It is through Rasta I learned what it has all been for (well in most regards). I felt at home. Jah lion. That is Rasta. . . .one God, one aim, one destiny and one love. Peace, love, ras'pect.

Dear DarRen,

Reading your story, I feel envious of your focus, your sureness about this path. Over the years, I have flirted with many religions and nothing drew me in. Where I see god-ness is in the beauty of the natural world—the crocus, the daffodils, the foxes, the lions, the birds. It is the miraculous raw beauty and pattern that I connect with. And the relationships we get to have with all of this, and each other. Maybe that is one of the things about prison that so deeply disturbs me. At least while you were at the Resource Center, you were able to sit in the grass and watch the movement of the sun across the distant lake. If prisons must be, let's flood them with beauty and color and art and music and dance and flowers and animals (not spiders or bats, clearly). I could design a prison that was about healing rather than punishment! What does it mean to be a Rasta inside the prison? What will it mean to be a Rasta when you are free?

Peace and Ras'Pect, Judy,

It is good that you see the beauty of the lions! Me too.

You know, a bunch of things happened at about the same time. I finally got the hearing aids I needed; this seem to help out a lot. With my mental health, I was not as paranoid. I met several people who were key in my growth—a chaplain, a crisis worker and a psychologist. I learned new skills from each and was able, for the first time, to admit that I was a victim of physical and sexual abuse as a kid. They began a group called Extended Clinical Monitoring. I got in it. We sat in a circle and discussed issues under the guidance of these people. The common quality in each was compassion, forgiveness and core beliefs about being in peace with the universe and operating on the principles of love. I didn't fully understand but I never forgot. As this knowledge began to take hold in me, compassion and love began to soften my heart. The ghosts of my past began

"Trapped by Freedom"

causing me guilt. I prayed for relief and Jah spoke to my heart. "Truth. Speak the truth; be the truth and live it." This was hard to do. My life had not been centered around truth.

I've wondered how long it will take for me to ultimately go from survivor to healer? Right now I am too often still defensive and suspicious but I assume that would change once I'm free. My mission in going forward and doing Jah work is to promote love and unity; to help the downtrodden see their higher selves. I'm interested in working with children and I'd like to see some programs be put into place inside the inner city: parenting classes, anger and stress management, some sort of economy class that teaches the value of the dollar, how to budget, save, plan, prepare. I'd like to see pride in who you are. I'd really <u>love</u> to do something with sexual abuse victims.

I feel in my heart that I no longer have it in me to cause harm to another. At my core, I'm not violent. I've never sat around and thought of ways to hurt people. I have no desire to hurt anyone. At my core, I'm alone and afraid and don't know how to deal or express. I had no tools to address the secret thoughts or feelings that were a whirlwind inside me. Now I feel more peaceful. I feel love. I seek to heal; to continue to grow and evolve. My life as a Rastafarian has led me to this point. I paint and write, hoping that someone will see and hear—and avoid sitting inside the Wisconsin prison system—any prison system. There are not many examples of men leaving here and staying out. There aren't many with my sentence structure who make it. I feel hopeful I will be one who does.

I folded this letter of hopefulness and put it in the back pocket of my jeans. The spring morning was perfect. The nearby lake sparkled with tiny rainbows on the crest of each ruffle of water and I wondered if loons had been calling earlier. Spring is their season here. I thought of the waste. Human beings locked in tiny cells; human beings who could contribute in such powerful ways to all of our lives. Are there some who, on being released, would commit another crime? Sure. But I wondered to what extent recidivism is *caused* by our prison system. So many questions.

I decided to skip the campus meeting I was supposed to attend and walked by the lake instead, along the boardwalk where I could see the emerging cattails and watch the tiny fish busy in the glistening water. The sun was warm.

Dear DarRen,

Good to hear there is a sunbeam in your cell, a place for warmth on these warm/cool spring days. And thank you for sending the painting. I can well imagine the desire to be a bird flying free. Do you become that bird through your painting?

"Bird"

CHAPTER 22

When I Am Inside a Painting, I Am Not in Prison

Dear Judy,

There was a time when I refused to think of life outside of prison. More than ever I do now feel hopeful. Until I was put in seg this last time, I hadn't realized how much I had fallen in love with my painting. I truly missed it and that was amplified by the fact that I was locked in all day and I could not hear music and I couldn't fall into TV land.

Television and radio are diversions in prison. There are classes like parenting, anger management, high school completion, or basic skills. Sports and in-house competitions are important. One prison offered an inmate rodeo for years. Religious activities are offered. About 50% of prisoners have work assignments. Some are involved in activities like the in-prison hospice volunteers.

But I think the arts, in particular, may offer the most potent ways to sooth the pain and loneliness. They offer emotional release and expression. Painting gives DarRen a pathway toward healing in the world he lives in with no visual stimulation and minimal color (other

"Passion or Pain"

than racial difference). I also know it is possible to write beyond what you (consciously) know, to come to greater insight. (How risky is it to keep a personal journal in a world where anything can be taken from you at any turn and then used against you?)

There are prisons where inmates create dance and theater productions and learn about themselves through "living" Shakespeare. It seems to me that these sorts of engagements are essential if the real focus of incarceration is on increased self-understanding, mindful decision-making and lasting rehabilitation.

> *. . . When I am painting, my cellmate does not exist. When I am inside a painting, I am not in prison. So if a roommate exists, that means I am in prison and then I'm asking, "Why are you trying to bring me back while I am trying to get away."*

"Graffiti on the Wall"

Prisoner healing touches more than the incarcerated individual. Extended families and communities are hurt as well. Those who work in the system too often have high levels of alcoholism and divorce and estrangement, perhaps reflections of the cruelty of our current system. And the victim survivors? I have to wonder if they feel healed by today's system. Jackie Millar[3] was healed from the inside out, she says, by coming to love the two boys, now incarcerated men, who shot her execution style. She has forgiven them and visits them yearly.

> . . . *Plus art is deeply personal. When I paint I'll sketch out the picture and then begin painting and I'll usually sit and work on it until it's finished; for most paintings this means two or three*

---

3   Millar, Jackie and Judith Gwinn-Adrian (2007). *Because I am Jackie Millar.* Los Angeles: Golden (The Press)

days. Sometimes a week. I'm driven to see it come to life; to see the lights, the darks, the colors. The shapes. The emotion.

I think of my mother. She was an artist for the final years of her life, after my father's death. I wonder if she painted to heal as well.

. . . I have always loved color. At school I was encouraged to paint and such. Two things made me lay it down for a long time. First, I drew a picture for my granny. It was yellow and black; the only two colors I had. It was a mix of graffiti and landscape. There were some hills that had black clouds and a bright yellow sun. Below it was a subway car with "I Love You" spelled out in bubble letters. Graffiti was in at that time. Granny said it was nice and gave it back.

"It's for you."

"Nawl, it looks like some of that voodoo stuff." That was a crack at my father side of the family. I never sent her anything after that until recently I done a blue and yellow portrait of her for her birthday. I haven't spoken with her since she's gotten it. But my mother said she loved it. I was relieved.

Did my father's mother look like me? I've never seen a photo or a painting of her. She died in childbirth. DarRen had extended family surrounding him most of his young life. He said he loved being among his people in the hood. I needed to find out who my people were. Are relationships and connections another part of healing?

. . . I won some contest at elementary school that was city-wide and they exhibited my picture at Carthage College in Kenosha. My art teacher took me to see it. There was a man there, an art instructor. He was clearly a homosexual or at least what I thought homosexuals were, based this on his speech pattern and body movements.

Boys crying in our house was a no-no. I was about nine or ten and in the fourth grade. Mrs. B was the teacher, my only black teacher. She put me on to Mozart and I discovered Johann Bach. His first name seemed like a black name to me at the time. She was mean, but I liked her and I felt as if she truly cared for me. She had given me some homework. I forgot what it was except it was a written assignment. It was long. My baby sister was about two at the time and was doing what she did best. Pester me. She was off limits (everyone in the house was fair game to be hit except her). I wanted to hit her but knew my mom would flip her lid.

Mean, but he liked her. Made me smile. I remembered two teachers from middle school. One was the pottery teacher who taught my favorite class. I saw him working in the local library one Saturday morning and asked why he did that. I didn't fully understand when he said he needed a second job to live in my neighborhood. And then there was my math teacher. She was mean to everyone, except me. So strange. I barely spoke in any classes and wasn't good in math, but something inside of her connected with me, of all the students in the class. She was mean but I liked her.

*. . . I just kept on doing my homework and finally my baby sister threw something—a toy of some kind—and knocked over some red punch and got my schoolbook and assignment wet. I was so angry. I felt so helpless. I hated disappointing Mrs. B. The first day in her class she gave a talk about the value of a book, not just a school book, **a book**. She talked about slaves teaching themselves and each other to read. She ended with, "I expect you'll respect these books. There will be no marks or stains of any kind when you give them back."*

Books. They were so important in my home growing up and I read all the time, squirreled away in my back bedroom at the top of the back steps that led to the side door into the kitchen. I remember when my father brought home a book called *No More Bad Dogs* to help us all train the German shepherd puppy that had joined our household. Next time I saw that book, the dog had chewed off the corner and much of the back binding. For years, that book sat, crooked, on the shelves with the other books. Just a reminder of one bad dog.

> . . . I sat at the kitchen table and I cried. My mother came into the kitchen. She asked me why I was crying and, through my sobs, I told her. She mocked me; called me a sissy and told me she was not raising sissies and to stop acting like a girl. That had a serious impact on me because of everything else that was happening—the punishments. I do not think it was said with meanness; I think it was said as most other things, with a little playfulness and a goal to make sure that we were tough. I didn't like being called by a girl's name but I couldn't stop crying. She said, "Well I guess you choose to be a girl then, so I have to give you a girl's name. Diane." Then she called the rest of them kids into the room and announced that my new name was Diane. I don't think I felt anything; I had, in that moment, just given up.
>
> My mother had seen me drawing. She said that the picture was very pretty. I began to smile. Then she said that men that are artist are sissies or fags and asked me which I was which just built on the whole Diane thing. And she may have actually believed that artists were homosexuals.
>
> I'm sure them calling me Diane, the actions that went along with that, and my misunderstanding of what was taking place had a lot to do with my putting my art aside. I didn't want to be around people who may have been homosexuals. I'd had more than my share. I didn't see art as an important part of me at that time, and for a long time after. I stopped drawing until I got to high school and found out that there was no relationship between artist and homosexual.

I understand why DarRen wished he could work with urban families to teach them things like parenting skills. I'm not so naïve as to think I could go in and teach such capacities there, but I believe he could. Recently I saw an African-American man about DarRen's size, with dreads, who is employed in one of Madison's community centers.

"Tu"

He was working with the five-year-old kids. A group was gathered around the tattered donated couch he sat on, as he read aloud to them. He was Velcro to those children. His smiles were their smiles. It crossed my mind that if someone was hurting one of those children, they would possibly tell this trusted man.

> . . . *Later, at my trial, my judge said that my case was going to be a warning to all gang members. There had been blood on my shirt after Mr. Fish was hurt. I cut it up and burned half of it; I put the other half in my pocket. The judge said I was more concerned with preserving my so-called gang colors than I was with preserving human life. When I cut the shirt in half it was not about saving the colors of the shirt. I had painted the shirt. It was air brushed and on the back of the shirt was this diamond in blue and black with a "R" in the middle. R was for Ren, my nick name. But it was suppose to be the symbol of a air brushing business me and several people I'd met in Green Bay were trying to start. It was to be named F.I.R.M. (From Inside Ren's Mind).*

There is no question that DarRen was a deeply troubled and mentally ill young man: a victim and a victimizer. I wonder what the judge saw? Why did he feel there was no hope for growth or change or rehabilitation over the course of an entire lifetime as he gave the one hundred year sentence? What was inside the judge's mind?

. . . In prison, a special friend from the outside helped me reconnect with painting and drawing as a way to distract and soothe. No one had ever taken time to explain simple things like that.

I talked with this transsexual, B, when we were in the prison library. B is also a artist and was asked by my special friend to lend a hand as I reconnected with art. That was and has been a challenge. I'd never been around a transgender before and was about to sever all ties until I was <u>told</u> that we should not be friends and I seen these same people picking on B. No one picks on my friends but me. And I don't like bullies. I let it be known that I'm no one's defender but any acts of violence that are not responses to violence, I'll take personal and may interject. My point was received. In any case, B has some very interesting art. I can see the conflict in the work. I hurt B's feelings not long ago though when I was invited to double cell. That's not going to happen. We only discuss art so we both know what can be expected.

I began to understand art was a calling in my life. I knew I was connected. When I was first at the secure mental health Resource Center, at six something AM, they'd take us outside for a smoke break. While we were out there, the sun was rising over the lake and for the first time in years I could see natural water. I could watch the sun rise. I cried. There were days when I would go out by myself and walk barefoot in the grass, sit in it and sketch.

In that prison I would invent, all the men and women would see natural water and hear birds sing and walk barefoot in the grass if they wished. There would be color and purposeful creative activity and humanity. There would be engaging physical work, hard work. Mozart and Johann Bach's music would play (and some joyful rap as well). There would be skill building, like learning to use computers— imagine getting out of prison today having never touched a computer key? There would be teaching and learning and preparation to succeed after release. And those who didn't play well would get <u>more</u> color and music and learning. (I've never understood expelling children who didn't do well in school—they need more and better school, not less.) There would be healing.

. . . Inside me there is a feeling, a feeling that I want to show more courage in my painting. There is a deep sadness that seems to just lurk in the shadows. At times, I want to paint just what I see it in my mind. I have tried a few times and I end up changing certain things for fear that some of those things are too dark.

I'm imprisoned by my secrets. As my heart softens, it gets harder to hold it in. It eats at me more than ever. I'll never be free of it. All the lies. All the abuse. The mistrust. Even when

"The Lion of Judah Is Rising"

I'm free, I'll still be imprisoned in a way. But I may be able to help free someone else. The emotion is hidden in all of my paintings— nearly all.

The portrait of me with the lion up top—look at my eyes. You see it? You see the hidden emotion?

Look at the Sugah Shack. It is my version of the original by Ernie Barnes. When I was a kid watching Good Times, *I loved the paintings and I thought J.J., played by Jimmy Walker was the artist, but either way I was glad to see a black artist who was not gay* and was not doing graffiti. But, look in the painting. At first it looks like a party. Look deeper. It always struck me how the people in the paintings were doing things that are considered fun but that they never looked happy or looked like they were having fun.

"Sugah Shack"

That was me. The closed eyes. The drunk in the corner. The sadness is there.

I have tried to talk about the sadness at times and it has been laughed off. I had told friends a few things and they did not believe me. I did not push the issue; I liked that in a way. But at the same time I felt like the friends were denying a part of me and dealing with some fantasy or some version of me.

"Boy in Closet"

The hot box painting. If I were standing in that spot in the painting, I'd be facing the back of the closet. To (my right in the painting) were large boxes with clothes in them. The center lines, vertical and horizontal, are the cracks in the door and under it. It was a sliding door that folded in the middle so it would allow a little light in. The carpet was brown and when the light is on I could see that. I tried to add subtle emotion but did not know

"Animal in a Cage"

how. I wanted to make the eyes look as if they were on the verge of tearing up. But I'm much more of a crybaby now than I was then.

I got a set of Masterstroke bristle filbert brushes. Someday I'm going to get the round set. When I got them bigger brushes, it meant fewer strokes. They hold paint and moisture better than my old ones. This allows for better blending. The benefit of not being trained in a school of arts is that I will draw on anything; everything is used—paper, cardboard. The paintings of me with the lion and the one of Tu are on cardboard. I've done more painting on canvas this year; I had more access.

I have paint on nearly every piece of clothing I have. I use to have a set that I reserved for painting. I was recently told that getting paint on my prison greens is a violation: destroying state property. And a new rule; if you get sent to seg, all hobby supplies must be sent out of the prison as part of the punishment; they cannot be returned. You will have nothing when released from seg.

"The Tribute Party to Ernie Barnes"

My life has shaped me to be who I am. Without the darkness my light would not appear to be so bright. If my background was changed from dark to bright white or yellow, that would reveal that my light is only a dingy shade of grey.

You know those baby tents that hitch up to a bike; they have wheels on them? I could very easily see me with one of those, keeping art supplies in there. I can't wait to sit in Jah nature and paint Jah beauty. Painting. That's where I fit in.

It is fascinating to look inside the mind of a person who sees the world through line and pattern and connection and color. My mother was able to do this. We would be driving someplace and she would say, "Look at that, four blue cars in a row." Little things. But color was central to her world. In my mind, I picture who DarRen might have been if his granny had seen his talent, pulled him under her wing, and enrolled him in a magnet school for the arts. I wonder. . .

CHAPTER 23

My Son

Dear DarRen,

I was sitting on the front steps of one of the college buildings and just as I read your words about the baby tents pulled behind bikes, a young couple rode past with two of them behind their bikes and I presume two kids. I can completely envision you with one of those—not carrying your son because he is about your size!—but riding a bike on early spring days like this with painting supplies in the tent and you stopping to capture the spring pastels of the natural world. Maybe someday we could put together an artist's retrospective (is that the correct term) of your work. You have mentioned how many of your family members own your paintings. Have you ever painted your son's portrait?

Judy,

The reason I haven't painted my son to this point is that I am not talented enough. He is perfect and I cannot capture the perfection. I have written about him though.

My Son

I remember the last time.
It has been engraved in my mind.
I remember the last time.
The elongated oval of your eyes.
Big brown and sparkling.
I remember the last time your long slender arms
*   wrapped around me.*
The warmth of your embrace.
I remember the last time.
Your warm smile.
Spreading across your face at the sight of me.
I remember the last time.
For a short while, a very short while, we
*   re-familiarize ourselves with each other.*
I remember the last time.
Almost in secret I study every part of your body,
*   photographing it in my memory.*
I remember the last time we said our good byes.
I remember how sadness moistened your eyes.
Inside I held tightly so that I wouldn't cry.
Though I don't see you often, when I do I hate to
*   say goodbye.*
Son, you are never far from me.
Because I remember the last time.

. . . I was locked up March 23. About November 11 or 12 she brought my son in a car seat. My eyes filled with tears. I looked

down and seen this beautiful gift from Jah. I questioned in my head was he mine. At that moment I didn't care.

My momma said, "Yeah, he's yours."

I looked through the glass trying to see everything. In the County Jail there is no contact. I looked down and seen these long socks.

"How come you didn't get socks that fit better?"

"What do you mean?"

"Those are big."

"No, this boy got your feet."

She pulled off the socks and revealed his flippers. Son! I remember them first photos I got. He was such a beautiful and peaceful baby. I guess all fathers say that huh? But he was.

Those early years, I would see him two times a week. I held him nearly the entire three hours. I fed him. When he get a little older, I'd walk through the visiting door and he'd take off running with his arms stretched.

"Daddy!" Over and over. I'd bend down and he would jump and wrap his little arms around my neck and give me the best hug I've ever gotten. I felt thirty feet tall and made of diamonds.

Daily I dream of being free and seeing my son outside of this place. My wish is that he is well. That he never has to do time. That he follows his dreams and sees them come true.

My son is joy in my life.

"Granny"

"Rest in Love"

CHAPTER 24

Granny Knew

That spring, DarRen wrote about his granny.

I sent out a Request for Information from the prison social worker. "I'm hearing impaired but would like a special phone call to my grandmother. She's in hospice care and will die soon. I'd like to say goodbye. I'll need a phone that is speaker phone. Please."

The prison social worker's response, "Fill out 'request' form and also on bottom write in detail why you feel justified/entitled to call. I will present to the unit manager for denial or approval."

After reading the response, I was painfully aware of my circumstances. It also made it very real that my granny is dying. I don't know why. But reading this response illuminated Granny's impending death as oppose to my powerlessness.

Then shortly after,

. . . Today is May 28, 2012 and I woke feeling a little strange. That feeling stayed with me all morning. This afternoon, after meals, I was called out and allowed to make a special phone call

where I was informed that my granny, Lelioa Mae Morris, died this morning.

She was my first introduction to compassion and love. She and my father's mother are the greatest influences on who I am today. The things that they tried to teach me years ago were not lost on me, just at the time the soil was not ready for the seeds that were planted.

DarRen's mom invited me to attend Granny's memorial service— her mother's service. I had called her that morning, asking if I could drop off some of DarRen's paintings as I passed through Kenosha, not knowing that was the day the family was gathering to remember Granny, the woman who had been so formative in DarRen's life. The woman who fed him and kept him safe some nights. The woman who played *Trouble* and *Sorry* with the younger kids. Granny who lost her leg to the *sugah* and cried when DarRen told her she didn't have a foot on the side that was itching. Granny, who took care of all the children when DarRen's momma was recovering from the bullet wound.

When I arrived at the apartment with the paintings, I entered a flurry of women getting dressed for the service. Fussing with hair and make-up and just-right church attire. DarRen's mom was giving instructions on which dress she wanted to be brought from the closet; her wheelchair wouldn't pass through the bedroom door.

My invitation was reaffirmed.

I replied, "This is a family service. I shouldn't interrupt."

I was debating to myself. Do they really want me or are they being polite? Who was I to enter this intimate family event? Yes, I felt I was family to DarRen but did that also mean I was family to everyone who surrounded him? They barely knew me; why did they care about me? Was I a link to DarRen who was so distant from them all, geographically? After all, he had been away from family for more than half of his life. What could I offer? I didn't know. But the offer felt more than sincere; it verged on a command.

"If you don't want to go, just say so. But you are family, so you are invited."

"Well, what will I wear? I've just got jeans."

"You can wear one of my dresses," DarRen's mom stated. "Go into that bedroom and look for the white dress hanging in the closet. And in the top drawer there are some white stockings."

I did as I was told.

"Look, she is swimmin' in that dress." Chuckles and shy sideways looks.

The dress was too big but I put my wrinkled jacket over the top. "How is this?"

"Get her a slip."

Why had I chosen that day to wear my multicolored, Aztec design underwear? Happily the design was on the front only. I put on the half-slip but it wouldn't stay up.

"If I had a pin, I could fix it. Or how about this?"

No slip and I held my purse in front of me.

"It will do. You look nice."

I was the woman in the white dress—was I the woman in the white dress from the painting DarRen had done for me when we first began corresponding? Was I family now? I turned to DarRen's mom.

"So do you. Beautiful dress and I love your new braids."

DarRen's mom rode with me to the church, her wheelchair folded in the back of my car. After she got out and into her chair, two men carefully carried her up the front steps to the church. I later learned that this tiny, white, aged church had been built by DarRen's grandfather. It was about the same size and age as the nearby white clapboard homes—worn but tidy. Part of the wallboard toward the street was rotting. There was a bullet hole through one of the mock stained glass windows. I stared. Was that actually a bullet hole? Yes, it came from the outside in. How did I know that? I don't know. Was I afraid? Of what, I had to ask myself. Of a bullet or of becoming a member of this extended family whose story I knew so intimately?

The service began. Someone had leaned DarRen's painting of Granny against the front altar. "Rest in Love." His aunties gathered together on one side of the room. The minister was calling and singing, saying that this was a celebration of Granny's life. This man in black had known her. He talked long about the painting and about DarRen.

We need to get this man out. We need him in the community. We need him to help guide the young men.

> *I remembered DarRen's words, I recognized the moment*
> *in the service when the singing began and the time for*
> *eating was getting close—that was the time when, as a boy,*
> *DarRen would have arrived.*

The only other light-skinned person in the room was DarRen's granddaughter with her blue eyes and blond hair. One and a half years old. She sat through the nearly 3-hour service munching a few crackers and practicing clapping to the music.

The celebration ended and people milled around, waiting for the food to be ready in the basement. DarRen's mom sat in the wheelchair to the side of the long-ago varnished pews. DarRen's sister, son, granddaughter, and I sat nearby. A few family members cautiously came over to me. One relative wanted the prison address, which I wrote for her on a used envelope. One wanted a photo with me because I was family. She later mailed a copy to DarRen.

"Are you the baby's grandmother?"

"No," someone answered for me.

"She's DarRen's lady friend."

Very narrow stairs wound to basement. Those who were taller had to crouch to walk down. I stood tall, or short as the case actually is. I said I'd wait to eat because the minister had asked those who were serving the food if there was going to be enough. The response, "We will stretch it to feed everyone. No, you eat. You eat, too."

Fried chicken. Green beans. Soft drinks. And cookies.

"Where are my cookies, Judy?" I had handed DarRen's mom the plate of food she had sent me to get for her and now she was teasing me. Oatmeal raisin was her favorite, she said. I headed back down the winding stairs to the community room.

She called after me, "I'm diabetic so don't bring me no soda, I can't have sugar."

I met the auntie who had special style and had dressed little DarRen in pink for one Easter service, although she said it was salmon. He complained, he said, until he saw the responses of the girls. Suddenly he wasn't pink, he had once written, he was golden.

His auntie wore a large church hat so we had to converse to one side where she could look out. DarRen's son told me he could use a new van. People nearby looked at me with playful smiles. I smiled back.

Who were these people who so readily embraced me? This large extended family. With a history of secrets. I felt included.

I wrote DarRen about the invitation and my initial reluctance. I wrote about the service, his painting, and honoring of his granny. I told him I stood for him in that family gathering, a surrogate who was treated kindly. I asked about the stories we were writing together and whether that was a violation of these relationships. He thoughtfully replied.

Dear Judy. I do not tell stories. Not a story, not their story. I am doing what should have been done more than twenty-five years ago. I am sharing my experience. At some point it can no longer be about them. They have not always acted in my best interest. I am trying to learn how to do this now for myself and surround myself with people who can see me, not the reflection of me in some distorted fun house mirror. I've been trained to embrace this mantra: Protect the family. That is what I am doing. In this case that will be me taking off all my clothes and standing naked, allowing them to see the deep gashes in my soul. Not to shame anyone. Not to blame anyone. But in the spirit of what my granny said: Protect them babies. I am where I am and I am who I am. That will not change. But there are children being born every day all over the world and they do need protecting.

Protect them babies. DarRen was referring to Granny's final words, her final days. Toward the end, she was in and out of comas. Granny wasn't seemingly aware of where she was and spoke disjointed sentences.

But there was one mantra she repeated again and again as she was entering the passageway to death. There was at least one thing that haunted Granny in her move through that pathway. One thing she had had etched in her memory for so many years. Perhaps one action she wished she could have taken. In the haze, on her deathbed, she repeated,

> *Get them babies outta there.*
> *Get them babies out.*
> *Them older boys is messing with 'em.*
> *Save them babies.*
>
> *Get them babies outta there.*
> *Get them babies out.*
> *Them older boys is messing with 'em.*
> *Save them babies.*

Granny knew.

Visitation

I t is again spring. Of a new year. Visitation has been repeatedly denied every six months for close to three years now. The chapters of this book have been sent inside for DarRen to comment on, modify, and return. That means they have been read internally. I have to wonder to what extent the denials for visitation have been related to the words of this book. Nothing more dangerous than a black man with a pen, I was once told.

An attorney has been working for us, with the prison, on breaking this cycle of unreflective visitation rejections. We should hear this week, or next, what the final outcome is. There have been several meetings among prison social workers, security personnel, a parole officer and DarRen. (Why was DarRen suddenly assigned a parole officer when he has no official chance of parole?) This is profoundly different than earlier requests for visitation. I am hopeful.

May 1, 2013. I used to believe that positive results came from doing good. I won't generalize and say that is always incorrect, but in dealing this prison system, it has proven true.

Visitation denied.

I am angry. At first, I was sad and then I realized that, by having allowed the prison to know that DarRen and I wanted to visit (play chess, eat chocolate, catch up on family stories), they now have a way to extend their punishments beyond the walls of their house. I have decided we have given them too much power. From this point on, I am not going to expect that they will ever allow visitation. We will continue to reapply every six months but the denials won't be as hurtful.

The reason given on this Removal/Denial/Approval form (why is their default to begin with the negative?): "The Warden has reasonable grounds to believe you have attempted to bring contraband into a penal facility and/or pose a threat to the safety and security of visitors, staff, inmates, or the institution."

Since the denial is about me visiting, I have to assume the comment is about my giving something to DarRen that violates the rules, which could not (and would not) happen. If it is about his behavior in general, then the comment means they believe I am so feeble I would merely follow his lead. Maybe they believe he is a threat to me.

They haven't told us specifically why we were again denied. And they won't.

DarRen once said he is beyond the reach of luck. You have to wonder. But then this isn't exactly about luck.

This is not where I wanted the story to end. It is today's reality.

But I am thinking that "posing a threat" to today's prison industrial complex is precisely where DarRen and I should be standing. Where we should all be standing. Over recent years I have talked, off the record, with district attorneys, parole officers, prison-reform advocates, and even judges. To a person, they confide that the long-armed U.S. justice system is broken and out of control. To a person, they say they do not know what to do about it. And, to a person, they then shrug as if there is no recourse.

I believe change can happen. I have to believe that. Maybe the stretch of the pen—this pen—is part of that answer. Many people are writing about the needed changes.

In the big picture, I am hopeful that prison reform will someday come. In the moment, however, thousands of boys and girls become men and women, sit in cells they will never call home. And we all lose.

PAINTINGS AND DESCRIPTIONS

"Rose Garden Envelope" (11" x 18", acrylic on cardboard, 2012, #000260) DarRen's letters often arrived with designs or decorations on the envelope. This rose garden envelope was my favorite.

"Day of Rest at Home" (18" x 14", acrylic on canvas board, #000071) This painting was based on my memories of my time in Jamaica. A picture on my granny's wall. I am not sure if it was a photo or a professional photo. I was thinking of what it would be like to be at home, sitting there, enjoying a smoke and drawing.

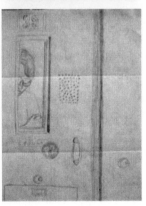

"J in DS2 (Disciplinary Segregation, Stage 2)" (8.5" x 11", pencil on paper, #000236) J is a guy who, in expression of thought and action, is about 14 years old. When I crossed paths with him he was being teased by other people in the seg unit, not for being slow, rather for being in prison for having sex with a teenage girl when he was in his early twenties. Sometimes he would pace back and forth. Other times he would silently stand at the door for hours holding himself and staring at the ground. I use to wonder what was happening inside him that would bring him to this point. Then I realized I had been there just like all of the other people that ever done a long stint in seg. It changes you. It gets inside you and rubs all of them secret places that we all hide and run from. Here in seg, there is no running from it. So it chews on your soul, slowly like the last meal of a man scheduled for execution.

"Gaptooth Girl" (5" x 7", acrylic, 7/21/11)

"Sketch of Girl by Bridge" (Pencil on paper)

"Boy in Closet" (Acrylic on canvas paper, Dec. 2009, #000072) As a boy, my brothers had some unique punishments for me. I do not recall the first time or what led to it. I remember the house (apartment). I was about 8 when we moved there. When I was about 9, we had both downstairs apartments and that was the first time I was thrown in there. I had developed a fear of the dark. So much happened to me in the dark; I remember being terrified. Once I kicked on that door and it popped open and what I faced outside that door made being inside of it less horrible. How it was set up—the line down the center of the back of me would be the crack from where the two doors came together. My brother had learned to use tools in shop class and that allowed him to place a pole outside the door that prevented me from opening it. After a while, I made up games to distract me from the heat—it was really hot. I think there was a boiler in the basement under this closet. I also needed to keep my mind off of the bugs in there with me.

"Night Watchman" (7" x 9", acrylic on canvas, #000176) The painting came from a black and white, grainy photo. I liked the pensive stare and so I gave him color. I made him real.

"Eagle Wolf" (18" x 24", acrylic on canvas board) I've done this painting three times. This was the last. I liked the idea of this great being landing and able to show you some of where he/she has been or seen. The truth. Can you imagine if people told the truth, lived the truth like animals and if animals lied like people. What would that do for the spirits?

"Evil, AKA Carl" (10" x 15", acrylic on watercolor paper, 2011, #000184) I woke up this night with darkness seeping from my bones. I lay here unable to sleep. Running from a devil and chasing evil. Why was I born. Why do I live. Why didn't I die... Death, it seems like water to a man dying of thirst. I already have so much blood on my hands, why not my own. Darkness in my thoughts. Darkness in my bones. There's only one way I'll ever get home. A place where there's no Carl. The fourth letter is D... so dead. Carl is dead.

"RIP 2PAC" (20.5" x 25", acrylic on cardboard, 9/11/11, #000199) I used this cardboard to paint on and had some paint left over, so painted a memorial to 2PAC in the center. The 2PAC painting was spur of the moment. I don't have a good drawing board. The tape will not stick to it and they have very stupid rules on what we can have here. So when I know I'll have projects to send out, I snatch up cardboard being discarded and make me a box which then becomes my drawing board. As you'll notice there are a lot of outlined rectangles or squares made by pieces I taped to it and painted and the colors spilled off creating the outline. I had a bunch of paint left over from a picture that I didn't want to go to waste so I took them colors and painted the picture as best I could from a magazine my cell mate at the time had on the desk.

"K, Full Belly, Sleepin'" (5.5" x 6.5", acrylic on cardboard, 1/22/13, #000274)

"Artist in His Studio" Columbia is the only max prison where we can open the window. My current cellmate has an issue with the light on most of the day and most of the night so I take one of my personal towels and drape it off of the side of the bed and he retreats into the darkness. I take the trash can, set it on the desk, and place a few books in it for weight at the base. We cannot have easels. I lay masonite board over the can top. I fill an empty (plastic) coffee jar with water so that I can rinse my brushes. I set up what it is I am working on atop this makeshift easel and I step out of my cell and step into my studio! The space if very tiny; it is good for me that my cellmate is the type of person who will lay in front of his TV because this gives me the freedom to move without bumping into each other. The sketch was done in one sitting, without any (or very little) refining.

"Awesome" (14" x 18", acrylic, April 25, 2012, #000232) This painting is awesome. I did not want to let it go. Have you ever had someone so completely understand you? I have and it was great. She's gone. Things are different. I dream of what was and feel hopeful of what could be. We are all our own people. But still I dream.

"Free" (6" x 12", May 18, 2012, #000238) This painting is based on a woman I've seen and heard other men judge for her behavior. They consider her to be slut-ish. I don't see her that way. I don't know her and never held a conversation with her. But from afar, she seems to be the contrary. She's comfortable with who she is and therefore free. Who and what she is. . . a matter of opinion.

"Unknown FaceBook Woman" (8" x 10", acrylic on posterboard, Fall, 2012, #000265) A very pretty woman yet in this mix of beauty and innocence there seems to be this hovering sadness. That is the attraction of such a piece to me.

"Jah Heals All Pain" (18" x 24", acrylic on canvas board, #000170) Several months back, when an inmate sang his song about pain, I envisioned a man that was down trodden but seeking redemption, hoping that there was something to hope for. I was deeply hurt and hurting in a way I hadn't felt in a long time. But I held hope that Jah was going to heal my pain. The short dreads symbolized the beginning knowledge or recognition that there is a God and that we are connected. INI. . . The Angel with the flag, Angel of Jah, is there to remind me of Zion. The promise that the god spirit in me is empowered to achieve. . . and the Shield of David to protect INI. I was trying to show hurt, despair and, yet, hopefulness.

"The Lion of Judah Is Rising" (20" x 32", acrylic on canvas paper, April 20, 2011, #000109) My only surrender is the Most High Jah Rastafari. Each day I seek out the spirit of the conquering lion. HIM Spirit fills my lungs, starting a fire inna my soul. Its smoke comes from my center, through the pores of my flesh seeping from my high tension wires. This is a self portrait.

"Trapped by Freedom" (14" x 18", acrylic on canvas panel, 6/1/10, #000132) Since I first created this painting, my insight into the basic concept of it has grown as I have grown. The man emerging from (being pulled into) the heart. The bittersweet feeling of loving and being loved is tainted by the limits and strains of prison. I was saying that I am trapped by love, the very thing that I claim as my freedom—the inability to fully explore and express that love. This is the promise of a new day, a wiser (the dreads) stronger version will be born when I look up, metaphorically, placing my thoughts and emotions on a higher plane. I am placing myself in a position to watch the sun rise and find the key in the light I could not find in the dark.

"Bird" (5" x 8", acrylic on paper, #000091) Leaf after Leaf Drops off, flower after flower, some in the chill, some in the warmer hour; Alive they flourish, and alive they fall, and Earth who nourished them receives them all. Should we, her wiser sons, be less content to sink into her lap when life is spent?

"Passion or Pain" (5" x 7.5", acrylic on cardboard, January, 2013, #000279)

"Graffiti on the wall" (5" x 7", acrylic card, 2/14/13, #000286) By Ren

"Granny" (8" x 11", acrylic on canvas, 6/28/10, #000155) This is my Granny Lelioa M. M. She was hugs, kisses, fun, games, explaining what I done wrong and why it was necessary for me to do the things she asked of me. She was home cooked meals and full bellies. She was at times a safe night's sleep. She was the first representation of love that I can remember. She was love and pure joy. Her whole being use to light up when the grandkids were around. She was stubborn, diabetic. She had gangreen, she was a leg short. She was the reason I stopped painting and drawing as a kid. She was an unknown. She is my granny.

"Tu" (5" x 7¾", acrylic on cardboard, #000278)

"I wake up stranglin
Tangled in my bed sheets"
I know there is a boogie man.

"Tu"

"Sugah Shack" (18" x 24", acrylic on canvas panel, 10/27/10, #000172) The painting was by Ernie Barnes; Sugah Shack is my version of the original. As a kid I use to go to local galleries and museums and I never seen black artists. So for me seeing the paintings on "Good Times"—I loved the paintings and I thought J.J. played by Jimmy Walker was the artist, but either way I was glad to see a black artist who was not gay and was not doing graffiti. It always struck me how the people in the paintings were doing things that are considered fun but that they never looked happy or looked like they were having fun. That was me.

"Animal in a Cage" (16" x 12", acrylic on canvas panel, #000073) It's reflective of my struggles to deal with segregation in Waupun prison. At times I didn't act like a human because I was not being treated like one. After one of many beatings (by the very people who were supposed to help me), I sat in that moment, gas still clinging to my body and burning. Cold and hungry, I sat on that concrete slab and wondered, would it ever end? Why had my life been a constant struggle since day one. See camera in upper left hand corner.

"The Tribute Party to Earnie Barnes" (11" x 14", acrylic, #000159) When I painted that one I had the sacred chalice and the imperial fiyah ablaze. I could see the music and so I added musical notes and a shapely sistah singing from her soul, like them powerful soulful singers of yesterday—the Labelles and Franklins or my girl, Millie Jackson. And it was a party to honor Earnie Barnes, the original painter of the *Sugar Shack*.

"Rest in Love" (Acrylic, June 9, 2012, #000244) All praises be unto His Imperial Majesty, Jah. On June 9, 2012, my kin people gathered and celebrated and said goodbye to My Granny as she was sent back to where she came from, physically, the earth; spiritually, Jah, to begin the process of transforming. Someone mentioned that he was my Granny's favorite. That was part of her charm. She made each of us, in her own way and at different times, feel as if we were her favorite and in those moments, we probably were. I remember my first plane ride was with my Granny to San Diego. The large white Christmas tree she put up ever year. Sitting on the deep freezer that use to be in the dining room or sitting in the orange high chair in the corner next to the stove. I remember when Steve, me and Ken used bread to catch and burn "Phil." I remember how we would gather in the kitchen, sweet treats and ice cream, laughing and joking. I remember when I was nicknamed Pumpkin or Nutty Professor, or the only whuppin I ever got from my granny was because I stuck my tongue out at her. I remember she loved playing Sorry and kickin' the pieces to the other side of the room. Though she was known for her cooking, she also was open hearted and loving not just to family either. She was fun. She was funny She could be firm. She is loved and as she moves on, I hope and pray that as we wait for the next sun rise that she rests in love. Read 1 Corinthians, Chapter 15. Side note...I hope that as we are all remembering my Granny, we remember that she was about family. In my generation and the one before me, some bad things happened to some of us. Hopefully remembering the good will set us on the path of healing and forgiving. As times get harder and the end draws near, we will need our family. Not to just gather when someone sleeps, but creating a space for my son, his children, my cousins and their children where they can find that joy, that security and warmth that we felt. I have not seen most of you for the 18 years I've been here. No guilt. No blame. Just remember my Granny and transform from kin people to family—to and for each other. May Jah Bless you all.

"Jamaican Model" (18" x 24", acrylic on canvas, March 6, 2013, #000288)

"Island Gyal" (14" x 18", acrylic on canvas panel, #000290)

"That Quick Glimpse" (10" x 18", acrylic on paper, #000282) The first time I met J, I was at Wilson School in Kenosha playing ball with Vonn and a few other homeboys. It was a hot summer day. We had the car pulled up on the grass, music pumpin' while me and Vonn served them cats on the court. I looked up and saw this white woman, bright blond hair (I wasn't into blonds and my girl at the time, D, had skin that was the closest thing I've ever seen to the actual color black). She had on this dark shades and a teal blue short set and black sandals. She had this little boy that stumbled along side of her. It was just like the movies. This was only the second time I'd had that sort of reaction, right away I was drawn. It was more than looks but she was about a block and a half down and I didn't have my glasses on so I had no idea what she really looked like. As she got closer, I called out. She kept walking. I described the color top and called out again. She ignored and kept walking. I gave it another shot. She slightly turned her head and gave me a peak and very coolly pulled her dark shades down, then quickly pushed them back in place. I jumped in the car and drove across the street along side her. She ignored and kept walking. I pulled ahead and parked in someone's driveway blocking her path. I got out the car. Now it was my turn. My skinny self got out the car still sweating and no shirt on, all cut up. Just knew I was looking good. I slide in again. She said, "I wondered if you'd keep yelling at me from over there or if you'd actually come over here if you really wanted to say something to me. Well now that you've forced your way into my walk with my son, what is you have to say that is so important?" I was thrown off by this jazzy woman. But not deterred. From that moment we spent the rest of the day together until about 10pm. She was about 28 and I was 16. Thought she may have believed that I was 19. There are many mental images of her I go over. But that first is my favorite. . . that quick glimpse over the rim of her darkers.

"Shaka Zulu, Strong Black African Warrior" (5" x 7", acrylic card, April 5, 2013, #000296) I love the eyes on this painting. It reminds me of the book I seen when I was a kid with the Africans in it, where it showed us we didn't have to pretend to be Native American braves; we could be African warriors.

WHAT CAN YOU DO?

Get involved nationally and/or locally. There are many projects in different parts of the country, like those listed below, that are focused on prison reform at the present time.

- In Wisconsin, a group called WISDOM is working on alternatives to incarceration for a safer and healthier Wisconsin. Their 11 x 15 campaign is aimed at reducing the Wisconsin prison by one half (from 22,000 to 11,000) by 2015. (A part of this drive is that Wisconsin has the highest black male incarceration rate in the United States, according to the 2010 decennial census.)

- In Madison, Madison Area Urban Ministry is an interfaith social justice organization working toward criminal justice system reforms and many other related issues (housing, jobs, education) for prisoners returning to the community. http://www.emum.org/

- In Madison, Books to Prisoners sends books to prisoners in the state of Wisconsin free of charge, believing that books are tools for learning and can help open minds to new ideas and fresh possibilities. http://rainbowbookstore.coop/b2p

- In Milwaukee, The Benedict Center is an interfaith, nonprofit criminal justice agency working with victims, offenders and the community to achieve a system of justice that is fair and treats everyone with dignity and respect. It provides community-based treatment alternatives to incarceration for women so they can live safer and healthier lives for themselves, their children and the community, emphasizing restorative community alternatives to imprisonment, to ensure fair and equitable justice for all. http://benedictcenter.org/

- Nationally, Michelle Alexander (author of *The New Jim Crow*) is leading efforts to help us understand the impacts of the War on Drugs and what that has meant to incarceration levels. http://newjimcrow.com/

- On the Internet, news articles about our nation's criminal justice system are shared on this site reflecting the organizer's belief that we have a national incarceration crisis (a belief in lock 'em up and throw away the key) and we must ask ourselves, "at what expense?" https://www.facebook.com/PrisonReformMovement

- And support the current governmental efforts to get "smart on crime." Reverse mandatory minimum sentencing and racial sentencing disparities. Offer compassionate early release for prisoners facing extraordinary or compelling circumstances, provide more drug/alcohol and mental health treatment and community supervision programs, and eliminate life sentences for those 17 and under. Help children of incarcerated parents understand what is happening in their families and help them succeed in school. U.S. Attorney General Eric Holder has said. "Today, a vicious cycle of poverty, criminality and incarceration traps too many Americans and weakens too many communities…many aspects off our criminal justice system may actually exacerbate this problem, rather than alleviate it."

- To help DarRen personally, painting supplies are not provided in prison. He must purchase them and does so from kind donations from friends and family. If you'd like to help, please send money orders (only) to: DarRen Morris [#236425], Columbia Correctional Institution, P.O. Box 999, Portage, WI 53901. All support is greatly appreciated, be it words, prayers, positive thoughts, helping hearing impaired or sexually abused children, or financial donations.

AUTHORS' BIOGRAPHIES

DarRen Morris: Seventeen. That was my age when I was sentenced and I have now served more than half of my life in maximum security Wisconsin prisons.

My sentence? Life in prison. My crime? I was party to the unintentional death of an innocent man.

Although I was involved in this death, I am not a murderer. I know this in my heart, in my regret for this loss of life, and through my daily actions.

I am an artist. I paint and donate my works of art. In the years to come I want to create art that will help save youth from making thoughtless choices. I also want to create art that will help you on the outside understand what we face on the inside—the very real need for prison reform in Wisconsin and elsewhere—the very real need to involve more people in working toward prisoner rehabilitation rather than punishment.

Most of us on the inside are both perpetrators and victims. Hurt people hurt people.

Help me lessen the hurt.

Correspondence may be sent to: DarRen Morris [#236425], Columbia Correctional Institution, P.O. Box 900, Portage, WI 53901

Positive words preferred.

Judith Gwinn Adrian: I teach undergraduate and graduate classes at Edgewood College, Madison, WI, and support the work toward holistic alternatives to incarceration.

When I completed my Ph.D. (University of Wisconsin-Madison, 1993) in adult education, I understood that adult learning is about change and about the belief that all of us continue to grow throughout our lifespans (and beyond. . . who knows). We are all teachers and all learners. There is always hope and always opportunity to make things better.

Correspondence may be sent through: inwarmblood.com

CPSIA information can be obtained at www.ICGtesting.com
Printed in the USA
LVOW07s2111210415

435488LV00001B/320/P